JAPANESE DIRECT MANUFACTURING INVESTMENT IN THE UNITED STATES

JAPANESE DIRECT MANUFACTURING INVESTMENT IN THE UNITED STATES

Mamoru Yoshida

PRAEGER

New York
Westport, Connecticut
London

Library of Congress Cataloging-in-Publication Data

Yoshida, Mamoru.
  Japanese direct manufacturing investment in
the United States.

  Originally presented as the author's thesis
(doctoral—University of Miami)
  Bibliography: p.
  Includes index.
  1. Investments, Japanese—United States.
2. Corporations, Japanese—United States. I. Title.
HG4910.Y58   1986   332.6'7352'073   86-22689
ISBN 0-275-92347-9 (alk. paper)

Library of Congress Catalog Card Number: 86-22689
ISBN: 0-275-92347-9 (alk. paper)

First published in 1987

Praeger Publishers, 521 Fifth Avenue, New York, NY 10175
A division of Greenwood Press, Inc.

Printed in the United States of America

The paper used in this book complies with the Permanent
Paper Standard issued by the National Information Standards
Organization (Z39.48-1984).

10 9 8 7 6 5 4 3 2 1

Contents

List of Figures

List of Tables

Foreword

Japanese enterprise is a fascinating phenomenon — especially to Westerners. It embodies a distinctive set of values that command both attention and admiration.

Traditionally, Japanese enterprise has been viewed in terms of its cultural homogeneity and cohesiveness and its human relations characteristics that have so thoroughly integrated people management into the strategic success formula of the firm. Books such as *Theory Z* and *The Art of Japanese Management* have been big sellers as people in the West — indeed, in the world — have become intrigued, if not captivated, by the expanding competitiveness of Japanese enterprise. The image of these firms in some instances is nearly collosal. They are seen as monolithic and pervasive, racing, as it were, to a destiny of global market dominance.

A complimentary perspective sees Japanese enterprise as the embodiment of a Japanese political consensus aimed at establishing an economic commercial hegemony over several selected world markets such as photography, automobiles and electronics. This view sees Japanese enterprises as benefiting from protected home markets that, in many cases, have been large enough and internally competitive enough for them to become world-class producers. It sees Japanese enterprises as benefiting from home-government subsidies for their research and development and from less-than-stringent environmental controls in Japan that allow them to undercut producers in foreign markets whose products bear heavier social costs. It sees them as the beneficiaries of the Japanese peoples' distinctive work ethic that underwrites their commercial success and a social policy preference that is slow to reward further a working society with increased leisure time, retirement security, and the like. It reinforces foreigners' perceptions of Japanese enterprise as monolithic, pervasive, and dominance driven.

Perceptions such as these provide for "convenient characterizations," and in the early days of the West's fear of and fascination with Japanese enterprise, they functioned in quick and effective fashion in conveying some fundamental concepts. But today's emergent Japanese multinational enterprises are a distinctive breed in different ways — as are the management systems that give them direction and meaning.

Japanese enterprise is in the throes of a fascinating evolution. Fiercely competitive domestically and, generally, having been extremely successful in export markets, Japan's enterprises, not unlike many U.S. companies in the 1960s, find themselves evolving into multinational enterprises — some deliberately, some begrudgingly. They are being seriously challenged by their very success. The development of foreign markets, many of these firms are finding, involves a continuum rooted in exports and culminating in globally rationalized production and marketing. Japan's multinational enterprises are generally early in this evolutionary process. By and large, they are presently market seekers with foreign-based production serving foreign markets. And they are being "stressed," culturally, structurally, and operationally, as they are moving from exporters to foreign-based market seekers to internationally integrated enterprises.

Professor Mamoru Yoshida, in this remarkably timely and insightful book, has profiled a point in time critically important to the maturation of Japanese multinational enterprise. He examines the crucial nexus between parent and subsidiary in several key dimensions, including the investment rationale, the government's role, or lack of it, regarding the initial movement of production overseas, and the establishment of subsequent managerial and financial control mechanisms. His data base consists of companies' experiences and was established first-hand by Professor Yoshida himself. He offers insightful analyses and integrates his issues and findings with the recently growing body of literature on Japan's multinational enterprises.

I am sure those who read Professor Yoshida's *Japanese Direct Manufacturing Investment in the United States* will find it informative and useful. They will probably find it intriguing too. For the thoughtful reader, it likely raises as many questions as it answers. This, perhaps, is its main contribution.

Duane Kujawa
University of Miami
April 24, 1986

Acknowledgments

This study is based on my doctoral dissertation completed at the Graduate School of International Studies, the University of Miami. For this, I had the privilege of being chosen as one of four finalists by the Academy of International Business in its 1984–85 Dissertation Competition. I would like to express my gratitude to the following members of my dissertation committee, who have read the manuscript and provided constructive comments: Dr. June Teufel Dreyer, Dr. Roy J. Hensley, Dr. Duane Kujawa, Dr. Harold Strauss, and Dr. Julian I. Weinkle. Dr. Kujawa was my principal advisor during the entire period of my doctoral program from 1981 to 1985. He is a dedicated educator and researcher with a superb sense of humor. His moral support, encouragement, and constructive criticism, coupled with his own extensive research on multinational enterprises, helped me immeasurably throughout my undertaking of this study and are greatly appreciated.

This research would not have been possible without the participation of Japanese corporate executives and managers as well as officials from the Ministry of International Trade and Industry (MITI) and the Federation of Economic Organizations (Keidanren). I am very much appreciative of their amiable cooperation and generous contribution of their time and knowledge to this study. I would also like to acknowledge my gratitude to the executives and managers at the U.S. subsidiaries of the participating Japanese companies who kindly arranged my interviews at their corporate headquarters in Japan.

During my field work in Japan I was fortunate to receive assistance and valuable information from many individuals. Among them, I am particularly indebted to Dr. Noboru Yamamoto and Dr. Noritake Kobayashi at Keio University. Their kind assistance and invitation to a meeting of the Workshop on the Study of Japanese Multinationals (Takokusekikigyo Kenkyukai) in Tokyo were valuable and instructive.

I would also like to express my gratitude to the following individuals who were kind enough to share their expertise during my preliminary research for this study: Mr. Hajimu Hori at the Japan Trade Center, New York City; Ms. Susan MacKnight at the Japan Economic Institute of America, Washington, D.C.; Mr. Albert L. Seligmann at the United States–Japan Advisory Commission, Washington, D.C.; and Dr. Yoshi Tsurumi at Baruch College, the City University of New York.

Finally, I am particularly grateful to Florida Atlantic University for the grant and encouragement for my research endeavor during the academic year 1984–85.

JAPANESE DIRECT MANUFACTURING INVESTMENT IN THE UNITED STATES

1   INTRODUCTION

RESEARCH PROBLEMS AND OBJECTIVES

There has been a tremendous increase in the number of Japanese firms investing in manufacturing operations in the United States in recent years, especially since the early 1970s. At the end of 1983, for example, 334 U.S. manufacturing firms were owned wholly or in part by Japanese investors, of which only 14 were established as Japanese subsidiaries prior to 1970. These 334 firms owned 521 manufacturing plants in the United States.[1]

Why did the Japanese investors set up manufacturing subsidiaries in the United States? Is such investment, as popularly believed, basically a defensive action by individual firms in order to protect their established U.S. markets from the rising protectionist sentiment in the United States?

Granted that differences in corporate culture exist between Japan and the United States, it is conceivable that Japanese companies may have difficulty in managing manufacturing operations in the United States. Attitudes and expectations of non-Japanese members introduced into their organizations through such direct investment make it difficult for these companies to continue their traditional decision-making and control systems. The cultural difference coupled with the geographical distance between the two countries may pose a significant administrative challenge on the part of the parent companies in Japan.

Then, how do these parent companies in Japan coordinate the operations of their manufacturing plants in the United States with their home and other overseas operations? Are these plants basically

1

free-standing units with a considerable degree of decentralization of authority in corporate policy decisions? Or, are they part of tightly controlled and integrated systems conceived on a global basis by the Japanese parent companies?

Japanese firms' drive for foreign direct investment in recent years has attracted much attention in the United States. *Business Week,* for example, had a special coverage of the topic in 1980 and 1981. The reports put forward the phenomenon as "Japan Inc.'s global investment surge" and "Japan Inc. goes international with high technology."[2] The concept of "Japan Inc.," according to Destler and others, emerged by the early 1970s and was espoused at the U.S. Department of Commerce and by some on the White House staff. In this view, they note, the Japanese "had developed a powerful, rapidly growing, purposively managed, and relentlessly self-interested economic juggernaut which was posing a fundamental challenge to U.S. economic supremacy."[3]

How does the recent increase in Japanese firms' direct manufacturing investment in the United States relate to the perceived collaboration of government and business in Japan? Is such investment a part of the firms' enterprise strategies reflective only of business, or are there government considerations as well? Or, is it a result of some fundamental change in the government-business relationship in Japan?

This study attempts to answer these and other related questions and thereby examines the nature of Japanese direct manufacturing investment in the United States. Primary data for this study were collected through extensive personal interviews this author conducted in the summer of 1984 in Japan with executives and managers of 15 Japanese companies as well as officials from the Ministry of International Trade and Industry (MITI) and the Federation of Economic Organizations (Keidanren).

There are two major research objectives. The first is to investigate the decision-making processes and control systems of Japanese companies in high-technology industries with regard to their direct manufacturing investments in the United States. The reason for selecting the high-technology industries is twofold. First, international competition and/or cooperation in the industries will likely be intense among the industrialized countries in the coming decade. Recently, there has been every indication of such increased competition, especially between Japan and the United States.[4] Second, the current Japanese industrial policy stresses structural adjustment of the Japanese economy toward "knowledge-intensive" (i.e., high-technology) industries.[5] The policy would have a significant effect on the behavior of Japanese firms in their domestic and international activities. This last point leads to the second objective of the current study, which is to provide some new insights into the much-debated subject of the government-business relationship in Japan, specifically the nature of Japan's industrial policies and their probable effects on the business strategies of Japanese firms.

Although numerous studies have been published on such aspects of Japan as management, economy, society, and politics, limited information is available that focuses on Japanese direct manufacturing investment in the United States, especially the investment decision-making process and the control system, including parent-subsidiary linkages in international management areas. This study attempts to fill this void.

ORGANIZATION OF THE STUDY

Chapter 2 reviews existing research studies relevant to the subject matter of this study. It is divided into four sections: industrial organization, foreign direct investment, investment decision making, and the control system. Topics included in these sections provide the background information for the research framework of the current study.

Chapter 3 presents the research design and approach. An environmental model is used to analyze both internal and external factors affecting Japanese companies' decisions to invest in U.S. manufacturing operations. The findings from the present research are presented in Chapters 4 through 6. In each of these chapters, the research findings are related to and contrasted with those from relevant research studies existing at the time of the current research.

Chapter 4 examines the investment decision-making process of the 15 Japanese companies interviewed. The chapter is divided into three sections: the initiating forces, the feasibility study, and entry strategies and decision making.

Chapter 5 explains how these parent companies in Japan administer the manufacturing activities of their subsidiaries in the United States. This chapter is divided into two sections: corporate structure and the control system. Here, structural linkage between the parent and the subsidiary is analyzed by taking into consideration the headquarters' organizational structure, locus of policy formulation, communication methods, and evaluation practices.

Chapter 6 describes interactions among macroeconomic and microeconomic actors in Japan. It traces the gradual changes in government-business relations in Japan, which in part have accounted for the sharp rise in Japan's overseas direct manufacturing investment in recent years. The chapter consists of four sections: relaxation of foreign exchange controls, MITI's new direction, private initiatives, and Japan's direct manufacturing investment.

Finally, Chapter 7 summarizes and synthesizes the research findings. It provides discussions on the implications of the current research findings for policy makers and research ideas for further studies.

2   BACKGROUND

This chapter reviews major prior studies on the following four topics relevant to this study: industrial organization, foreign direct investment, investment decision making, and the control system. The review attempts to set the stage for the current study by presenting some concepts and theories advanced by other researchers and deemed important in analyzing Japanese direct manufacturing investment in the United States.

First, Japan's industrial organization will be analyzed in order to illuminate the environmental and institutional conditions that affect the behavior and the decision-making style of Japanese corporations. Here, the government-business relations and the nature of macro-micro economic management and coordination will also be reviewed.

Next, the nature and reasons for foreign direct investment will be examined, with a particular attention focused on Japanese direct manufacturing investment. Here, foreign direct investment will be viewed from both macroeconomic and microeconomic perspectives.

Then, the behavioral aspect of investment decision making will be explored in order to highlight the process of how a decision to invest in manufacturing abroad is reached at the level of the firm. The focus here will be on concepts that characterize the Japanese decision-making style.

Finally, the concept of control system will be studied, especially in the context of parent-subsidiary relations. Here, the focus will be on the parent company perspective — how the parent company monitors and administers the activities of its manufacturing plants abroad.

INDUSTRIAL ORGANIZATIONS

To understand the behavior of Jananese companies, it is important to understand the unique aspect of Japanese industrial organization as well. The domestic business, economic, and political environments in Japan have been quite different from those in the United States. Such differences in environmental factors are likely to be reflected in corporate strategies and activities, which in turn result in different patterns of foreign direct investment. Thus, differences in the pattern of firms' behaviors cannot be dismissed as irrational simply from the perspective of one particular culture. As Drucker notes:

> The most fruitful starting point for institutional analysis and for understanding the behavior of people in institutions might be the assumption that they are behaving rationally and that they rationally optimize their realities. The assumption might be that different behavior is best explained in terms of different realities and that it is the job of the institutional analyst to find out what the realities are.[1]

Japan's postwar economic success has attracted considerable attention to the inner workings of her industrial organization and management practices, particularly with respect to her industrial policies and the government-business relationship. As Kaplan has noted, close communication and coordination of economic activities between the business and the government have developed since the time of the Meiji Restoration in 1868.[2] Japan's government-business relationship centers around the organized business, the bureaucracy (especially MITI), and the government (the Liberal Democratic Party). Yanaga, in 1968, illustrated this three-power relationship as follows:

> The most important functions of the bureaucracy involve the protection and promotion of business and industry, in whose behalf it formulates long-term economic plans, makes forecasts, sets goals, and establishes priorities. Organized business provides members for the cabinet, the Diet, and government advisory councils and administrative commissions. It hires retired government officials as corporation executives and trade associations officials. In return for political contributions by organized business, the party in power strives to create a political climate conducive to carrying on profitable business enterprises. In this role, the party in power is in effect the political arm of organized business in much the same manner that the Japan Socialist Party is the political arm of labor. It is the party in power that selects the Prime Minister and the Cabinet members who head the administrative departments and exercise decisive influence on budget formulation.[3]

The coordinating mechanism in Japan's economic management was somewhat strengthened after the end of World War II, as the governmental policies were inevitably focused primarily on efforts to rebuild the domestic economic basis. Johnson studied the postwar economic miracle of Japan, focusing on the Japanese state-guided market system. He observed that MITI had played a significant role in coordinating the roles of the state bureaucracy and privately owned businesses to make the market work for developmental goals. This coordinating mechanism (a state-guided market system) was a rational choice in response to Japan's situational conditions. Johnson further elaborated on this point:

> The priorities of the Japanese state derive first and foremost from an assessment of Japan's situational imperatives, and are in this sense a product not of culture or social organization or insularity but of rationality. These situational imperatives include late development, a lack of natural resources, a large population, the need to trade, and the constraints of the international balance of payments.[4]

A national priority in Japan has been consistently placed on nurturing the economy. With the conscious efforts of business and government, Japan transformed into one of the major industrialized countries by the late 1960s. During this postwar period of economic development, the current structure of Japan's industrial organization has evolved. It has some distinctive features characterized, among other things, by industrial groups.

Unlike the prewar *Zaibatsu* (big financial combines owned and controlled by holding companies of a few wealthy families) system, the postwar Japanese industrial organization has been moving toward democratic choice and decision making. Except for a limited number of large corporations, corporate ownership now tends to be widely diffused and publicly held. Industrial groups in the current industrial organization in Japan are based on cross-holding of shares and interlocking directorship. Within each group, key companies are closely connected horizontally with each other, and each of these key companies has subsidiaries and affiliates of various size that are horizontally connected as group-member firms.[5]

Dodwell Marketing Consultants classified Japanese industrial groups into the following types:

1. Groups of Zaibatsu origin: Mitsubishi, Mitsui, and Sumitomo.

2. Groups centering around leading banks: Fuyo, DKB (Daiichi Kangyo Bank), Sanwa, Tokai, and IBJ (Industrial Bank of Japan).
3. Groups that are established around large industrial concerns: Nippon Steel, Hitachi, Nissan, Toyota, Matsushita, Toshiba-IHI, and so on.[6]

As of March 1982 the six major groups (Mitsubishi, Mitsui, Sumitomo, Fuyo, DKB, and Sanwa) had presidential councils. A typical council of presidents (*Shacho-kai*) is composed of the presidents of the top companies belonging to an industrial group. It is presumably the highest decision-making body for that group. However, it is not clear how a presidential council actually functions as a decision-making body for an entire group. Dodwell Marketing Consultants observed that

> the members of a presidential council, however, do not want the council to be identified as a "policy-making body" for the whole group. They think that the presidential council should not be associated with the image of the holding company of the prewar Zaibatsu. According to them, the council is only a meeting to be held regularly for fostering friendship between the presidents of the group; every member is independent and no one is bound by the decisions or recommendations made by the council. The reader is left to judge the credibility of this statement as the discussion carried on by the councils have never been disclosed.[7]

Sasaki attempted to explain the coordinating mechanism of Japan's economic activities and how the major industrial groups fit into this mechanism.[8] Figure 2-1 illustrates this coordinating mechanism. The numbers 1 through 6 represent stages of coordination from micro to macro levels.

First, major group-member companies coordinate the resource allocation and activities of their related companies and subcontractors through their financial and administrative controlling power. Sasaki argued that this intragroup vertical coordination had been strengthened after the inception of capital liberalization in the late 1960s. He cited, as an example, the case of the Japanese automobile industry. In the early 1970s, Toyota and Nissan increased their stock ownership percentages in their parts suppliers in order to protect their vertically integrated production systems from the threat of takeover of these subcontractors by foreign capital.[9]

Second, interindustry horizontal coordination is made possible within each major industrial group through their cross-holdings of ownership

FIGURE 2-1
COORDINATION OF ECONOMIC ACTIVITIES IN JAPAN

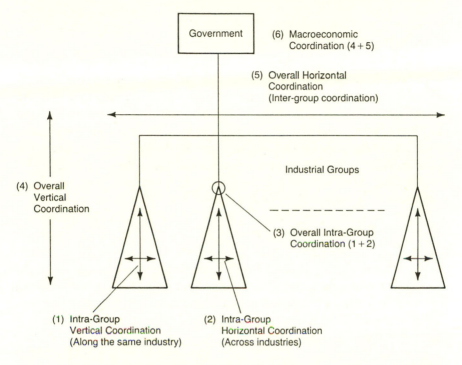

Source: Adapted with permission from Naoto Sasaki, *Management and Industrial Structure in Japan,* Copyright 1981, Pergamon Press.

shares of their member firms in several different industries. Third, overall intragroup coordination becomes complete through the vertical and horizontal coordination stages.

At the fourth and fifth stages, administrative guidance by MITI takes effect on intergroup coordination. At the next stage, the Industrial Structure Council, an advisory organ to the ministry, plays an important role in deliberating long-term economic policies relating to Japan's industrial structure.

Because of its unique aspect, therefore, the industrial organization in Japan seems to be a relevant factor that should be taken into consideration when analyzing the behavior of Japanese firms. The next section reviews some major studies on foreign direct investment, especially with regard to Japanese foreign direct investment.

FOREIGN DIRECT INVESTMENT

A variety of hypotheses have been proposed to explain why foreign investors should necessarily invest within a market instead of exporting to supply that market. Studies on foreign direct investment in the past have mainly been confined to those of U.S. and European companies. However, as Japanese firms began to increase their overseas investments in recent years, several major studies were already undertaken to describe the characteristics of Japan's foreign direct investment and the particular behavior of Japanese multinationals.[10]

With regard to U.S. foreign direct investment, Hymer paved the way for further research by showing in 1961 that those industries in which foreign direct investment most prominently occurred tended to be oligopolistically structured.[11] Building on Hymer's work, Kindleberger surveyed various theories of foreign direct investment and asserted that in a world of pure competition foreign direct investment could not exist.[12] Under the classical economic model of perfect competition, no one firm can affect the price of a product nor the market as a whole. There is no product differentiation among producers and sellers of given products. In such a market environment, a local firm has a clear advantage over a foreign firm, since to serve the local market the latter would incur large costs of transportation and communication. Therefore, Kindleberger attributed the reason for foreign direct investment to various market imperfections such as imperfections in goods markets or factor markets, scale economies, and government-imposed disruptions.[13]

Aside from the macroeconomic explanations of foreign direct investment, Vernon attempted to explain the phenomenon at the level of the firm. He proposed a product life cycle hypothesis and argued that a firm with a competitive advantage based on its product technology would eventually be pushed into investment in overseas production.[14] As the product technology of a firm matures, international competition increases in the product market. To defend its market abroad, the firm will be forced to undertake foreign direct investment. Thus, Vernon took into account the interdependence of firms in international markets and provided insights into a logical sequence of the development of a firm from purely domestic operations to international trade and then eventually to overseas production.

It is often observed that firms in an oligopolistic industry tend to move in tandem in order to maintain stability within the industry. Knickerbocker illustrated the follow-the-leader behavior in foreign direct investment among U.S. firms in oligopolistic industries. He showed that when one U.S.-based firm entered a given foreign market, its major competitors also entered that market within a short period of time.[15] Flowers noted similar behavior among European and Canadian firms investing in the United States.[16]

Daniels, in 1971, studied the profile and the investment decisions of 40 Canadian and European companies with respect to their direct manufacturing investments in the United States. He argued that the international oligopoly could be a predictor for such direct investments and that the U.S. facilities of these firms had in many cases enhanced the investors' ability to export to the United States.[17] This latter conclusion should be interpreted with caution, since his data included some companies engaged in assembly operations that do not substitute for trade, and these data were not disaggregated.

Does the pattern of Japanese foreign direct investment differ from that of Western multinational corporations? Observing the North-South (developed and developing countries) problems in economic development and trade, Kojima proposed a normative theory of foreign direct investment from a macroeconomic (national as well as international economic) perspective.[18] His theory is based on the traditional economic theory of comparative advantage originally advanced by Ricardo and then elaborated by others through the framework of the Heckscher-Ohlin-Samuelson theory of trade. The basic tenet of his theory is that foreign direct investment *should* be undertaken to achieve allocative efficiency in various resources through a proper adjustment in the international division of labor. The direction of his approach is analogous to the framework suggested by Harry Johnson, who investigated the welfare implications of foreign direct investment in the international economic system.[19]

Kojima integrated the theories of international trade and investment and categorized foreign direct investment into two types according to its effect on international trade: the trade-oriented foreign direct investment that complements international trade and the anti-trade-oriented foreign direct investment that substitutes for international trade. He explained the distinction between the two as follows:

> Direct foreign investment leads to structural adjustment and changes in the components of import and export, if it transfers a package of capital, technology and managerial skill from an industry which has a comparative disadvantage in the investing country to the recipient country, where it develops a comparative advantage. . . . The point is that direct foreign investment in these circumstances works in a complementary fashion to changes in the pattern of comparative advantage. On the other hand, if direct investment moves out from an industry in which there is a comparative advantage in the investing country when it has no prospects of developing a comparative advantage in the recipient country, it leads to a loss of efficiency by blocking the reorganization of international trade. This is direct foreign investment that decreases trade.[20]

He termed the first type the "Japanese Direct Investment Model" and the second the "American Direct Investment Model." Because he perceives that the primary motivational factor for foreign direct investment between advanced industrial countries is a variety of trade barriers, he suggests that Japanese firms would be better advised to refrain from rushing into full-scale direct investment in U.S. manufacturing.[21]

Another approach to the study of Japan's foreign direct investment was advanced from both international economic and political perspectives by Roemer, who studied U.S.-Japanese competition in international markets.[22] In his concept of politicoeconomic hegemony, a country's international economic strength was measured by the aggregation of its strengths in various spheres of competition. He advanced a four-stage theory of an advanced capitalist country's reliance on trade and investment as instruments of international economic competition as follows:

> A developed capitalist country which becomes involved in significant international economic competition is seen as passing through four stages. . . . In the first stage, the country's share in world exports of manufactures starts to rise. In the second stage, the rise in its trade share slows (or its trade share becomes stable), and its share in world direct foreign investment in manufactures starts to rise. In the third stage, its trade share in manufactures starts to fall, but its investment share continues to rise. In the fourth stage, its trade share continues to fall and its share in manufacturing foreign investment starts to fall also.[23]

He predicted in 1975 that Japan would begin to develop into an active investor in manufacturing operations abroad. He argued that Japan would rely much more on direct investment and less on trade than she had in the past and that the pattern of her investment would become characterized by large oligopolistic investments in all sectors, including the advanced sectors.[24]

Tsurumi identified some characteristics of Japanese direct manufacturing investment in the United States since 1971 (Period II) as opposed to the one prior to 1971 (Period I), based on the data he collected on Japanese firms' entries into U.S. manufacturing for the period of 1958 through 1973.[25] He reported that in Period II large manufacturing firms replaced small ones as the dominant forces on the U.S. scene and that contrary to the pattern of Japanese investment in Asia and Latin America, Japanese trading companies were not actively involved in manufacturing subsidiaries in the United States. He reasoned such behavior on the part of Japanese manufacturing firms thus:

> Unlike the defensive measures they employed in coping with import substitution attempts of developing countries, however, Japanese investors in the United States and to some extent, in Europe, aggressively entered the United States and other industrialized markets as the logical sequel to investors' export successes. And these investors' entries were based on their strengths arising from specific product- and process-related technologies which they had earlier perfected in Japan.[26]

At about the same time Tsurumi reported the result of his research findings, Yoshino studied the Japanese version of the multinationalizing trend in business. Although he recognized a pattern of Japanese foreign direct investment in manufacturing industries similar to that of U.S. multinationals, he came to the following conclusion:

> Japan's inability to generate major innovative technologies will almost certainly limit the multinational spread of her industries and will particularly inhibit any large scale entry of Japanese manufacturing activities into the U.S. market. For the foreseeable future, then, Japanese enterprises will scarcely challenge the dominance of U.S.-based multinational enterprises.[27]

Another study on foreign direct investment of Japanese firms was undertaken by Ozawa in the latter half of the 1970s. He developed a macroeconomic picture of Japanese foreign direct investment by weighing the roles of Japan's public policy and market forces. He argued that the behavior of the majority of Japanese investing firms was different from the U.S. and European multinational enterprises and that Japanese foreign direct investment was "not an aggregation of microeconomic behaviors of the firms but both internal and external macroeconomic constraints on Japan's industrial production at home and her overseas trade conditions."[28]

According to Ozawa, Japan's multinationalism is taking a unique evolutionary path, since Japan struggles to escape from "the Ricardian trap of industrialism" — the uncertain supplies of overseas resources and the irremovable scarcities of labor and industrial space at home — led by her high-powered economic growth, a phenomenon that does not exist in the United States.[29] He contended that the growth of Japan's foreign direct investment had just begun to be promoted by the Japanese government, essentially to meet Japan's national interests. Thus, he recognized a sharp contrast between the U.S. government attitude toward its own multinationals and the Japanese government's integration of foreign direct investment in both its overall economic growth strategy and its foreign economic policy.[30]

As the preceding review of major studies has revealed, various theories have been advanced to explain the phenomenon of foreign direct investment. In general, the analytical emphasis has gradually shifted from an economic approach (the market imperfection model) to an institutional approach (the behavior of multinational corporations). The emergence of non-Western multinationals requires the institutional approach, which can incorporate comparative aspects of industrial organizations in different countries where these multinationals originate.

As reviewed, Kojima presented the normative theory of foreign direct investment based on the comparative advantage theory and implied that Japan's foreign direct investment followed this normative pattern. Ozawa indicated the involvement of the Japanese government in directing the flow of Japan's foreign direct investment. Roemer attempted to explain the increase in Japan's foreign direct investment based on the systemic determinism of capitalist countries. Tsurumi and Yoshino followed the institutional approach, examining the behavior of Japanese multinationals.

Upon reviewing the existing literature on Japan's foreign direct investment, however, readers are left with several intriguing questions that cannot be answered through casual observations of the phenomenon. How, for example, did Japanese investors come to their decisions to open their manufacturing plants in the United States? What was the influence of the Japanese government — through certain direct measures and/or indirect measures (administrative guidance) — on the investment decision-making process of these investors? The following section reviews some existing studies on the investment decision-making process in general and the Japanese decision-making style in particular.

INVESTMENT DECISION MAKING

Reasons for foreign direct investment at the level of the firm vary in accordance with how the decision maker perceives the objective reality of the domestic and the international business environments. Individual firms make their investment decisions in response to various internal and external opportunities, pressures, and constraints perceived by them. Here, investment decision making can be viewed as a part of the strategic planning of international firms.

Robinson lists four major constraints that companies take into consideration in selecting their most effective strategy for achieving their corporate objectives:

1. The domestic environment, which poses particular economic and political pressures on companies.
2. The socioeconomic environment of the host nation, which presents a unique structure with different institutions and goals.
3. The structure of the international economic and political system, which determines the rules of the game in international trade and investment.
4. Company resources, which include financial resources, personnel, technical knowledge, goodwill, intangibles (patents, copyright, trademarks, and trade secrets), the distribution system, and political leverage.[31]

He further explains that four other variables, in interaction with the four constraints as perceived by corporate management, produce a set of perceived pressures and perceived risks, which in turn create self-imposed restraints. These variables are past company experience, existing company structure, the quality of the communications systems, and personal likes and biases.[32]

Decisions to undertake foreign direct investment differ from domestic investment decisions. Robinson lists four reasons why this is so.[33] First, foreign direct investment is more expensive and involves more variables than does domestic investment. A company investing abroad, for example, needs special legal, financial, and area skills. Furthermore, the firm has to go through time-consuming international communications and travel. Second, decisions to invest abroad are less likely to be stimulated by an internal company market survey and more likely to be the result of external pressure on the firm. Third, they are more likely to be the result of selective analysis of market opportunities than that of universal and comparative analysis. Fourth, they are less subject to quantitative analysis due to greater uncertainty.

Aharoni undertook the first major analysis of the decision-making process for foreign direct investment. Based on his interview survey of U.S. manufacturing firms, he concluded that the firms' behaviors were irrational when compared with economists' preconception of the maximization-of-income assumption. According to Aharoni, the decision-making process is characterized by "the continuous dynamic social process of mutual influences among various members of an organization constrained by the organization's strategy, its resources, and the limited capacity, goals, and needs of its members, throughout which choices emerge."[34]

Aharoni emphasized the social nature of decision making and commitment created by a strong initiating force as well as by the time, efforts, and money spent by the organization to collect information. He observed that

> the very act of collecting information creates many individual commitments and often organizational ones as well. In order to collect information, it is necessary to communicate with people, to make certain decisions, and often to give tacit promises. In the process, commitments are accumulated until a situation is created which leads inevitably to investment.[35]

The decision-making process, especially in a relatively large organization as in the case of multinational corporations, is a product of the very complex communication process among individual decision makers within the organization. Past studies have identified some unique features in the Japanese decision-making style. Some of these features, which may affect the investment decision-making process of Japanese firms, are evident in the *Ringi* and *Nemawashi* systems.

The Ringi system, characterized as bottom-up group decision making, has been identified as unique to the Japanese decision-making process. A *Ringi-sho* is a proposal that is drawn up normally by a lower manager at a corporate division and passes through related divisions and departments, eventually reaching the top management for final approval.

The process involves a number of people, so that the location of responsibility for the decision made often becomes diffused. Yoshino observed that the role of the corporate president under a strict Ringi system was that of "legitimizing decisions made by group consensus by affixing his seal of approval."[36] Thus, the concept of Ringi circumscribes the leadership, authority, and initiative of the top management in a Japanese organization.

Another concept introduced to explain the Japanese decision-making style is Nemawashi, the practice of broad consultation before taking action. It is an informal process in which an essential decision is often made prior to a formal process of writing and detailing the decision. Both Ringi and Nemawashi, thus, imply that the Japanese decision-making process is consultative and participative and that it takes quite a while for a Japanese corporation to come up with a final decision. Clark reasoned such decision-making practices in Japanese organizations as follows:

> The idea that everyone may be involved in a decision is much easier to subscribe to in a Japanese company, with its relative homogeneity, its absence of extreme distinctions between management and labor, and its high proportion of graduates in economics, law, and other studies which emphasize social relations, than it is likely to be in a Western company with its differentiated work force, sharp distinction between management and labor, and dependence on specialized skills.[37]

The process of decision making described here produces some positive results within an organization. For example, the process enhances understanding of the decision problem among a large number of employees and can create corporate wide commitments to implement the decision. However, since Japanese firms have grown in size during the rapid expansion of Japan's economy and have been faced with increased competition at home and abroad, they may have begun to view the traditional decision-making process as inefficient and ineffective in responding quickly to the rapidly changing international business environment and in managing their corporate activities in line with a set of consistent goals and objectives.

The decision-making process at the corporate level is a complex subject and needs to be analyzed in conjunction with a specific decision problem. The process may take either bottom-up or top-down form, depending on particular decision problems in addition to such factors as personal attitude and commitment and the involvement of the top management. Existing studies on the decision-making process of

Japanese companies have not focused on any specific decision tasks. The current research study, therefore, fills this gap by examining the decision-making process of Japanese companies with respect to their decisions to invest in manufacturing operations in the United States.

Investment decisions are followed by implementation. This implementation stage involves both parent and subsidiary. Thus, to understand the nature of Japanese direct manufacturing investment in the United States, the parent-subsidiary linkage is an important issue to explore. For the present study, a major concern is the control system employed at the headquarters of an investing company. The next section reviews some studies on the concept of the control system in general.

THE CONTROL SYSTEM

An effective control of activities is the key to success, or even survival, for any type of organization. As Robinson states, control consists of "the relationships and devices designed to assure that strategy (or policy) decisions are made by designated authority in conformance with corporate goals, that tactical (or operating) decisions conform to the selected strategies, and that actual operations are in harmony."[38] In other words, the control system can be viewed as including a monitoring system in which a corporation ascertains that each unit of the organization is functioning well as planned to attain its corporate objectives. The system also has to provide timely information on any deviations in the results of the corporate activities from the original plans so that the management can devise and take corrective actions.

Planning and control are the inseparable ingredients for an entire system of control, and they constitute an important aspect of administration of modern business organizations. As an analytical framework, Anthony conceptualized three phases of planning and control: strategic planning, management control, and operational control.[39] Strategic planning, the first phase, is "the process of deciding on objectives of the organization, on changes in those objectives, on the resources used to attain these objectives, and the policies that are to govern the acquisition, use, and disposition of these resources."[40] Here, strategic plans are analogous to major long-term plans or master strategies, the purpose of which is to clarify the direction of the company's future courses of actions. Strategic planning is possible only after a careful and adequate assessment of the corporation's strengths and weaknesses. Strategic plans are affected by and altered in accordance with the changes in the economic, political, legal, social, and technological environments in which the firm operates. Management control, the next phase, is "the process by which managers assume that resources are obtained and used effectively and efficiently in the accomplishment of organizational objectives."[41] It involves various managerial plans and techniques to implement the corporate master strategies. Operational control, the final phase, is "the process of assuring that specific tasks are carried out effectively and efficiently."[42] It encompasses implementation and evaluation of daily operations.

In reality, however, the three phases of planning and control are not mutually exclusive. They are interrelated in a complex way, for as Schwendiman observed, "Policy-making (strategic planning) is not only the result of deliberate consideration of long-run problems facing the organization but is also often influenced disproportionately by day-to-day decisions, frequently made on an ad hoc basis by lower level administrators rather than by designated policy-makers."[43]

In managing its subsidiary abroad, the parent company needs to decide how the authority and power of planning and control should be allocated between the headquarters and the subsidiary. This is the familiar question of centralization versus decentralization in organizational structure. Stated differently, it is a question of how to design the structural linkage between the parent and its subsidiary.

According to Chandler, structure is the design of organization through which the enterprise is administered. He contends that structure follows strategy and that the most complex type of structure is the result of the concatenation of several basic strategies. He argues further that the design has two aspects essential to an organization in assuring the effective coordination, appraisal, and planning in carrying out the basic objectives and strategies and in utilizing the total resources of the enterprise: the lines of authority and communication between the different administrative offices and officers and the information and data that flow through these lines of communication and authority.[44]

Quality of decisions, whether they are strategic decisions at the top-management level or operational decisions to implement corporate plans, depends on quality of information on which the decisions are to be based. Designing an appropriate organizational structure is one of the most important considerations for assuring the quality and the timeliness of information for decision making. As a business enterprise becomes large in size or expands in terms of its product lines or the geographical coverage of its marketing and manufacturing activities, it has to introduce some new form of organizational structure to cope with the complex flows of information.

In 1972, Stopford and Wells observed three phases of structural adjustments in U.S. firms as these firms expanded their businesses abroad. In the initial phase, all the new foreign subsidiaries were tied to the parent companies by loose financial links. The foreign subsidiaries at this phase enjoyed substantial autonomy in their corporate activities and decisions. Stopford and Wells reasoned this initial autonomy at the subsidiary level was as follows:

> The initial autonomy of the first few foreign subsidiaries reflects the fact that most U.S. manufacturing firms stumbled into manufacturing abroad without much design. The early investments in foreign manufacturing made by most firms were defensive reactions against the threat of losing markets that in the first place had been acquired almost accidentally. Only later did conscious strategies for growth on a global scale emerge.[45]

As the subsidiaries grow and accumulate resources, pressures to introduce a formal control system begin to emerge at the corporate headquarters. In the second phase, an international division begins to coordinate all the foreign activities of the enterprise. The international division in U.S. firms typically operates as an independent part of the enterprise. The top management begins to realize that the enterprise would be able to reap the benefit of its multinational spread of business activities by coordinating production and marketing on a global basis and by setting strategic and other major policy decisions at the headquarters. As the needs to integrate all the activities of the enterprise grow, new forms of organizational structure begin to evolve. These firms are typically based on product lines and/or geographic regions: worldwide product divisions, area divisions, and a mixture of product and area divisions.[46]

In contrast to the pattern of structural adjustment over time that was observed in U.S. corporations by Stopford and Wells, Yoshino observed a different pattern among Japanese firms investing in overseas manufacturing plants. He noted in 1976 as follows:

> In a Japanese enterprise, at the early stages of the firm's foreign manufacturing, day-to-day operations of the subsidiaries had to be closely controlled by the export division of the parent company. . . . Managers of local subsidiaries had only limited discretion over major decisions, because the subsidiaries were created to complement the firm's export and the major

competitive strength of Japanese subsidiaries abroad initially was closely tied to the tremendous economies of scale in production enjoyed by the parent companies in Japan.[47]

Yoshino also observed that the international division in a Japanese enterprise appeared to be much less autonomous and independent than its U.S. counterpart. He concluded that de facto corporate-wide integration took place in Japanese enterprises through formal and informal communication channels based on the traditional Ringi system.[48] Under the system, the managers' responsibilities tend to be ill defined so that each major decision is made by the collective body of managers from various divisions and departments within an organization.

Yoshino's observation suggests that Japanese multinationals have control systems different from those of U.S. multinationals. Research studies on the control systems of Japanese companies are limited, especially those relating to parent-subsidiary linkages for international operations. Thus, the current study also explores this issue in order to gain further understanding of the nature of Japan's direct manufacturing investment in the United States.

This chapter has presented the major research studies relevant to the current study of Japan's direct manufacturing investment in the United States, especially regarding those factors and concepts that might explain the investment decision-making process and the control system of Japanese investors. It has also reviewed Japan's industrial organization and government-business relations in order to gain a basic understanding on the possible effect of macro-level actors on corporate behaviors. Several other important studies, which have not been introduced in this chapter, will be discussed in later chapters in conjunction with reporting of the findings of this study.

3   RESEARCH DESIGN

This chapter summarizes the research design, which is based on the background review of existing research studies presented in Chapter 2. Although this study is based largely on personal interviews conducted in Japan in the summer of 1984, it employs several other research methods as well. These research methods and the research framework as well as the profile of the Japanese companies interviewed in Japan are explained in this chapter.

RESEARCH FRAMEWORK

This study employs an environmental model to guide the research effort. The model is similar to a conceptual framework used by Farmer and Richman for their comparative analyses of differences in business practices in different national environments.[1] In their study, environmental characteristics were organized broadly into four groups: educational, sociocultural, legal and political, and economic characteristics. They used the framework to analyze the effect of various factors in these environmental characteristics on corporate activities and management processes. Figure 3-1 presents a model constructed for the current study showing an overall relationship among major environmental factors and actors that may affect the decision-making process of Japanese firms for their direct manufacturing investments in the United States. The model is not intended to reinforce the concept of Japan, Inc. nor to test existing hypotheses; rather, it attempts to illustrate in a simple diagram the

FIGURE 3-1
MAJOR ENVIRONMENTAL FACTORS AND ACTORS AFFECTING THE DECISION-MAKING PROCESS OF JAPAN'S DIRECT MANUFACTURING INVESTMENT IN THE UNITED STATES

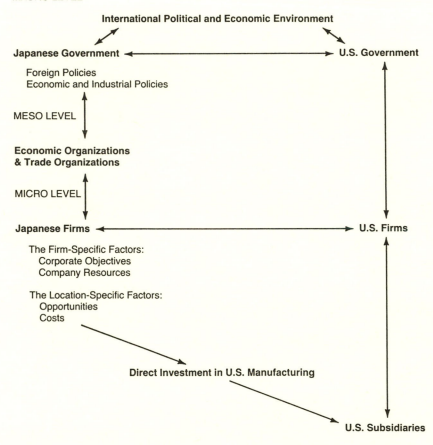

MACRO LEVEL

International Political and Economic Environment

Japanese Government ←→ U.S. Government

Foreign Policies
Economic and Industrial Policies

MESO LEVEL

Economic Organizations
& Trade Organizations

MICRO LEVEL

Japanese Firms ←→ U.S. Firms

The Firm-Specific Factors:
Corporate Objectives
Company Resources

The Location-Specific Factors:
Opportunities
Costs

Direct Investment in U.S. Manufacturing

U.S. Subsidiaries

Source: Constructed by the author.

complex reality of interactions among various actors and factors in national and international environments. It also attempts to focus the research attention on the linkage between macro- and micro-oriented theories. Japan and the United States can be viewed as individual political and economic systems and, at the same time, as subsystems of the international political and economic system. Individual firms are identified as micro-level actors. Economic organizations and trade associations in Japan represent meso-level actors (intermediaries), and various ministries and other institutions of the Japanese government are macro-level actors. In addition, a number of other actors can be identified in this model, for example, international organizations such as the Organization of Economic Cooperation and Development (OECD), the International Monetary Fund (IMF), and the United Nations at the multilateral level, and transnational institutions such as the Japan-U.S. Economic Council, the Advisory Council on U.S.-Japan Economic Relations, Japan-U.S. Businessmen's Conference, and Japan-California (U.S.) Association at the bilateral level.

Influences from and policy decisions at the macro level affect behavioral choices at the micro level through the individual firms' utilities and subjective probabilities of the expected outcomes of their decision alternatives. The micro-level actors can also affect policies to be formulated at the macro level. The meso-level actors are assumed to play the role of "gatekeepers" between the macro and the micro actors. In this sense, the model resembles the conceptual model of political systems developed by Easton, who introduced the concept of gatekeepers.[2] According to Easton, gatekeepers can be either individuals or institutions, whose function is to restrict and filter both the types and the quantity of the specific demands that reach the point of decision by authorities. Public opinion by itself does not constitute a demand unless and until it is articulated, organized, and pressed on the government. Naturally, different systems have different gatekeeping processes.

Aside from the interactions among the macro- and micro-level actors, an internal environment affects the decision-making process at the level of the firm. The internal environment includes such firm-specific factors as company resources (financial, technical, human, etc.) and corporate objectives. Coupled with information on the location-specific factors, the management decides whether to invest in U.S. manufacturing. During or subsequent to the investment decision, the management should also design a system to facilitate administration and communication between the headquarters and the manufacturing subsidiary.

The model utilized for the current study, therefore, is a holistic one. This type of approach in research studies has not been without criticisms. Heller and Wilpert cite one such critique made by Moberg and Koch:

> In as much as contingency or situational approaches replace previous methodological monisms . . . , there has been an ill-judged tendency to move towards what Moberg and Koch . . . see as grandiose and precocious attempts to aggregate different structural approaches and present them as integrated theories. Such holistic demands, they argue, would destroy the very basis of contingency thinking by falling into the universalistic trap instead of contributing to a mid-range theory of organizations between "universal truths" and "everything depends."[3]

Nevertheless, a holistic approach seems relevant for research in Japanese decision-making and control systems. For example, based on the review of the literature in management science and studies of right- and left-cerebral hemispheres, Doktor suggests that differences in Japanese and U.S. management practices may be attributable to differences in cognitive models of causation, which may be related to different languages. He states that

> in reviewing this literature, it appears that most Japanese embrace an "environmental" model of causation as opposed to the more American orientation, derived from our Greek intellectual heritage, which is that events occur in "response" to the action of one or more prior events. This difference between the "environmental" and the "responsive" model of causation can be applied to organizational settings.[4]

One's behavior is based on one's cognitive model of the relationship between the environment and self. The process of this observation changes or distorts an objective reality and leads one to conceive a subjective reality. Based on this subjective reality, one makes decisions for the future. In an organizational setting, the decision-making process can also be affected by the decision maker's cognitive model about the relationship between the organization's internal and external environments.

RESEARCH METHODOLOGY

As stated in Chapter 1, this study attempts to accomplish the following two research objectives: investigate the investment decision-making process and control system of Japanese parent companies that have established manufacturing plants in the United States and examine the Japanese government-business interactions or inactions in relation to such direct manufacturing investment.

The purpose of this research is to discover new facts and to advance the current state of knowledge. To accomplish the two research objectives, this study employs several data collection methods, including the personal interviews conducted in Japan by this author. The use of multiple methods of data collection reduces the chance that the data collected are artifacts of a particular method of data collection used. As Lin explains:

> A researcher's confidence in any pattern of relations to be tested or found is increased as more and more different methods of data collection yield a similar result. Thus, for example, if a relationship between two variables is found in both a questionnaire survey and an interview survey, then more confidence can be given to the theoretical structure from which the relationship derives.[5]

The primary information on Japanese-owned manufacturing plants in the United States comes from the 1980 benchmark survey and annual updates on Japanese-affiliated manufacturing establishments in the United States compiled by the Japan Economic Institute (JEI), a Washington-based research firm. The JEI reports list those U.S. manufacturing establishments in which Japanese companies have at least 10 percent of ownership interest. As of December 31, 1983, there were 334 manufacturing companies in the United States affiliated with Japanese companies. These companies had 521 manufacturing plants in operation or under construction at the end of 1983.[6]

The JEI reports identify, for each manufacturing plant, the name of the manufacturing company, its location within the United States, the name(s) of and the percentage ownership shares(s) of the owner(s), the type of entry (startup or acquisition), its major product lines with the four-digit Standard Industry Classification (SIC) codes, the approximate number of employees, and the year of opening or acquisition of the plant. The owners of these U.S. manufacturing plants include Japanese, U.S., and other foreign nationals. For the purpose of this study, one Japanese owner was identified for each manufacturing plant as a primary Japanese investing company (the largest Japanese owner of the manufacturing plant). Then, all the primary Japanese investing companies were classified into the following three categories according to the size and corporate affiliation — thus, all of the 521 manufacturing companies were identified with these three categories:

1. Group Member Firms: Companies that are affiliated with 16 major industrial groups (Mitsubishi, Mitsui, Sumitomo, Fuyo, DKB, Sanwa, Tokai, IBJ, Nippon Steel, Hitachi, Nissan, Toyota, Matsushita, Toshiba-IHI, Tokyu, and Seibu) and are listed on the Japanese stock exchanges.[7]
2. Other Listed Firms: Companies that do not belong to the 16 major industrial groups but are listed on the First Section of the Tokyo Stock Exchange.[8]
3. Unlisted Firms: Companies that do not satisfy the criteria for the first and second categories above. These companies are presumably small to medium and/or family owned.

For interindustry analysis, product lines of manufacturing plants were categorized according to two-digit SIC codes. Several of the 521 manufacturing plants were manufacturing multiple products covering more than one industry. In these cases, each plant was matched with one industry that approximated the main industry category of the primary beneficial owner of the plant. Then, all the variables listed above were coded and cross-tabulated for a preliminary analysis.[9] A portion of the analysis of this entire population of Japanese-affiliated U.S. manufacturing plants is presented, as relevant, along with the research findings from the interview survey, in Chapters 4 through 6.

The interview survey was undertaken to investigate the inner workings of the decision-making process and control system of Japan's direct manufacturing investment in the United States. Due to the nature of the research problem at hand, a mail survey of a large number of companies and other organizations was considered inappropriate. The problem was to determine an appropriate sample of Japanese companies and macro- and meso-level actors for personal interviews.

In line with the environmental model presented earlier, actors from three different levels of policy formulation and implementation were selected: MITI from the macro level, Keidanren from the meso level, and 15 Japanese companies from the micro level. The Ministry of International Trade and Industry was selected among other ministries and agencies of the Japanese government because it still plays a vital role in formulating Japan's industrial policies. Selection of Keidanren was also based on the same reasoning, for as Kaplan states, "Speaking mainly for big business, the Keidanren leadership, the elite of the Japanese business establishment, exerts considerable influence on government policy."[10] (Appendix A lists the titles of these interviewees and the dates of the interviews.)

Selection of the 15 firms for personal interviews was based on the primary Japanese investing companies of U.S. manufacturing plants in high-technology industries. Definitions of high-technology industries vary considerably among different analysts. Richie and others, for example, developed three definitions of high-technology industries based on several criteria such as research and development (R & D) expenditures, the use of scientific and technical personnel relative to total employment, and product sophistication.[11] The U.S. Department of Commerce suggests industry-based and product-based definitions.[12] Schmenner, based on his study on location decision of U.S. manufacturing companies, groups high-technology industries according to three-digit SIC codes. The components of the high-technology industries according to Schmenner's classification are as follows:

SIC Code	Industry
357	Computers and office equipment
366	Communication equipment
367	Electronic components
376	Guided missiles and space vehicles
38X	Instruments (measuring, analyzing, controlling, photographic, medical, clocks)[13]

Schmenner's classification method was chosen for this study, since the data on three-digit SIC codes of products manufactured at Japanese-affiliated plants in the United States were readily available from the JEI reports. (No Japanese-affiliated subsidiaries were engaged in manufacturing activities in the industries identified with the SIC code number 376.) Accordingly, 52 Japanese firms were identified as primary Japanese companies investing in 78 high-technology plants in operation or under construction as of the end of 1983 as well as 7 high-technology plants that had been sold or closed since the 1980 benchmark survey of JEI. These 52 firms were then stratified largely into two categories, large firms (group-member firms and other listed companies) and small firms, according to size and corporate group affiliation.

There were 32 large and 19 small companies. From this population, ten large and five small firms were selected for personal interviews. However, as will be noted later, it became known during the field work in Japan that one high-technology manufacturing affiliate was owned by an unlisted firm, which was loosely connected with a large listed company. Therefore, the actual interview survey covered nine large and six small firms.

In order to make inquiries on possible influence, consultations or coordination among group-member firms in the investment decision-making process of large firms in particular industrial groups, five large firms belonging to different industrial groups were selected: two firms each from a different group of Zaibatsu origin, one from a group centering around a leading Japanese bank, and two from groups established around large industrial concerns. Presentation and discussion of the research findings are based primarily on the two categories of the companies interviewed — large and small firms — except for those issues where identification of group affiliation is deemed important.

Initial contacts were made by telephone with Japanese employees at the U.S. subsidiaries of these 15 primary Japanese investing companies in order to identify appropriate personnel for the survey and to arrange for actual interviews to be conducted at their corporate headquarters in Japan. The response rate was 100 percent, which may reflect the importance that corporate executives and managers placed on the research topic. In the meantime, a questionnaire was prepared, initially in English and then translated into Japanese. A copy of the questionnaire was sent to each of the participating firms in Japan. The prospective interviewees were instructed to fill out the questionnaire prior to the scheduled interviews.

The questionnaire consists of 40 items, which are divided into seven major sections: (1) the initiating forces, (2) investigation, (3) decision making, (4) implementation and control, (5) evaluation practices, (6) company information, and (7) interviewee information. (Appendix B contains a sample questionnaire.) The questionnaire is designed to collect basic information on the decision-making process and control system of the 15 Japanese firms investing in manufacturing operations in the United States. Some of the questions are relevant only to the initial and most recent direct manufacturing investments undertaken by these companies.

As indicated in the questionnaire, a 25 percent rule was used to survey only those U.S. manufacturing plants with more than 25 percent ownership shares held by these Japanese investors. Two question items in the final section of the questionnaire were adopted, with some minor modification, from the study on managerial decision making by Heller and Wilpert.[14]

The purpose of the questionnaire was to facilitate the proceeding of interviews by covering basic questions in written form and by familiarizing the interviewees with the survey topic well in advance of the actual interviews. Combined with the results of the personal interviews, individual responses to the questionnaire are presented and discussed in various parts of the text.

Open-ended interview questions were also generated not only to collect information on corporate objectives, strategies, and structures, but also to supplement the questionnaire items on the investment decision-making process and control system at the level of the firm. They were to be used as a guide for conducting the actual interviews smoothly and efficiently. Interview questions were also prepared for MITI and Keidanren to seek their opinions and identify the level of their influence on Japanese firms' direct investments in the United States. The purpose of the interviews was to find a synthesis of macro-micro behaviors and interactions in Japan's economic management under current environments. (Appendix C contains a list of the questions used in the personal interviews.).

An interview survey is often affected by biases introduced in the interactions among the respondents, the survey instrument, and the interviewer. Responses may lack accuracy and objectivity, especially when the survey deals with the respondents' decisions made in the past. One recent study on corporate investment decisions conducted by the U.S. Department of Commerce warns researchers of such biases:

> Empirical studies that test the assumptions of the theoretical models, however, are difficult to design and therefore subject to attack on various methodological grounds. Because many of these studies rely on interviews with business decision-makers about planned or past relocations, they suffer from the desire of the interviewees to maintain confidentiality and, in some cases, to rationalize a prior action that may or may not have been undertaken on the basis of purely objective analysis. Many of the considerations that are part of the investment location decision cannot be quantified or predicted and may include personal preferences of company management, inertia, limited knowledge of opportunities, and culture-specific biases.[15]

For the current study, therefore, the responses of the interviewees were cross-checked with company records (annual reports and profiles) and other published materials in order to ascertain plausibility and validity of these responses. Each interview generally lasted two to four hours, and in some cases follow-up interviews were conducted. Findings from the field research and interpretative discussions in light of other studies are presented in Chapters 4 through 6. By agreement with the companies interviewed, company names are not disclosed in the text. In reporting financial or other numerical figures, therefore, aggregated data or averages are used as appropriate to avoid disclosure of individual firms.

PROFILE OF THE FIRMS INTERVIEWED

This section provides general information on the 15 Japanese companies that participated in this study. Personal interviews were conducted in Japanese with executives, managers, and staff employees at their corporate headquarters in Japan. The information presented here includes corporate size, international activities, and interviewees of these 15 firms.

Corporate Size

Size of a firm can be measured in a variety of ways. Table 3-1 compares the size of the nine large and six small Japanese companies in terms of the amount of capital (contributed capital), the annual sales volume, and the number of employees. A distinct difference in corporate size can be observed among the large and the small companies in all of these three measures. It can also be observed that some variations in corporate size exist even among the nine large firms.

Table 3-2 shows a comparison of average capital and annual sales per employee of the large and the small companies. It gives interesting additional information on the difference in corporate size. First, there is a striking difference in average capital per employee. The small firms are less funded to a significant degree — $2,000 per employee compared to $9,538 for the large firms. This can be expected, though, since these firms do not have wide arrays of capital sources that are normally enjoyed by firms listed on stock exchanges. Second, the large firms command

TABLE 3-1
SIZE OF THE FIRMS INTERVIEWED
(In Million Dollars for Capital and Annual Sales)

	Total	Large Firms	Small Firms
Capital			
Less than $20	6	0	6
$20–$100	3	3	0
$100–$300	3	3	0
$300 or over	3	3	0
Total	15	9	6
Annual Sales			
Less than $1,000	6	0	6
$1,000–$5,000	6	6	0
$5,000–$10,000	2	2	0
$10,000 or over	1	1	0
Total	15	9	6
Number of Employees			
Less than 1,000	4	0	4
1,000–5,000	2	0	2
5,000–10,000	4	4	0
10,000–50,000	3	3	0
50,000 or over	2	2	0
Total	15	9	6

Note: Conversion rate of $1 = 230 yen was used.

Source: Company records and *Yukashoken Hokokusho.*

TABLE 3-2
AVERAGE CAPITAL AND ANNUAL SALES PER
EMPLOYEE OF THE FIRMS INTERVIEWED

		Large Firms	Small Firms
1.	Average capital	$248,000,000	$3,000,000
2.	Average annual sales	$4,406,000,000	$224,000,000
3.	Average number of employees	26,000	1,500
4.	Average capital per employee	$9,538	$2,000
5.	Average annual sales per employee	$169,461	$149,333

Source: Company records and *Yukashoken Hokokusho.*

higher average annual sales per employee than do the small firms —
$169,461 in comparison to $149,333. These differences in corporate size
translate into the difference in available corporate resources, which may
affect the company's strategic decisions, including its decision on direct
manufacturing investment. The corporate size, in conjunction with other
variables such as product diversification, market segments, and
distribution channels, may affect the company's organizational structure
as well.

International Activities

The extent of international activities varied among the companies
interviewed. Items 1 and 2 in Section 6 of the questionnaire attempted to
measure the level of the company's commitment of resources to its
overseas manufacturing activities. Item 1 asked the number of
manufacturing plants as well as that of factory workers in various regions
of the world. Item 2 asked the size of the manufacturing activities
overseas and in the United States relative to the company's domestic
manufacturing activities in terms of the following four variables: assets,
gross sales, net profit, and number of full-time employees. To the latter
question, only 5 of the 15 companies responded in full. Four of the
remaining firms did not provide any information on this, citing
confidentiality or unavailability of such figures. The remaining six firms

TABLE 3-3
NUMBER OF OVERSEAS MANUFACTURING PLANTS
OWNED BY THE FIRMS INTERVIEWED
(By Geographic Region)

	Total	*Large Firms*	*Small Firms*
United States	46	41	6
Asia	56	53	3
Europe	23	23	0
Latin America	21	20	1
Total	146	137	10
Number of overseas manufacturing plants per firm	10	15	2

Source: Compiled by the author.

provided only incomplete figures. Usable information is reported in Table 3-3, summarizing the number of overseas manufacturing plants by geographic region.

The average number of overseas plants per firm was approximately 15 for the large firms, and 2 for the small companies. The large companies had 53 manufacturing plants in Asia and 41 plants in the United States. All of the nine large companies had one or more manufacturing plants in Asia and the majority of them had plants in Latin America as well. The six small firms had one manufacturing plant each in the United States, and the majority of these companies did not have overseas plants in any other regions.

The number of factory workers at manufacturing establishments in the United States varied considerably among the companies surveyed. One large firm had only 35 employees in its three manufacturing plants located in the United States. The total number of plant employees for the other large companies, most of which had more than one manufacturing plant in the United States, varied from 400 to 2,000, while the average per plant ran from 100 to 700. All the small firms with one exception numbered employees anywhere between 25 and 60. One small company had 400 employees at its U.S. manufacturing establishment. As will be discussed in later chapters, this company's investment is more like a portfolio investment rather than a direct investment, since this Japanese investor exercises minimum control over management of its U.S. manufacturing company.

Commitment of corporate resources to overseas manufacturing also varied considerably among the companies. Three large companies had anywhere between 14 and 20 percent of their total assets committed to their overseas manufacturing plants. Four small firms committed between 5 and 13 percent of their total assets.

Since the level of foreign commitment was not ascertained conclusively through the questionnaire and interview survey, the extent of dependency on exports was computed as a surrogate measure based on information obtained from *Yukashoken Hokokusho* (financial statements filed with the Ministry of Finance, (MOF), in Japan, which is equivalent to 10-K reports U.S. companies are required to file with the U.S. Securities and Exchange Commission) for the large firms, all of whose securities are listed on the First Section of the Tokyo Stock Exchange, and from company profiles (company publications mainly for public relations and recruitment purposes) for three small firms. (Data were not available for the remaining three small companies). Table 3-4 summarizes

TABLE 3-4
EXPORT-DEPENDENCY RATIOS OF THE FIRMS
INTERVIEWED

Ratio	Total	Large Firms	Small Firms
60 to 80 percent	2	2	0
40 to 60 percent	2	1	1
20 to 40 percent	5	4	1
Less than 20 percent	3	2	1
Unknown	3	0	3
Total	15	9	6

Note: Export-dependency ratios were computed by dividing total export sales by total sales.

Source: Company records and *Yukashoken Hokokusho.*

TABLE 3-5
JOB TITLES AND DIVISIONAL RESPONSIBILITIES
OF THE PRIMARY INTERVIEWEES

Title and Division	Total	Large Firms	Small Firms
President	2	0	2
Executive vice-president	2	0	2
Director or manager*			
Corporate Planning Division	6	5	1
International Division	2	2	0
Product-Based Division	1	1	0
Export Division	1	0	1
Public Relations Division	1	1	0
Total	15	9	6

*Some companies use different names for particular divisions. For example, Overseas Department is used for the International Division; and Corporate Planning Office, Staff Office of Planning, and General Planning Department, for the Corporate Planning Division.

Source: Compiled by the author.

the information on export-dependency ratios of these nine large and three small firms.

Two large companies had a very high export-dependency ratio. Approximately 70 percent of their total annual sales for the fiscal year ending in 1983 were export sales. Two other large firms had a low export-dependency ratio of about 10 percent. The percentages for the remaining five large companies were anywhere between 25 and 42 percent. Three small firms depended on export sales for 14 to 56 percent of their total annual sales. Again, such levels of international activities and commitment of corporate resources abroad may have an important bearing on these Japanese companies' investment decision-making processes and control systems.

Interviewees

Principal interviewees from the 15 Japanese firms had been in their companies from 16 to 30 years. The average number of years with the company was 22.3 years. Table 3-5 summarizes job titles and divisional responsibilities of these primary interviewees.

The primary interviewees were selected according to the inputs of their U.S. subsidiaries in response to this author's request for qualified and appropriate executives or managers who would be able to participate in the interview survey. Thus, for the purpose of this study, it is quite significant to know which divisions and at what level in the corporate hierarchy the interviewees represent at their corporate headquarters. This provides important additional information on the corporate structure and the locus of decision making with respect to the U.S. subsidiaries of these 15 companies. This point will be discussed later in conjunction with the reports of the research findings.

To find out the attitude of the Japanese executives and managers toward "change," the interviewees were requested to address themselves to the question of the rate of change in their own industries in the next five years with regard to the following three areas: technology, organization, and human relations. The interviewees were also requested to consider whether the anticipated changes in the three areas would be "too slow" or "too rapid" for them. Their responses, in a five-point scale spreading from "very slow" to "very rapid," are summarized in Table 3-6.

Technological changes were expected to be quite rapid in comparison to the changes in organization and human relations. However, the

TABLE 3-6
INTERVIEWEES' ASSESSMENT OF CHANGES IN THE NEXT FIVE YEARS: TECHNOLOGY, ORGANIZATION, AND HUMAN RELATIONS
(In Percentage)

		Large Firms			Small Firms		
	Total	Tech-nology	Organi-zation	Human Relations	Tech-nology	Organi-zation	Human Relations
What rate of change do you expect?							
Very slow	0.0	0.0	0.0	0.0	0.0	0.0	0.0
Slow	5.1	0.0	0.0	0.0	0.0	0.0	40.0
Moderate	30.8	12.5	37.5	50.0	0.0	60.0	20.0
Rapid	38.5	0.0	50.0	50.0	60.0	40.0	40.0
Very rapid	25.6	87.5	12.5	0.0	40.0	0.0	0.0
Total	100.0	100.0	100.0	100.0	100.0	100.0	100.0
Will change be too rapid?							
Too slow	0.0	0.0	0.0	0.0	0.0	0.0	0.0
Slow	23.1	12.5	25.0	37.5	0.0	0.0	60.0
Moderate	43.6	12.5	50.0	50.0	40.0	100.0	20.0
Rapid	25.6	62.5	12.5	12.5	40.0	0.0	20.0
Too rapid	7.7	12.5	12.5	0.0	20.0	0.0	0.0
Total	100.0	100.0	100.0	100.0	100.0	100.0	100.0

Note: The percentage of interviewees endorsing the indicated position is based on responses from the interviewees at eight large and five small companies.

Source: Compiled by the author.

TABLE 3-7
INTERVIEWEES' ASSESSMENT OF MANAGERIAL
ABILITY OF CORPORATE MANAGERS IN THE NEXT
TEN YEARS
(In Percentage)

	Total	*Large Firms*	*Small Firms*
Will corporate managers be different?			
Much better	41.7	37.5	50.0
Better	41.7	37.5	50.0
Same	16.6	25.0	0.0
Bad	0.0	0.0	0.0
Worse	0.0	0.0	0.0
Total	100.0	100.0	100.0

Note: The percentage of interviewees endorsing the indicated position is based on responses from eight large and four small companies.

Source: Compiled by the author.

majority of the interviewees did not consider the anticipated change in technology "too rapid." This implies that for them the rapid technological change does not pose a managerial problem to any significant degree. Yet, the respondents considered the expected changes in organization and human relations "moderate" to "slow." Especially at the small firms, 60 percent of the respondents considered the anticipated change in human relations "slow." In general, it is true that changes involving human aspects are slower than technological changes.

The interviewees were also asked to predict the managerial ability of corporate managers in the next ten years. Their responses, in a five-point scale ranging from "much better" to "worse," are summarized in Table 3-7. The majority of the respondents had a positive assessment that managerial ability of corporate managers would improve in the next ten years. In other words, their view was that the future managers would have to be equipped with strong managerial skills in order to cope with complex business environments expected in the future. In fact, the interviewees expected the improved managerial ability as a necessary condition for future corporate success rather than being simply optimistic about the future. With this information on the 15 companies and the interviewees as a background, the remaining chapters attempt to answer the research problems and objectives stated earlier.

4 THE INVESTMENT DECISION-MAKING PROCESS

This chapter reports the research findings on the process of investment decision making of the 15 Japanese companies interviewed. The chapter is divided into three sections: the initiating forces, the feasibility study, and entry strategies and decisions. The objective here is to probe into such questions as how the opportunity or the urgency of direct investment in U.S. manufacturing was brought to the attention of the top management at the home office, what rationales for such investment were raised and considered relevant, who participated in the feasibility study, what type of information was gathered during the investigation, on what decision rules the final decision to invest was based, and how the final decision was reached at the level of the firm.

Eight of the nine large Japanese parent companies had more than one manufacturing plant in the United States. Another large and all of the six small Japanese parent firms had only one manufacturing plant in the United States. In two of these latter cases, some on-site expansion of manufacturing facilities had taken place. In addition to the product lines in the high-technology industries as defined in Chapter 3, these manufacturing plants were engaging in manufacturing or assemblying of various product lines, including color TV sets, audio equipment, industrial chemicals, and other consumer and industrial components and products.

Questions regarding the investment decision-making process were addressed to the interviewees in the form of a questionnaire for their companies' initial and most recent, where applicable, direct manufacturing investments in the United States. Therefore, 15 initial and

41

8 most recent direct manufacturing investments in the United States by the 15 Japanese companies were examined. Personal interviews supplemented and expanded their answers to the questionnaire. The findings are presented here with discussions in light of other related research studies.

THE INITIATING FORCES

This section discusses who proposed the possibility of direct manufacturing investment in the United States and with what reasons. The section is divided into two subsections: the source of the investment proposal and the reasons for direct manufacturing investment.

The Source of the Investment Proposal

The genesis of a suggestion for a possible manufacturing investment in the United States can be difficult to pinpoint. Aharoni, in his study of the foreign direct investment decision processes of U.S. firms, encountered such difficulty in identifying the initiating forces:

> In any specific case it is generally very difficult, if not impossible, to pin down one reason for a decision to look abroad, or to find out precisely who was the initiator of a project. The decision results from a chain of events, incomplete information, activities of different persons (not necessarily in connection with the particular project), and a combination of several motivating forces, some of them working in favor of such a decision, some against it. . . . The impact of any one of these forces depends on the social system it encounters. It depends on various feelings and social and organizational structures, on previous events in the company's history, and on other problem areas facing the company at the time this force is encountered.[1]

The Japanese companies also reacted to various forces that had originated from different sources at different times. In six of the nine large firms interviewed, a possibility of direct manufacturing investment was, in general, proposed by the middle management from the product-based division (*Jigyobu,* a decentralized division based on a particular group of product lines — explained in detail in Chapter 5) at the headquarters in Japan. At one of these firms, however, the corporate president with a strong will initiated its first manufacturing investment in the United States. At one other of these six companies, the initial investment was originated at its marketing division and the most recent investment at its product-based division.

At one large company, other than the six large firms mentioned earlier, both the initial and most recent direct investment opportunities were communicated to the home office by a Japanese managing director stationed in the United States. Since this managing director cannot attend a regular meeting of the Council of Managing Directors (*Jomukai*) at the headquarters office in Japan, he maintains a close person-to-person communications link with another managing director residing in Japan. At this company, therefore, investment opportunities in the United States are generally filtered through this transpacific communications linkage. At one remaining large firm, the initial investment was proposed by a Japanese engineer living in the United States, and the most recent investment was originated and implemented by the sales subsidiary in the United States.

On the other hand, in most of the six small firms, the initiating forces came generally from the top management. In two of these firms, as was true at one large company cited earlier for its initial investment, the top management became strongly committed to the idea of local production so that the decision to invest was, technically, made even before the feasibility study was carried out. The actual investigation in these cases was, therefore, used to justify the top management's desire to establish a manufacturing base in the United States. At another small company, an investment opportunity in a high-technology venture was brought to the attention of the corporate management by a U.S. entrepreneur.

As stated, the exact sources of the initiating forces were difficult to locate and varied among the companies and also between the initial and the most recent investment of the same firm in some cases. Several factors seemed to be responsible for these variations — for example, the objective of the direct investment (defensive versus aggressive), the structure of domestic and international activities of the company, the personality of the top management (especially that of the corporate chairman and/or president), and other company-specific and product-specific factors. In general, stimuli for manufacturing investments in the United States were received by those individuals at the top- or middle-management level with experiences in international business activities at the headquarters or those engaged in marketing and information-gathering activities in the United States. Then, suggestions for the possibility of direct manufacturing investment were communicated informally to production managers and/or to the other members of the top management. Aside from the initiating force, however, in order for an investment proposal to be considered seriously, the proposal must accompany strong motives and rationales. This point is discussed in the following section.

Reasons for Direct Manufacturing Investment

To find out why the Japanese companies decided to invest in manufacturing operations in the United States, the interviewer requested the respondents to rank the relative importance of 14 possible reasons for their initial and most recent investments, using a four-point scale ranging from "very important" to "not important." Therefore, all of the nine large and the six small firms rated the relative importance of the 14 items for their initial U.S. manufacturing plants; in addition, eight of the nine large companies rated for their most recent manufacturing plants.

Those items not considered during the investment decision-making process were assigned the same score as "not important." In addition to the 14 possible reasons, the interviewees were asked to specify other reasons considered important for their investments, if any. Only one large company indicated another "very important" reason — this Japanese company could not export to the United States the product it currently manufactures at its U.S. plant prior to the establishment of this plant due to its contractural agreement with its U.S. distributor. Table 4-1 summarizes the ratings of the 14 possible reasons for direct manufacturing investments in the United States by the 15 Japanese investors in terms of average, rather than normalized scores.[2]

As expected, reasons for direct manufacturing investment in the United States varied in importance, depending on particular conditions and situations at the level of the firm. In most cases, an investment proposal was considered in light of multiple reasons. One or two dominant reasons often translated into a specific mission of the investment and affected the mode of investment. In turn, the mission of the manufacturing venture affected the structural linkage between the home office and the U.S. manufacturing plant. This last point on the structural linkage will be discussed in the next chapter.

As can be observed from the average ratings for all 14 items, the large firms tended to consider more items as important reasons for their

TABLE 4-1
REASONS FOR DIRECT MANUFACTURING INVESTMENTS IN THE UNITED STATES

		Average Rating		
				Small
		Large Firms		*Firms*
Reason	*Total*	*Recent*	*Initial*	*Initial*
Number of cases	23.00	8.00	9.00	6.00
Look for the large U.S. market	3.35	3.50	3.56	2.83
Establish closer relations with customers in the United States	3.17	3.13	3.44	2.83
Secure access to technology	2.39	2.25	2.11	3.00
Overcome trade restrictions	2.39	2.50	2.78	1.67
Take advantage of currency fluctuations	2.04	1.88	2.33	1.83
Diversify risks	2.00	2.25	2.00	1.17
Look for political stability	2.00	2.13	1.89	2.00
Look for a well-established infrastructure	2.00	2.00	1.78	2.33
Save shipping cost	1.65	1.88	1.67	1.33
Follow competitors	1.52	1.63	1.44	1.50
Save land cost	1.43	1.63	1.33	1.33
Secure access to raw materials	1.35	1.63	1.22	1.17
Secure access to capital	1.26	1.63	1.11	1.00
Save labor cost	1.17	1.25	1.11	1.17
Total average rating	1.95	2.12	1.98	1.80

Note: The average ratings are based on a four-point scale: 4 = very important, 3 = important, 2 = less imporant, and 1 = not important or not considered.

Source: Compiled by the author.

investments than did the small companies, and they had more multiple reasons for their most recent investments than for their initial investments, with the average ratings of 2.12 for the most recent investments and 1.98 for the initial investments of the large firms compared to the average rating of 1.80 for the initial investments of the small firms. Major reasons for investments are discussed further here, integrating responses from the questionnaire and the personal interviews. The personal interviews were in fact instrumental in uncovering reasons for particular responses to the questionnaire.

The large market size of the United States was considered as the most important reason by the majority of the companies interviewed. Out of the 23 initial and most recent investments, 19 were motivated by this factor as one of the "very important" or "important" reasons. In three of ten technology-seeking investments, which will be discussed later, this factor was not a major concern at all.

A large market is an indication of potential for generating ample profits; it also provides an investing firm a margin of error in estimating production volume. The large market size is also critically important for those companies that depend more on economies of scale in production than on unique product differentiation. As Yoshino observed: "For firms in mature oligopolies, the most serious entry barrier was in the form of scale. As a first condition, therefore, to investing in the United States, an enterprise had to have a substantial enough market position there to enable it to produce on a large scale."[3]

However, the market can also be served by exporting rather than by local production. Therefore, the real reasons that compelled these firms to start manufacturing in the United States must be something other than the market size alone. Although market potential is a necessary condition for a successful business venture, it may not be a primary force for a firm to establish a manufacturing plant in a foreign country.

Most of the firms considered establishment of close customer relations as a primary reason for their direct manufacturing investments in the United States. In fact, 18 manufacturing plants were established due to this reason coupled with some other reasons. One large company, which embarked on full-scale manufacturing operations in high-technology products in the United States, explained its conviction that it would be able to enjoy the same locational advantages as its competitors in the United States. Here, one important advantage is direct market stimuli for product development and technological innovations through its manufacturing presence and close interactions with its customers.

A close customer relationship is an important factor in both maintaining and expanding the firm's market share, especially in nonstandardized and technology-intensive products. Because the needs of customers change constantly and competition is keen within the U.S. market, a quick response to such changes will determine success or failure of the company's market penetration. After-sale services, replacement of parts, technical assistance, modification of product designs to suit the customer needs, and so on, all become an integral part of marketing products. Such close attention to customer needs cannot be attained effectively through exports from a distant place.

Securing access to technologies was one of the compelling reasons for Japanese direct investments in 10 out of 23 U.S. manufacturing plants surveyed. Franko also noted this motivational factor among European multinationals for their direct manufacturing investments in the United States.[4] Some anecdotes about those Japanese investors with this investment reason are provided next.

The initial investment of one large firm was an equity participation in a new manufacturing venture originally conceived by a U.S. engineer who was a technical director of a U.S. company at the time. This U.S. firm was a contractor to the U.S. National Aeronautics and Space Administration (NASA) and was experiencing shortage of funds to continue product development because of the budget cuts by the U.S. federal government in the late 1960s. The engineer had a vision of establishing a corporation with a superior technology on his own but lacked capital to pursue his own venture independently. He brought his plan to the attention of his one-time college professor, a Japanese engineer then residing in the United States as a section chief of the Japanese company. These two engineers conducted a preliminary study on whether or not the plan would be feasible for business and convinced themselves of its future potential.

With his strong belief in the project, the Japanese engineer proposed the investment plan to the middle management of the Japanese firm. No action on the proposal was taken by the Japanese management. The engineer reasoned that the middle management was not able to understand his investment proposal, since the technology involved in the project was too advanced for the Japanese market and did not seem to fit for mass production. Then, he approached the top management at the corporate headquarters. At this time, his proposal was readily accepted, since the top management had been looking for some new technologies. A meeting was held among the parties involved in Tokyo, and four months later a new corporation was formed in the United States with 43 percent of the equity capital provided by the Japanese corporation.

A similar story was noted during the interview with one small company. In this case, a U.S. entrepreneur approached the corporate executive with his idea of a new venture in production of advanced electronic components. As this Japanese firm was implementing its corporate strategy of diversification into high-technology business, the top management responded positively to this outside investment proposal.

At another small company, a chain of events, which led this firm to establish a manufacturing base in the United States, occurred rapidly in a short period of time. This corporation initially sold its electronic instruments in the United States through a large Japanese trading company. However, it became increasingly dissatisfied with the trading company's inability to provide accurate and timely feedback of information on the needs of its U.S. customers. To solve this problem, the top management decided to establish the company's own sales arm in the United States. In the late 1970s, a representative office was opened as an information-gathering post on the West Coast. One year later, a sales subsidiary was incorporated. Then, within a few years, the subsidiary started assembly operations on the premises. This Japanese firm has been trying to capitalize on its manufacturing presence in the United States. It recruited some U.S. engineers and managers for its U.S. plant and started a program of sending its young employees from the home office in Japan to the U.S. subsidiary for management-training purposes.

One large company acquired a 100 percent ownership interest in an existing U.S. firm. One of the primary reasons cited by this firm for acquisition was to diversify its own business into new product lines developed by the acquired firm. A Japanese managing director stationed in the United States spotted the opportunity to acquire the U.S. firm, whose product lines generally complemented those of the Japanese corporation. Therefore, the acquisition would also make it possible for these two firms to cooperate on R & D activities. Furthermore, it would serve another purpose in this case: Because the Japanese company had not been dependent on exports in the past (it had an export-dependency rate of less than 10 percent), it had not developed a strong marketing force in the United States. The acquisition of this medium-sized U.S. firm enabled the Japanese corporation to obtain quickly a direct market access in the United States.

In addition to the technology-seeking manufacturing plants, four of the nine large Japanese companies have already established their subsidiaries that specialize in R & D activities in the United States. Since U.S. firms are increasingly reluctant to license their technologies to Japanese firms,[5] more and more Japanese firms will likely move to establish R & D and/or manufacturing bases in the United States. Several major Japanese firms other than those interviewed have also started or have been contemplating establishing research laboratories and plants in order to overcome U.S. moves for a technological blockage against Japan.[6]

Trade restrictions (or anticipated trade frictions) were cited as a primary reason for direct manufacturing investments in the United States by some of the large firms interviewed. Trade disputes have been growing stronger between Japan and the United States since the late 1960s, although the points of contention have been changing from textiles in the earlier days to automobiles and then to semiconductors in recent years.[7] Since Japan is more politically and economically dependent on the United States than vice versa, Japanese firms tend to become oversensitive to the threat of closing the U.S. market from their exports. This insecurity tends to be further aggravated by constant reporting on Japanese-U.S. bilateral economic frictions by Japanese newspapers and other media. To ameliorate the bilateral relations, some Japanese companies and business leaders have become increasingly involved with public relations activities in the United States. This point will be discussed further in Chapter 6.

A trade dispute in semiconductors was anticipated in the late 1970s, and so two of the large companies decided to begin manufacturing in the United States. One of these firms initially started assembly operations with a limited scale but recently made a decision to establish a vertically integrated (full-scale) manufacturing plant, with a stated belief that assemblying was not enough to forestall the protectionist sentiment in the United States.

"Buy American" practices exist at all levels in the United States — local, state, and federal. However, they have not been increasing at the federal level since the conclusion of the Tokyo Round of Multilateral Trade Negotiations in the late 1970s. The Japan-U.S. Businessmen's Conference brought up this subject in its annual meeting in July 1984 and noted that

> the Federal Buy American Act requires some government agencies to purchase domestic products even if they are 6 percent more expensive than the imports (12 percent differential in high unemployment areas, and 50 percent if national security items are involved). Thirty-six U.S. states have some kinds of Buy American policies or practices and in five of them, purchase of foreign-made steel or some other specific products is virtually banned.[8]

One large company, which supplies electronic components to U.S. customers, cited the Buy American practice at the industry level as one of its primary reasons for the decision to invest in U.S. manufacturing. According to the interviewee, products to be manufactured locally would have "Made in U.S.A." labels and thus become acceptable to U.S. customers.

Trade restrictions or frictions were not cited as a reason for investment by any of the small companies. However, during the interview, one corporate executive of a small firm also mentioned a Buy American campaign he had observed at a trade convention in the United States in the mid-1970s. He had certainly been intimidated by the organized campaign and had begun to consider it necessary to start some sort of local production in order to market his company's products in the United States.

The Japanese yen was revalued in a significant way after the collapse of the Bretton Woods Agreement in the early 1970s. This and subsequent revaluations narrowed the gap in production costs between Japan and the United States. Combined with the oil shocks in the 1970s and the resultant double-digit inflation in Japan, prices of certain natural resources and energy became considerably cheaper in the United States than in Japan. Some of the large and small firms interviewed, especially those with a strong conviction in the idea of establishing a manufacturing plant in the United States, were able to justify their investment plans owing to a substantial increase in the value of the yen under the current flexible exchange system.

As the Japanese yen gets stronger vis-à-vis the U.S. dollar, products manufactured in Japan and shipped to the United States become less price competitive. One large company mentioned an advantage of having a U.S. manufacturing plant in such a case. Depending on the conversion rate, the company would be able to adjust production volume between the headquarters and its U.S. subsidiary's plants to mitigate the effect of currency fluctuations.

The other reasons for direct investment listed in Table 4-1 were considered secondary by the majority of the firms. However, it should be noted that six large companies considered international diversification of business risk as an "important" reason for their nine investments in U.S. manufacturing. Two of these firms meant the diversification in terms of their product lines, and the other four companies in terms of their manufacturing bases. This may imply that these companies began to draw up their supply (production) strategies on a global basis and, thus, are beginning to resemble major U.S. multinational corporations.

THE FEASIBILITY STUDY

Feasibility studies were carried out in a varying degree of thoroughness with different objectives and involved various personnel of the firms interviewed. At one large company, for example, a preliminary investigation was performed at the product-based division at the home office, and then a written proposal was submitted to the top management. After the proposal was reviewed and accepted at the Board of Directors' meeting (*Torishimariyakukai*), a project team was formed to draw up an operational plan.

At another large company, the corporate president had a strong determination to open a local maufacturing plant in the United States. In the late 1960s, he instructed a production manager at the home office and the company's U.S. subisidiary to conduct jointly an investigation on whether or not local production would be feasible. The result of the study was negative due to the expected high costs of production in the United States. A study report was submitted to the Jomukai (the Council of Managing Directors) at the home office in Japan. Despite the negative prospect, the president and the chairman of the company, both of whom were founder-executives, did not give up their plan. Another investigation followed to find a way to implement the plan.

Two large firms reported that their feasibility studies had been performed solely by their sales subsidiaries in the United States. At one of these large companies, the president of the sales subsidiary (a Japanese director transferred from the headquarters) went further and set up an assembly plant in the United States without a proper notice to the headquarters plant affected by such assembly operations. Because the production plant at the home office depended on export sales of finished products and was operating under a rigid production schedule, the plant manager and other employees did not welcome the sales subsidiary's requisition orders of intermediate products for assemblying in the United States. This created some animosity and ill-feeling against the U.S. subsidiary on the part of the employees at the headquarters plant — a situation was not resolved until a few years later, when the top management at the home office subjected the U.S. manufacturing plant to the product-based division, the Jigyobu, at the headquarters through restructuring the ownership and control relationship among the home office, the U.S. sales subsidiary, and the U.S. manufacturing plant. This point will be taken up again in the next chapter on structural linkage and the control system.

At another large firm, a Japanese managing director stationed in the United States carried out feasibility studies on both the initial startup manufacturing venture and the most recent acquisition of a U.S. firm. A team of three Japanese engineers assisted him in evaluating the technical aspects of the acquired company.

In most of the remaining large firms, however, the feasibility study was undertaken by a project team. Since the direct manufacturing investment in these cases involved a large amount of capital and, thus, required a careful analysis from various angles, this form of investigation was a logical way of dealing with the decision problem. Typically such a project team was composed of five to ten individuals gathered from such functional fields as production, sales, accounting and finance, and corporate planning. These members of the project team from the headquarters were joined by some key employees at the sales subsidiary in the United States.

The type of information gathered throughout this investigation stage varied significantly depending on the mode of entry — acquisition or startup. There were three cases of acquisitions among the 23 cases examined. In these three cases of acquisitions, the major concern was in assessing the level of technology of the target company. Engineers from the home office, or a patent specialist in one case, investigated the product and process technologies as well as the quality of the labor force of the target company. The target company's records were also checked for any outstanding lawsuits or significant legal claims. During the process of investigation, the Japanese investors were also concerned about the market share of the target company's products, including the potential ability of the company's marketing force and the future market prospect of the products. In these cases of acquisitions of U.S. firms, the Japanese investors relied on U.S. investment bankers for much of their information and technical services rather than on the Japanese banks doing business in the United States. Because corporate acquisitions have rarely taken place in Japan, the Japanese banks have not yet developed expertise in this area.

For startups, the foremost concern of the majority of the firms interviewed was labor-related issues, including quality and availability of engineers, level of union activity, and past records on management-employee relations in a particular locality within the United States. In contrast to their familiar ground in Japan, where loyalty of employees to the company is almost assured under the socially evolved permanent employment system, these Japanese firms see as a major problem the management of non-Japanese employees with different personal values in a multiracial society. They are also apprehensive about how to maintain the reputation of good-quality products earned through conscious efforts in perfecting their process technologies, as they have earned at home in the past.

Other factors most frequently analyzed during the investigation stage were the market size for the products to be manufactured, total capital requirements for the investment (including expenditures during the development stage of a new company), infrastructure of a community, tax and other incentives to be granted for investment, and existence of subcontractors for procurement of intermediate products and supplies. In the case of startup ventures, the company's own technology level was also reassessed to see if it would be suitable and viable for local production. For those firms contemplating direct manufacturing investments in production of semiconductors, for example, an adequate infrastructure of a local community meant ample supply of clean water and electric power as well as good roads leading to a nearby airport.

Most of the firms interviewed were also concerned about whether a particular local community had a welcoming attitude toward their direct investments. Based on local reactions to some recent Japanese direct investments in the United States reported by correspondents of a major Japanese business newspaper company, Ishizuka lists three major concerns for the Japanese investors: local people may fear that the Japanese may be beginning to invade U.S. industries; Japanese employment practices may be seen as stressing too much company loyalty and discipline; and Japanese are seen as foreigners, but Europeans are not.[9]

During the feasibility study, information was also collected from outside parties. Some firms sought location-specific information from Japanese banks, mainly the Bank of Tokyo, doing business in the United States. Other Japanese firms, which had already established their manufacturing plants in the United States, were also consulted to seek information on their experiences. In addition, three companies hired either U.S. consulting firms or individuals as consultants in order to obtain location-specific information.

Typically the feasibility study lasted from 6 to 12 months. Generally a formal report of the feasibility study was prepared and submitted to the top management for reviews and deliberations. In the report, the planning horizon for the possible investment was set at a minimum of three years and a maximum of ten years, and in the majority of the firms it was set at five years.

ENTRY STRATEGIES AND DECISION MAKING

Several strategic decisions must be made with regard to which products are to be manufactured, what production processes are to be selected, what mode of entry (startup or acquisition) is to be used, what level of ownership control is to be pursued, and how the U.S. manufacturing plant is to be linked structurally to the entire corporate system. At the companies interviewed, these and other related strategic decisions were typically made at different points in time during the entire decision-making process for direct manufacturing investment.

Another question remained to be answered: Who made the decision to invest? Did all the companies use bottom-up decision making? Did they consult their affiliated firms for their decisions to invest in U.S. manufacturing? Did they receive any type of administrative guidance from the Japanese government?

To answer the questions, this section is divided into five subsections: selection of product lines and production process, mode of entry and ownership structure, location decision, decision rules, and locus of decision making. Selection of the control system will be discussed in the next chapter, which examines the corporate structure at the headquarters level and its structural linkage with the U.S. manufacturing plant.

Selection of Product Lines and Production Process

In an attempt to find out the corporate decision regarding selection of product lines and production process for the U.S. manufacturing plant, each firm was asked to compare the nature of its manufacturing operations in the United States with that of its domestic and other overseas manufacturing plants. Products being manufactured at the U.S. manufactuing plants and at the other overseas plants were compared with those at the headquarters plants. The comparison was made in terms of their position in the life cycle of products, that is, more mature, newer, or the same. Likewise, production processes at the parent and the subsidiaries were compared in terms of the means of production, that is, capital intensiveness and labor intensiveness. In addition, the interviewees were also requested to compare the skill level of labor as well as the productivity of the manufacturing plants at both parent and subsidiaries in the same fashion.

It is somewhat difficult to compare overall characteristics of domestic and overseas manufacturing plants in general terms, especially in the case of a large firm with a variety of product lines. However, gaining even a rough idea of some comparative differences seems warranted, since a decision on what and how to produce is a crucial point in the decision-making process for foreign direct manufacturing investment. Table 4-2 summarizes the responses to these questions.

Six large and three small firms reported that products being manufactured at their U.S. plants were in the same stage in the product life cycle as those at their headquarters' plants in Japan. Two large companies and one small firm reported that their U.S. plants were manufacturing products in the more mature stage in comparison to their headquarters' plants. At two U.S. manufacturing plants owned separately by two small firms, even newer products than those in Japan were being manufactured.

All of the large corporations and three of the six small firms had manufacturing plants overseas in addition to their U.S. plants. In comparison with the products manufactured at these other overseas plants, these companies, with the exception of one large firm whose comparative data were not available, reported that their U.S. plants were manufacturing products at the newer or the same stage in the product life cycle.

Comparison of production processes generally matched with that of the products manufactured. The majority of the companies, which started up manufacturing plants in the United States on their own, reported no difference in production processes between their headquarters' and U.S. subsidiaries' plants. In comparison with their other overseas manufacturing plants, some reported that their U.S. plants were more capital intensive.

These variances in the nature of products and production processes among the parent, the U.S., and the other overseas manufacturing plants seem to relate mainly to the timing of the investments and wage differentials among the countries where the plants are located. The majority of the companies began their overseas manufacturing investments in mature products in developing countries in Asia and Latin America in the 1960s and early 1970s. Their manufacturing investments in the United States were undertaken subsequent to their investment in the developing countries. At this time, more automated, capital-intensive production processes became available. More importantly, introduction of such labor-saving production processes was a necessary condition to

TABLE 4-2
MANUFACTURING PLANTS IN THE UNITED STATES COMPARED WITH THOSE IN JAPAN AND OTHER COUNTRIES IN TERMS OF PRODUCTS, PRODUCTION PROCESS, LABOR, AND PRODUCTIVITY
(In Percentage)

At U.S. Manufacturing Plants	Total		Large Firms		Small Firms	
	Japan	Others	Japan	Others	Japan	Others
Products						
Newer	14.3	35.7	0.0	37.5	33.3	33.3
Same	64.3	35.7	75.0	50.0	50.0	16.7
More mature	21.4	0.0	25.0	0.0	16.7	0.0
Unknown	0.0	28.6	0.0	12.5	0.0	50.0
Total	100.0	100.0	100.0	100.0	100.0	100.0
Production Processes						
More capital intensive	7.1	42.9	0.0	62.5	16.7	16.7
Same	64.3	21.4	75.0	12.5	50.0	33.3
More labor intensive	28.6	7.1	25.0	12.5	33.3	0.0
Unknown	0.0	28.6	0.0	12.5	0.0	50.0
Total	100.0	100.0	100.0	100.0	100.0	100.0
Labor						
More Skilled	7.1	21.4	0.0	25.0	16.7	16.7
Same	57.2	42.9	50.0	62.5	66.7	16.7
Less skilled	28.6	0.0	50.0	0.0	0.0	0.0
Unknown	7.1	35.7	0.0	12.5	16.7	66.7
Total	100.0	100.0	100.0	100.0	100.1*	100.1*
*Productivity***						
Better	7.1	14.3	0.0	12.5	16.7	16.7
Same	21.5	42.9	25.0	62.5	16.7	16.7
Worse	64.3	7.1	75.0	12.5	50.0	0.0
Unknown	7.1	35.7	0.0	12.5	16.7	66.7
Total	100.0	100.0	100.0	100.0	100.1*	100.1*

*Due to rounding errors.

**In terms of labor productivity — production volume per man hour.

Note: The table summarizes the percentage of companies endorsing the indicated position, based on responses from eight large and six small companies.

Source: Compiled by the author.

maintain a competitive edge in the United States, where labor costs were high in general.

From the foregoing observations, it can be hypothesized that the more recent the investments, the more highly automated the production processes to be installed in order to assure product quality and to save labor-related costs. The selection decision also seems to relate to the Japanese perception regarding the quality of the labor force in the United States. This point will be discussed later in conjunction with the interviewees' perception regarding the skill of local employees and the productivity of U.S. manufacturing operations.

In some cases, comparison became complex. One large company reported, for example, that its U.S. plants (engaged in production of apparatus for medical use and synthetic chemicals on a small scale) were employing more labor-intensive methods of production than its highly capital-intensive plants for petrochemical production in Japan. One small company mentioned that its U.S. plant, a startup venture with a U.S. entrepreneur, was manufacturing custom integrated circuits (ICs) and was therefore more labor intensive (in skilled labor) than its highly automated plants in Japan.

One large firm commented that in today's competitive international markets, a corporation would not be able to survive by manufacturing mature products anywhere in the world. According to another large firm, a strong competition among Japanese manufacturers exists even within the United States. These competitive pressures would certainly compel many Japanese corporations to introduce new or improved products quickly. Their overseas manufacturing plants would also seem to be adjusted upward in products and production processes in order to meet these challenges in a rapid pace.

Regarding the skill of local employees and the productivity of U.S. manufacturing operations, the perception of the interviewees varied. About half of the Japanese companies reported that the skill of workers was approximately the same among their manufacturing plants in Japan, the United States, and other parts of the world. However, four large firms reported that the skill level of U.S. employees was lower than that of Japanese employees. Furthermore, six large and three small companies reported that they had been experiencing low productivity at their U.S. manufacturing plants.

In the case of one large firm that employs mostly Mexican Americans at its California plant, only 80 percent of the standard productivity in its Japanese plant was attained at its California plant using identical equipment. Another large firm noted a significant motivational problem in U.S. workers and their general attitudes toward the job in comparison with their Japanese counterparts, who normally identify personally with their company and are motivated for perfection in their assigned jobs. To avoid these production problems associated with U.S. workers, many of these firms have already installed labor-saving equipment or are planning to move ahead with more capital-intensive manufacturing operations in the United States.

Several research studies reported a similar difference in perception among Japanese companies with regard to the quality of U.S. labor and the productivity of U.S. manufacturing plants. For example, based on the questionnaire survey of 39 Japanese affiliates in the United States in 1979, the Nikko Research Center reported as follows:

> With regard to the productivity and efficiency of workers, questions were posed in the categories of skilled and unskilled labor. In the first category, 28 percent replied that it was similar to Japan, 56 percent said it was slightly lower and 10 percent thought it was slightly higher. For the latter category, however, only 18 percent thought it was similar to Japan, 54 percent slightly lower and 26 percent considerably lower, indicating an unusually low assessment. As a result, their overall judgment of American labor costs, taking the productivity into consideration, showed that 39 percent thought . . . [they were] slightly more expensive than in Japan, 31 percent about the same and 21 percent slightly cheaper.[10]

Kujawa conducted an interview survey in 1980 and 1981 with nine Japanese-owned manufacturing companies in the United States. He reported the Japanese interviewees' comparative assessment of workers in the United States and those at the parent in Japan as follows:

> [Six companies] felt their U.S. workers compared favorably with those in Japan on both a quality and quantity basis. . . . [Two firms} were pleased with their labor productivity "comparisons" and noted that, with more experience, their U.S. workers would likely pull up to the Japanese productivity-wise. Only [one company] reported a large productivity difference between its plant and a parent's plant in Japan. It was confident, however, that the gap could be narrowed via improved equipment and workers' efforts. All in all, the information presented here display a fairly positive experience with U.S. workers.[11]

The Japan External Trade Organization (JETRO), a nonprofit organization founded by the Japanese government, also conducted a field survey of 238 Japanese-owned U.S. manufacturing plants and operations between September 1980 and March 1981. It reported some comments as follows:

> In comparison with Japanese workers, the differences between excellent and run-of-the-mill employees are very pronounced. While there are more really excellent workers than in Japan, there are also many workers that simply are of no use. . . . There are considerable geographical differences in regard to the quality of labor. Specifically, quality was generally rated high in the north Atlantic states, the midwest and the Pacific northwest. In contrast, blue collar labor in the southern Pacific coast area was generally regarded as less productive. . . . Thus, overall, there was no major dissatisfaction regarding the quality of labor. Even in the few cases where labor quality was termed "poor", productivity was rated as between 70 and 80 percent of Japanese workers. This assessment, in fact, applied for all regions.[12]

In general, therefore, the findings of the current research support the other research findings cited earlier. However, as will be discussed later, quality of labor was a major factor in location decisions of the 15 companies interviewed for this study.

One small firm has been pursuing a positive gain from employment of skilled engineers at its U.S. manufacturing plant. With the help of headhunters in the United States, the company hired a few selected engineers with advanced skills at its U.S. manufacturing plant. The management objective was to manufacture newer products with better productivity, utilizing those highly skilled U.S. engineers. According to the executive of the firm interviewed, it tends to be rather difficult for small firms to attract the best-quality engineers in Japan and because of the particular employment practices and system prevailing in Japan (permanent employment, seniority system, paternalism, etc.), a Japanese company is normally expected to retain even unproductive and unskilled workers hired in the past. In contrast, labor markets in the United States are well developed and flexible. The Japanese executive finds them quite practical and pragmatic.

In relation to the selection decision on products and production processes, several large corporations mentioned that a major problem that remained to be solved would be how to compensate for not being able to take advantage of scale economies in overseas manufacturing ventures. One large firm explained, for example, a dilemma it encountered when it was studying the feasibility of a manufacturing venture in the United States. At this company, a major impetus for direct investment in U.S.

manufacturing was triggered by a rising protectionist sentiment in the United States. The international division at the home office recognized the need for local production in order to defend the company's position in the U.S. market. However, the product-based division at the headquarters was unwilling to undertake the manufacturing venture in the United States. Because the division was operating as a profit center and had a strong belief that manufacturing in Japan was most cost effective, it had an intense desire to produce at its headquarters' plants in Japan. The major questions to be answered by this company were, therefore, what scale of production would be appropriate and to what extent the local production should be vertically integrated in order to alleviate the trade frictions.

In summary, the strategies of the Japanese companies with regard to their selection of products and production processes are intricately related to their reasons for direct investment. In the case of a defensive investment induced by trade frictions, products to be manufactured are given, but the decision with regard to the volume of production and the level of production processes has to be made carefully. Selection of production processes is likely to be affected by the quality, the availability, and the cost of labor. In the case of investments in market-sensitive products, though, product selection becomes a major issue. This is also true in the case of direct investments motivated by the company's desire to diversify into new lines of business.

Mode of Entry and Ownership Structure

In the majority of the firms interviewed, startup was a preferred mode of entry into U.S. manufacturing. However, the investment decision was not made as a choice between startup and acquisition. Rather, each opportunity of either startup or acquisition was evaluated and decided upon separately as presented to the attention of the management. Furthermore, the investment objective was somewhat different between the two modes of entry.

Of 23 manufacturing plants surveyed, three cases are acquisitions. All three plants were acquired separately by three large companies. In addition to the plants surveyed in the questionnaire, as revealed by personal interviews two of the other large firms had acquired U.S. electronics companies in the same year they built their initial manufacturing plants in the United States. One of these large corporations, which has been expanding its manufacturing presence in the United States through startup ventures in recent years, explained that one of the major objectives of the acquisition was to learn U.S. management style, especially in human resources management.

In contrast, the objectives of the other companies in their acquisitions of existing U.S. firms were related mainly to the product technologies of the acquired firms. Seven of the nine large firms stated that startup was their basic policy in their direct foreign manufacturing investments. Acquisitions of U.S. corporations by some of these seven large companies were exceptions to the rule. None of the small firms acquired any existing U.S. companies. For them, as a corporate executive of one small company put it, acquisition was out of the question.

One large company, which acquired as its most recent investment a U.S. firm engaged in the production of electronic components, commented that it would not consider acquisition in the future. One interpretation of this position might be that the Japanese company ran into management problems at its acquired plant. Acquisitions seemed to be satisfactory to the other two firms. Both of these firms did not have a strong marketing force in the United States prior to their investments. The export-dependency ratio of these Japanese companies was about 10 percent, and their acquisitions of the existing U.S. firms were aimed at expansion or diversification of their own business and technological bases. Acquisitions also made it possible for these companies to effectuate a quick entry into U.S. markets. At the time of the decision to acquire an existing U.S. manufacturing plant, factors considered important by the companies were the product technologies and marketing know-how of the target company as well as the total acquisition cost.

For the majority of the firms interviewed, startup offered several advantages over acquisition of an existing U.S. company in establishing their manufacturing base in the United States. These Japanese companies enjoyed, for example, flexibility in location selection, factory layout with a future plan for a possible expansion, and complete control over the amount of initial and subsequent capital expenditures. More importantly, these companies were able to install equipment with production processes familiar to them. Starting from scratch, they could transfer or devise their own management systems with freshly hired U.S. employees. Because these firms had established their own distribution channels earlier through their U.S. sales subsidiaries, they could link their startup manufacturing plants with their sales subsidiaries at ease. These advantages were considered important from the outset of the decision-making process.

Therefore, for these companies startup offered less risk, in terms of organizational control, than did acquisition.

In his interview survey conducted in 1980 and 1981, Kujawa also noted a marked preference for startups over acquisitions among nine Japanese-owned and six non-Japanese foreign-owned manufacturing subsidiaries in the United States. His research revealed that six of the nine Japanese and five of the six non-Japanese foreign-owned case-study companies had startup manufacturing operations in the United States and that three of the six Japanese startup cases expressed their desires to mold company-specific workforce environments.[13]

Although the majority of the 15 firms in the present study preferred the startup form of entry because of multiple reasons cited earlier, the concern over labor management was expressed by some Japanese investors. Among the 15 Japanese firms interviewed for the current study, four large firms stated specifically that through startups they wanted to avoid inheriting past management practices, labor relations, and employees' particular habits of existing U.S. corporations. This preference for startup form of direct investment due to the management concern over employee relations might be uniquely Japanese. In his study mentioned earlier, Kujawa found that "none of the other [non-Japanese] foreign-owned firms noted the startup form was preferred because of the desire to build a company-specific workforce management system."[14]

There was another form of startup venture — a startup venture involving U.S. partners. Three manufacturing plants were established and owned partly and separately by two large companies and one small firm interviewed. In general, these Japanese firms assumed the role of venture capitalists. The main objective of their participation in these ventures was the unique technologies retained by the U.S. partners. One of the large firms stated that the venture was formed to combine two unique technologies developed in Japan and by the U.S. partner.

Of the 15 Japanese companies 14 held, directly or indirectly through their U.S. sales subsidiaries, 100 percent ownership interests in 20 of the 23 U.S. manufacturing plants studied. Included in this figure, three large companies secured 100 percent ownership interests in three U.S. companies acquired separately. The percentage of ownership share in the remaining three U.S. manufacturing plants varied between 30 and 65 percent. The majority of the Japanese companies in the current study, therefore, preferred 100 percent ownership.

In his survey of 2,749 Japanese-owned foreign subsidiaries in 1972, Tsurumi found that the strategy of majority ownership (including wholly owned) was preferred by large-sized Japanese firms and that the objectives of these large Japanese companies rested with consolidation of global activities, which meant parents' control over selection of production schedules and products of overseas subsidiaries, attainment of worldwide consistency in sales policies, and maintenance of secrecy of production processes and sales strategies.[15] Kujawa provides a further insight into the ownership strategy of Japanese investors as follows:

> If future Japanese direct manufacturing investment in the United States is going to become increasingly characterized by followers-turned-innovators . . . the preference for 100 percent ownership should strengthen. One caveat here, however, is that a firm which is following a catch-up strategy in the United States . . . may well trade-off full ownership for an alternative arrangement that buys it much-needed time.[16]

According to census data compiled by the Japan Economic Institute of America, the preference for 100 percent ownership as well as for startup over acquisition varied among those Japanese investors that entered into U.S. manufacturing activities in different industries. (Appendix D shows a summary of the census data on the mode of entry and ownership structure by industry.) Based on the same source of the data, Table 4-3 compares the mode of entry and the ownership structure of 521 U.S. manufacturing plants affiliated with three different categories of Japanese investors: group-member firms, other listed firms, and unlisted firms.

Of the 521 U.S. manufacturing plants owned wholly or partly by Japanese investors at the end of 1983, 263 plants, or 50 percent of the total, were acquisitions, and 289 plants, or 55 percent, were wholly owned. Most of the acquisitions (236, or 90 percent of the total plants acquired) were made by group-member firms and other listed Japanese firms (companies with large corporate size).

The group-member firms had the largest number of manufacturing plants with involvement of U.S. partners: 142 of the total 196 plants, or 72 percent with involvement of U.S. partners. This number includes 91 plants owned by Alumax, Inc., 45 percent of whose ownership shares are owned by a large Japanese company belonging to an industrial group of Zaibatsu origin. However, it can be observed that, excluding these 91 plants from Table 4-3, there is not much difference in the patterns of entry mode and ownership structure among the group-member and the other listed companies.

In general, as Appendix D shows, acquisitions were preferred by those Japanese companies investing in such industries as apparel and

TABLE 4-3
MODE OF ENTRY AND OWNERSHIP STRUCTURE OF
ALL JAPANESE-OWNED U.S. MANUFACTURING
PLANTS BY SIZE AND GROUP AFFILIATION OF
JAPANESE PRIMARY INVESTORS
(As of December 1983)

		Mode of Entry		*Ownership Structure*		
	Total	*Acquisition*	*Startup*	*Wholly Owned*	*Japanese Partner(s) Only*	*U.S.* Partners Involved*
Group member firms	253	154	99	100	11	142
Other listed firms	140	82	58	90	10	40
Unlisted firms	128	27	101	99	15	14
Total	521	263	258	289	36	196

*In the cases of "U.S. Partners Involved," there are two manufacturing plants with involvement of non-Japanese non-U.S. partners.

Source: Compiled from the census data published by Japan Economic Institute of America, Washington, D.C., "Japan's Expanding Manufacturing Presence in the United States: A Profile," April 17, 1981, and "Japan's Expanding Manufacturing Presence: 1983 Update," April 13, 1984.

textile products, chemicals and allied products, and primary and fabricated metals. In these industries, the level of Japanese ownership interest was low and the involvement of U.S. partners was the norm.

In contrast, Japanese corporations investing in the high-technology fields opted for different entry and ownership strategies. Table 4-4 summarizes the mode of entry and the ownership structure of 78 U.S. manufacturing plants in the high-technology industries owned by Japanese investors as of the end of 1983.

As the table reveals, 55 of the total 78 manufacturing plants in the high-technology fields, or 71 percent, were startups. Furthermore, 67 of the total 78 plants, or 86 percent, were wholly owned by Japanese parent companies. The current research findings on the 15 Japanese companies interviewed parallel with this marked preference for startups and 100 percent ownership among the Japanese firms investing in the high-technology industries.

Regarding the issue of the entry strategy (startup versus acquisition), Tsurumi argued as follows:

TABLE 4-4
MODE OF ENTRY AND OWNERSHIP STRUCTURE OF JAPANESE-OWNED U.S. MANUFACTURING PLANTS IN HIGH-TECHNOLOGY INDUSTRIES

| | | Mode of Entry | | Ownership Structure | | |
	Total	Acquisition	Startup	Wholly Owned	Japanese Partner(s) Only	U.S.* Partners Involved
Group member firms	29	5	24	25	0	4
Other listed firms	27	14	13	22	0	5
Unlisted firms	22	4	18	20	1	1
Total	78	23	55	67	1	10

Source: Compiled from the census data published by Japan Economic Institute of America, Washington, D.C., "Japan's Expanding Manufacturing Presence in the United States: A Profile," April 17, 1981, and "Japan's Expanding Manufacturing Presence: 1983 Update," April 13, 1984.

> Japanese firms would be pursuing the acquisition opportunities of U.S. and European firms as an expedient way of entering into a further expansion in the industrialized countries. . . . In particular, in these countries where the public stigma of working for "Japanese firms" still tends to pose difficult hurdles to Japanese investors, acquisitions of on-going concerns "as is" have been preferred by Japanese investors.[17]

The current study, however, did not reveal any evidence supporting his argument among the Japanese companies interviewed. Rather, the majority of the large and small firms expressed their strong preference for startup ventures in the United States, with various reasons cited earlier.

Location Decision

In the case of the acquisition form of entry, not much room is left for a separate location decision. However, selection of a plant site for a startup venture requires systematic considerations of its costs and benefits. The firms interviewed located their startup manufacturing plants in various parts of the United States. Most of the companies located one of their manufacturing plants in California. This is consistent with the census data. Table 4-5 shows location of the 78 U.S. manufacturing plants in the high-technology fields owned by Japanese investors by

TABLE 4-5
LOCATION OF JAPANESE-OWNED U.S. MANUFAC-
TURING PLANTS IN HIGH-TECHNOLOGY INDUSTRIES
(By Mode of Entry)

	Total	*Acquisition*	*Startup*
California	33	13	20
Georgia	6	0	6
New Jersey	5	1	4
Texas	5	1	4
Illinois	3	1	2
New York	3	1	2
Pennsylvania	3	3	0
Connecticut	2	0	2
Maryland	2	0	2
Massachusetts	2	0	2
Minnesota	2	1	1
Missouri	2	1	1
Washington	2	0	2
Alabama	1	0	1
Colorado	1	1	0
Florida	1	0	1
Kansas	1	0	1
Maine	1	0	1
Ohio	1	0	1
Tennessee	1	0	1
Virginia	1	0	1
Total	78	23	55

Source: Compiled from the census data published by Japan Economic Institute of America, Washington, D.C., "Japan's Expanding Manufacturing Presence in the United States: A Profile," April 17, 1981, and "Japan's Expanding Manufacturing Presence: 1983 Update," April 13, 1984.

mode of entry. Of the total 55 startup manufacturing plants, 20, or 36 percent, are located in California.

The interviewees were requested to rate the relative importance of 12 factors deemed to influence location decisions, using a four-point scale ranging from "very important" to "not important." Because location decisions are not applicable to acquisition cases, Table 4-6 summarizes the ratings of these factors only for startup manufacturing investments, including six most recent and eight initial investments by the nine large companies and six initial investments by the small firms.

For the majority of the companies interviewed, quality of labor force, proximity to markets, and lack of labor unionization were three guiding factors in narrowing down the number of possible plant sites in the United States. Although the lack of labor unionization was a "very important" factor for four of the nine large firms, it was not so important for the small companies. This can be expected, since unionization does not generally take place in a small factory.

Costs of land and labor were also major considerations for some firms, but only secondary considerations for the others. The majority of the large firms considered proximity to suppliers as an "important" factor, but that of the small firms did not. This indicates that these large firms intend to procure some materials locally for production at their U.S. manufacturing plants.

Such other factors as quality of life, tax and other investment incentives, and proximity to educational and research institutions were

TABLE 4-6
RELATIVE IMPORTANCE OF FACTORS INFLUENCING LOCATION DECISION

	Average Rating		
	Total	*Large Firms*	*Small Firms*
Number of cases	20.00	14.00	6.00
Quality of labor	3.40	3.64	2.83
Proximity to markets	3.10	3.14	3.00
Labor unionization (lack of)	3.10	3.43	2.33
Cost of land	2.70	2.71	2.67
Cost of labor	2.60	2.57	2.67
Quality of life	2.50	2.64	2.17
Special tax incentives	2.40	2.57	2.00
Proximity to suppliers	2.35	2.64	1.67
Proximity to educational and research institutions	2.30	2.14	2.67
Other state and local government incentives	1.95	2.07	1.67
Proximity to a Japanese community	1.65	1.71	1.50
Proximity to competitors	1.55	1.57	1.50
Total average rating	2.47	2.57	2.22

Note: The average ratings are based on a four-point scale: 4 = very important, 3 = important, 2 = less important, and 1 = not important.

Source: Compiled by the author.

indicated as factors of varying importance by the firms. Proximity to, or distance from, competitors and to a Japanese community was less or not important at all in the location decision.

Recently the Japanese business community made a concerted effort in requesting abolishment of the unitary tax system that had been adopted by more than ten states in the United States. Keidanren prepared a position paper and sent a delegation headed by Akio Morita, chairman of Sony Corporation, to the United States in early 1984.[18] The efforts of the delegation and those of other concerned groups led the states of Oregon, Indiana, Florida, and Illinois to scrap their worldwide unitary taxation systems. Following the official announcements of the abolishment, several major Japanese electronics firms announced their direct manufacturing investments in these states in mid-1984.[19] This type of private diplomacy may increase in the future — a point discussed more fully in Chapter 6.

Decision Rules

A majority of the firms relied on subjective judgments in making their final decisions to undertake their U.S. manufacturing investments, taking into account several quantitative and qualitative factors in varying degrees. Some of the large companies used their corporate standard investment criteria, including demand analysis, economic forecasts, and expected return on investment. Two other large corporations used sensitivity analysis, a mathematical technique designed to incorporate an allowance for uncertainty. A majority of the small firms did not make any explicit quantitative analyses at the time of their initial investments but considered their investments as test cases and set the maximum allowable amount of capital outlays at the time of their go decisions. Furthermore, the Japanese investors typically evaluated their investment projects case by case. They did not make comparative analyses of alternative investments.

A similar finding was noted by Kelly and Philippatos in their study of the foreign investment evaluation practices of 225 U.S.-based manufacturing multinational companies.[20] They found that the majority of the U.S. multinationals seldom compared and ranked foreign investments as advocated in normative microinvestment theory; instead, these companies analyzed each opportunity independently on a project-by-project basis and made a go or no-go decision. They also noted that more than 80 percent of their sample firms used subjective methods to evaluate foreign business risks and that only a limited number of them utilized sensitivity analysis to incorporate probability estimates.

Direct investments in foreign countries present the investors with scores of uncertainties in terms of social, economic, legal, and other culturally related factors. Thus, the actual investment decision-making patterns exhibited by the Japanese companies interviewed for the current study and the U.S. firms studied by Kelly and Philippatos seem to be quite understandable. However, as these companies accumulate knowledge and expertise in doing business abroad, they should become more sophisticated in analyzing various foreign direct investment opportunities. The current research revealed that the larger and more experienced Japanese companies tended to use more elaborate decision rules than did the smaller or less experienced firms.

Typically the Japanese companies proceeded with their U.S. manufacturing operations gradually and cautiously. To reduce the business risks during the first few years of the development stage, some of these firms started their assembly operations on the premises of their sales subsidiaries or by leasing their plant sites. By doing so, they could learn and become familiar with various factors associated with their manufacturing operations in the United States, and they were able to reduce some of the uncertainties inherent in the foreign environment.

Locus of Decision Making

The locus of decision making for the direct manufacturing investments varied among the Japanese companies interviewed. This variation, in general, seemed to have more to do with the personalities of the top management than with the size of the firm. In the case of some of the large and small companies with corporate founders still active as corporate executive officers, the decision tended to be made by these individuals with involvement of a limited number of other executives. In the other cases, the decision was made, more often than not, collectively at a Torishimariyakukai or at a meeting of the Jomukai.

Consensus building was carried out only at the top-management level in the case of five large and four small firms, and among top and upper-middle managements in the case of four large and two small companies. Generally, the upper-middle management was in charge of the product-based division, products of which were under consideration for manufacturing in the United States. Therefore, the locus of decision making was confined largely within the top-level management group with critical information obtained from, and appropriate considerations extended to, the product-based division to be affected by the undertaking of the direct manufacturing investment.

Each company was asked to indicate how long it took to reach the final decision to invest in U.S. manufacturing after the feasibility study had been completed. The amount of time varied from zero to four months. From this fact only, one might conclude that some firms decided on the spot, as in a top-down decision-making process, and that the other companies took time due to a lengthy process of consultative and participative decision making. However, this is not an accurate depiction of the decision-making process that actually took place in these companies.

At some companies, the decision to invest was firmly made by the corporate president or at a meeting of the Jomukai prior to the commencement of the feasibility study. The purpose of the study was to prepare a detailed operational plan. In the case of some of the large firms, Nemawashi was carried out among the interested parties of several key divisions throughout the feasibility study. After a final investment plan was drawn up, the Ringi process followed to confirm the consensus reached among the management involved. For example, at one large company, the Ringi process involved the management in charge of personnel, accounting, legal and public relations, production engineering, and product development.

In the case of direct investment, the locus of decision making tended to be centralized. How does this compare with decision making on other management tasks? The current research attempted to measure the effect of decision task on the decision-making style. Five methods of making decisions, which ranged from centralized to participative decision-making styles, were explained to the interviewees. (For detailed explanations of these five methods of decision making, see Item 2 in Section 7 of the questionnaire in Appendix B.)

The interviewees were asked to indicate which method of decision making was normally used for each of the 12 decision tasks. Then, individual responses were transformed into a continuous scale (a decision centralization score, or DCS) ranging from 5 (centralized decision making) to 1 (participative decision making) based on the respondents' percentages assigned to each decision style. Figure 4-1 illustrates this continuous scale (the influence-power continuum) and how to compute

FIGURE 4-1
THE INFLUENCE-POWER CONTINUUM

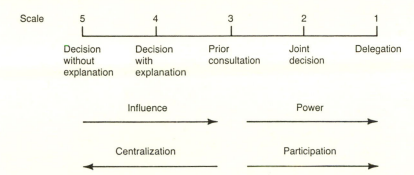

Note: If, for example, for a particular decision task a manager makes "decision without explanation" for 80 percent of the time and utilizes "prior consultation" for 20 percent of the time, his DCS value on this decision task is computed as follows: DCS = [(5 × 80) + (3 × 20)]/100 = 4.6.

Source: Frank A. Heller and Bernhard Wilpert, *Competence and Power in Managerial Decision-Making: A Study of Senior Levels of Organization in Eight Countries* Copyright 1981. (John Wiley & Sons, Ltd., 1981), p. 71. Adapted with permission of John Wiley & Sons, Ltd.

DCS values. A high DCS value indicates centralized decision making with little power and influence for the subordinates. A low DCS value suggests decentralized (participative) decision making with high degrees of power and influence of the subordinates.

The survey was intended to address middle-management personnel. The questionnaire was thus not applicable in a strict sense in the case of those firms whose interviewees represented only top management (executives). However, as the number of companies interviewed was limited, these executives were requested to answer the questions from their subordinates' viewpoints. Usable responses were collected from eight large and four small firms. Table 4-7 summarizes the responses.

The respondents at the large firms had a lower total average score (2.78) than those at the small companies (3.44). This may imply that managers at large corporations tend to utilize more participative decision making than those at smaller firms. However, it should be interpreted with caution, since the data were collected primarily from middle-management personnel at the large companies and top management (although responding to the questions from their subordinates'

TABLE 4-7
DECISION CENTRALIZATION SCORES (DCS) ON 12 DECISION TASKS

Superior's Decision Task	Large Firms Average DCS	n.a.*	Small Firms Average DCS	n.a.*
1. Increase your salary	4.13	0	4.45	0
2. Increase the number of employees working for you	2.69	0	3.33	0
3. Hire one of several applicants to work for you	3.00	6	3.38	0
4. Determine the style and layout of written letters in your office	1.88	0	2.40	0
5. Purchase a piece of equipment for your department at a cost within his budgetary discretion	1.88	0	3.20	0
6. Promote an employee to one of your subordinates	2.33	2	3.63	0
7. Give a merit pay increase to one of your subordinates	2.80	3	3.88	0
8. Change the money allocation for your department during the preparation of the company budget	2.85	2	3.38	0
9. Discharge one of your staff	2.50	6	3.50	1
10. Change an operating procedure followed by you	2.42	2	3.23	1
11. Assign you to a different job (on same salary) under his or her jurisdiction	3.40	0	3.63	0
12. Identify goals or standards of performance to be set for you	3.49	1	3.25	0
Total average	2.78		3.44	

*Indicates the number of respondents whose immediate superiors do not have the authority to make the final decision or when the decision task is not applicable for the respondents.

Source: Compiled by the author.

perspectives) at the small firms. Also, individuals at different levels of authority and maturity may perceive similar facts differently.

A detailed examination of Table 4-7 reveals further that at the large companies the DCS values range widely from 4.13 (high centralization) to 1.88 (participative), depending on particular decision tasks. This implies that depending on decision tasks, these Japanese companies utilize both top-down and bottom-up decision-making styles. Furthermore, individual responses and personal interviews revealed that some notable variations in decision-making styles existed among the 15 companies interviewed. This evidence in part implies that the traditional decision-making process based on group participation might have been gradually transformed into a mixed approach, where effectiveness and efficiency of decision making determine how the process should be structured.

Respondents at the majority of the large firms indicated that the decision tasks relating to hiring and firing of employees (decision tasks 3 and 9) were not applicable. This confirms Tsurumi's observation that one of the major differences between Japanese and U.S. corporations is the inability of Japanese managers to fire their subordinates. As Tsurumi states, "It is the collective entity known as the firm that hires all employees and decides on their fate."[21]

None of the companies, to the knowledge of the interviewees, had prior consultations with Japanese government officials with respect to their direct manufacturing investments in the United States. The decision to invest was reached at the corporate level, and subsequently the application of the intended project was filed at the Bank of Japan. All applications were automatically approved by the MOF and MITI. Although the interactions between the macro and the micro actors will be discussed further in Chapter 6, the following stories illuminate the locus of decision making at the level of the firm.

One large firm mentioned that except for enormously large overseas projects, prior consultation with government officials would not be necessary. Another large firm consulted with MITI officials regarding the ministerial approval for its planned direct manufacturing investment in the United States only a few days before the press release of its investment decision. Two other large firms pointed out that they had recently started informal discussions with MITI officials due to the increased bilateral trade disputes between Japan and the United States. Indeed, MITI has not been alarmed by the increase in Japanese direct manufacturing investments in the United States; rather, it seems to welcome such an increase in general in order to reduce political pressures from the U.S. government and industries. This last point will be discussed further in Chapter 6.

According to one large firm, it is important to communicate to the head of the company union the effect of the planned direct manufacturing investment on the existing manufacturing operations in Japan as soon as the final decision is reached at a meeting of the Jomukai. Although no explicit protests against foreign direct investments have been made by labor unions in Japan, such communication at an early stage certainly creates a good, trusting relationship between management and labor.

At the present time, none of the firms seemed to have developed a systematic policy of involving their domestic subsidiaries and affiliates into their direct manufacturing investment decisions. In all cases the investment decision-making process was confined within each corporate entity, and therefore the possibility of its direct manufacturing investment in the United States was not discussed even with its domestic subsidiaries and affiliates. However, one large firm mentioned that when its direct foreign investment had an adverse effect on some of its subcontractors, it normally went out of its way to find alternative production lines for them. This large company has a separate administrative division at its headquarters that handles various business-related problems and affairs of its affiliated firms.

Another large firm recently adopted a formal system of corporate strategic planning at its president's office, which would enable the company to set up a more coherent policy than in the past in order to maximize the total corporate strength by integrating all available resources of its headquarters and related firms. These points will be discussed further in the next chapter.

Corporate decision making, especially at a large company, is a complex process. The process becomes more complex in foreign direct investment than in the case of domestic investment, mainly because of added uncertainty. Among the Japanese companies interviewed, the top management played an important role in directing corporate resources to effectuate direct manufacturing investment in the United States. This may imply that the investment is seen as strategically important for the survival of the corporation and that the Japanese corporate executives have begun to assume an increased leadership role in strategic decision making, like their counterparts in the United States.

5   STRUCTURAL LINKAGE AND THE CONTROL SYSTEM

This chapter is divided into two major sections. The first section on corporate structure discusses various organizational structures adopted at the corporate headquarters of the Japanese companies interviewed, and examines how the structural linkage is maintained between the parent and the subsidiary. The second section on the control system reports the parent-subsidiary relations in more detail, focusing on the administrative control from the parent perspective.

CORPORATE STRUCTURE

The majority of the firms interviewed have adopted the multidivisional system (*Jigyobusei*) of management to organize their business activities, human resources, and communication channels. Under the system, a corporate entity is subdivided into several divisions (units) along its product lines. In a strict sense of the multidivisional form of administration, each division functions as a profit center responsible for revenue and expense generated from the divisional activities. Therefore, as a quasi-independent unit within the corporate entity, the head of a division is responsible for all facets of the business operations associated with the particular group of product lines assigned to the division. Consequently, the division has a vertical control over the divisional activities from manufacturing to sales of the products.

As the size of the firm grows in terms of the number of its product lines, customers, and employees, it becomes necessary to regulate and streamline the internal flows of information by adopting a new structure. As observed in the profile of the firms interviewed in Chapter 3, the large (listed) companies are significantly larger in corporate size than the small (unlisted) firms. However, a close examination reveals a significant difference in size even among the nine large and the six smaller companies, respectively. In addition, these 15 firms are operating at different levels of international expansion and sophistication, irrespective of the corporate size in some cases. At an initial glance, therefore, generalization seems unwieldy. With this caveat in mind, this section examines the corporate structures of these Japanese companies at their headquarters level and their structural linkages with their U.S. subsidiaries, drawing some illustrations of representative organization charts. The following discussions proceed, in general, from smaller to larger organizations in terms of employment size at the home office.

This section is divided into four subsections: small firms, large firms, from organizational fragmentation to coordination, and development of regional headquarters. The first two sections examine mainly the organizational structures of the small and large companies at their corporate headquarters, with a special attention given to those individuals and/or divisions in charge of international activities. The third section analyzes structural characteristics of these companies in terms of organization fragmentation versus coordination of various units of operations. The fourth section reports an emerging pattern of structural linkage between the parent and the U.S. subsidiaries in some of the large firms.

Small Firms

As mentioned earlier, the six unlisted firms are smaller in size and have a limited scale of overseas manufacturing operations in comparison with the other companies. The number of employees at these small firms ranges from approximately 200 to 4,000 and that of members of the board of directors is anywhere between 5 and 16. Their U.S. subsidiaries, with one exception, engage in parts production or assembly operations on a small scale. The main activity of these subsidiaries is largely confined to sales or service-oriented functions.

The exception is one small company that has a capital participation, with its Japanese sister company, in a startup manufcturing venture with a U.S. entrepreneur. The employment size at the U.S. venture is approximately 400. The U.S. corporation engages in production of custom ICs and is run by the U.S. management. The linkage is maintained by Japanese board members' attendance at the quarterly board meeting in the United States.

One of the small firms with approximately 200 employees at the home office has a single line of products (electronics parts). Its organization is structured with four functional units as depicted in Figure 5-1. This company was incorporated in the early 1960s as a spin-off subsidiary of another small unlisted firm. At this newly formed corporate entity, a system of divisional organization with division managers and section chiefs was adopted earlier but abolished in the early 1970s. At the present time, there is no functional demarcation between domestic and overseas sales among the employees in the Marketing Department.

The company's U.S. venture materialized in a rather haphazard way. The current president of the company and his U.S. acquaintance created the subsidiary in the late 1970s, which currently has an employment size of 60. With his U.S. acquaintance managing the U.S. subsidiary and the limited human resources at the home office, the corporate president in Japan is the only person maintaining the linkage between the home office and the U.S. subsidiary at the present time. An effort to coordinate the activities of the parent and the subsidiary has been unsuccessful because of serious communication gaps (the language barrier plus intricate

FIGURE 5-1
ORGANIZATION CHART OF A SMALL JAPANESE
COMPANY WITH A SINGLE PRODUCT LINE

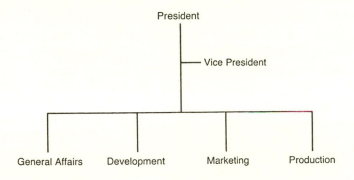

Source: Constructed by the author using the company's annual report.

differences in perception and value judgments) between the employees at both ends.

The president's dissatisfaction with the U.S. subsidiary has been growing in many directions. He now believes that the U.S. management is irresponsible and is considering the possibility of disinvestment or relocation of the subsidiary from the current location in the Midwest to the Pacific region where the company maintains a liaison office staffed with one Japanese employee. Because he is burdened with operational responsibilities at the home office and is without a support staff to assist him in the company's overseas venture, he seems to have been letting the problems persist.

Another unlisted company with about 300 employees has an organizational structure with two product-based divisions and several functional divisions with a large number of subsections. Its main organizational structure is summarized in Figure 5-2.

The company's International Marketing Division is divided into four geographically based sections: the United States, Europe, and two Far East sections. The company involves several divisions, including the International Marketing Division, to maintain and expand the linkage with its U.S. subsidiary. The company's vice-president has a strong interest in internationalizing its management process at the home office and is making a conscious effort to expose the company's Japanese employees to the U.S. employees hired at the U.S. subsidiary by transferring young Japanese employees to the subsidiary for management-training purposes and by holding at the home office in Japan a semiannual meeting attended by some key management personnel from the U.S. subsidiary as well as the board members, managers, and staff employees of the home office.

Although not shown in Figure 5-2, the divisions and departments are subdivided into numerous sections according to this company's original organization chart. There are 63 sections in total including 10 service, laboratory, and distribution sections. The Standardization Head Office in the chart consists of ten committees: budget, quality control, new products, public relations, safety and hygiene, fire and disaster prevention, design, proposal, cost control, and productive engineering.

The other unlisted companies use either an export division or an international division to handle their international trade transactions. At one small company with 280 employees, for example, an export division is attached to each of three product-based divisions. At another small company with 2,000 employees, an export and import department exists at the administrative level.

FIGURE 5-2
ORGANIZATION CHART OF A SMALL JAPANESE
COMPANY WITH TWO PRODUCT LINES

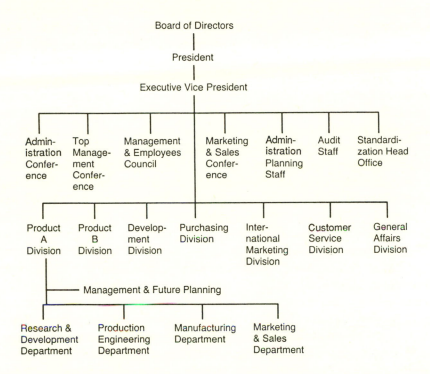

Source: Constructed by the author using the company's annual report.

In all cases, the linkage with their U.S. subsidiaries is maintained generally through one of the top management personnel familiar with international business. At one of these unlisted companies with 1,900 employees, for example, an executive vice-president at the home office in Japan has been assuming concurrently the presidency of the U.S. subsidiary with an employment size of 35. He once taught college physics and joined the firm to assume a management position with considerable responsibility for the company's international business affairs. He frequently visits the U.S. subsidiary, where expansion of business activities (a new plant to expand its technical services to customers) has been underway.

This company has aggressively been seeking technological tie-ups with U.S. firms and has, since the mid-1960s, established three manufacturing joint ventures in Japan with U.S. companies with advanced technologies. The company executive admits that the firm was influenced by and actively adopted U.S. management techniques from early on. Since its incorporation in the early 1950s, the company has created more than 20 subsidiaries in Japan and abroad, each specializing in one of the following four activities: equipment manufacturing, service, material production and processing, and sales. Its four overseas subsidiaries are located in the United States, Europe, and Asia and are mainly sales and service oriented. The corporate headquarters office handles various administrative functions as well as designing, testing, and assemblying of products. The company encourages competition among its related firms in terms of sales volume and profits; at the same time it promotes its group solidarity by stressing the growth of the combined group strength in comparison to the other major firms in the same industry in international competition.

This company has an international division, which is subdivided into four geographical areas: North America, Europe, Southeast Asia, and the People's Republic of China. Although it has not made any significant inroads into the market in mainland China, the management pays special attention to its business prospects in the country. With various functional duties handled at the international division with young staff employees, the corporate executive can devote his time to administrative matters associated with the company's overseas ventures and technical negotiations for licensing agreements with foreign corporations.

Overall, the majority of the small firms have adopted the multidivisional system, and the communications linkage with their U.S. subsidiaries is maintained by one or two executives at their corporate headquarters. There is one exception on this point, as noted earlier. One small company, with strong initiatives of the corporate vice-president, has been trying to open up a wider communication channel through meetings and employee transfers among the executives, managers, and staff employees of the headquarters in Japan and the management personnel of its U.S. subsidiary. It appears that this firm intends to internationalize its management practices at home by exposing as many of its Japanese employees as possible to U.S. management personnel. This practice might be quite costly for a small firm, but it can bring about some intangible values and assets to the company if it is well planned and directed.

Large Firms

All of the five group-member firms and the four other listed companies are listed on the First Section of the Tokyo Stock Exchange. The number of employees of these companies varies from 6,000 to 75,000, and that of the members in their boards of directors ranges from 11 to 28. All of these companies have adopted the multidivisional form of organizational structure and attach varying degrees of importance to their international divisions.

In general, the influence of a particular division within a firm is in proportion to the rank of its leader in the corporate hierarchy. Thus, one way of measuring the prestige of the international division in a Japanese company is to see if the head of the division is represented in the board of directors. Here, as status consciousness is particularly strong in Japan, the rank of corporate directorship — the top echelon in the corporate hierarchy — receives special attention both inside and outside the corporate entity. On this point, Tsurumi observed:

> The Japanese corporate culture, both internally and externally, deems the rank of corporate directorship and above as the peak echelon of the management hierarchy. Internally, for example, the appointment of a top manager to a new head position of any given function or department draws the attention of all members of the firm. Such an appointment is the explicit "body" language of the firm that communicates to its loyal members the increased importance of the specified activities headed by a ranking officer. Such "body" language calls for new dedication and cooperation from all corporate members.[1]

In five of the large corporations interviewed, the head of the international division is a managing director or an ordinary director. In addition, at two of these companies, another managing director is assigned to the U.S. subsidiary to assume its presidency. At the other four large companies, the international division does not have any member on its board of directors. However, at all of these four firms, a managing director or an ordinary director of the home office concurrently assumes a presidency in the U.S. subsidiary. This variance does not seem to relate to the corporate size or to the level of overseas activities. Furthermore, the international division at the majority of the large companies does not seem to assume the function of coordinating various overseas activities. The supporting evidence on this point comes from several sources and is enumerated as follows.

In the case of two large companies, a piece of the evidence was gathered at the time of this author's telephone conversations with Japanese personnel at the U.S. subsidiaries. As explained in Chapter 3, this author made initial contacts with Japanese executives and/or managers at the U.S. subsidiaries of the 15 Japanese primary investors in order to request participation of the parent companies in the current research and to seek their assistance in locating proper personnel at their headquarters in Japan who could answer the survey questions regarding the investment decision-making process and the control system at the headquarters level.

The Japanese personnel at the U.S. subsidiaries of the two large companies stated there was no one at their headquarters in Japan who had a complete picture of the investment decision and business-related matters of their U.S. operations; they kindly suggested that it would be better for this researcher to come to see their executives at their U.S. offices. However, given the specific objective of the current research (that of focusing on the parent perspectives) as well as time and budget constraints, this author explained that a personal interview at the subsidiary level would not be appropriate or feasible and asked if anyone at the international division at the home office would be available for participation in this interview survey.

One of the two subsidiaries' personnel replied that the international division was not involved with the U.S. operations. Instead, the management at the subsidiary was given the authority to conduct its business operations independently in the United States, and ultimate, that is strategic, decisions were closely monitored by the corporate chairman at the home office. An interview was finally arranged with a knowledgeable manager at the home office for general discussions on the corporate structure and the decision-making process.

A personal interview at the other of the two companies was arranged with two managers at the home office, one in charge of the overall operations of one product group (including the products being manufactured at the U.S. subsidiary) and another who had once assumed the vice-presidency at the U.S. manufacturing subsidiary in the past. This company had begun a major reorganization of its corporate structure in the mid-1970s and only recently created the International Operations Headquarters at the home office in order to improve coordination of its international activities.

The U.S. subsidiaries of the remaining seven large Japanese companies could locate appropriate interviewees at their corporate headquarters in Japan rather expeditiously. Interviewees at five of these seven firms were executives or managers from the division in charge of corporate planning, and those at the other two companies were from the international division (or the overseas department). Thus, overall, the international division at only two of the nine large firms had personnel familiar with or directly involved with the manufacturing activities in the United States.

Another piece of information supporting the conjecture made earlier was obtained during this author's field work in Japan in the summer of 1984. It was conveyed during the personal interview with Dr. Noritake Kobayashi, a professor at Keio University and chairman of the Workshop on the Study of Japanese Multinationals. According to Dr. Kobayashi, Japanese corporations in general do not have any division or department that coordinates their overseas activities at the headquarters level. His observation was largely based on a comprehensive study of 89 Japanese and 23 Western multinational corporations undertaken by the Workshop of the Study of Japanese Multinationals during the period of 1971 through 1978.[2] The study concluded that, in general, Japanese multinational corporations were in a less-developed stage in every aspect of international management — that includes recruitment and promotion of local personnel, production and procurement, organization, finance, training and management of Japanese employees for foreign assignment, planning, marketing, and R & D, in the order of serious to slight underdevelopment in international management practices of Japanese multinationals in comparison to those of Western multinationals.[3]

Tsurumi observed in 1976 the distinctive existence of the international division — or the KJ division, as he names it — in Japanese multinationals. He noted that the KJ division was formed in general not as a profit center and that functions of the division were limited to monitoring of subsidiaries abroad by means of keeping their records, evaluating their performance, and looking after their personnel needs.[4] Yoshino also observed a difference in the function of the international divisions of Japanese and U.S. multinationals. He noted that the international division of Japanese multinationals was less autonomous than its U.S. counterpart — the latter was generally formed as a self-contained unit to manage international business activities independently from the corporate central office. He attributed this difference to the traditional Ringi system prevailing in Japan that tends to obscure the exact location of responsibilities for major decisions.[5]

From the preceding observations, it appears that the majority of the large Japanese companies have serious problems in, or lack of coordination of, their overseas activities. This point will be discussed further in later sections.

Of the nine large firms interviewed, two companies did not disclose their organizational structures. Thus, the following analysis of the corporate structure pertains to the remaining seven large firms.

Two large companies have a similar organizational structure, and each has approximately 70,000 employees. Figure 5-3 shows a condensed organization chart of one of these two firms. This company has grouped its several product lines into five major autonomous divisions (Product Group A, B, . . . in Figure 5-3): industrial electronics, electronic components, consumer products, heavy-duty electrical equipment, and materials. The other company with a similar corporate structure has six major product divisions: power generation and transmission, industrial processes, industrial components and equipment, consumer products, computers, and electronic devices. In addition, each of these two firms has about 40 consolidated and 400 unconsolidated subsidiaries for the purpose of preparing its corporate financial statements.

The heads of the product divisions are members of the Board of Directors. Therefore, each product division operates quite autonomously as a profit center and commands a strong voice in corporate policy making. Although major corporate policies and action plans need final approvals at the board meetings, they are discussed frequently at an informal level, and consensus is normally reached through the process of Nemawashi among affected divisions and at the meetings of the Executive Directors Committee. As one company mentioned, the corporate president keeps himself up-to-date on what is taking place inside and outside the company by having frequent luncheon meetings with key personnel at the company's cafeteria.

The Board of Directors consists of chairman of the board, president of the corporation, executive vice-president, senior managing directors, managing directors, and ordinary directors. Each of the Corporate Policy Committee and the Executive Directors Committee consists of the top management except for the ordinary directors. In these two firms, the number of members on the board is 28, and those on each of the two committees number around 15.

FIGURE 5-3
ORGANIZATION CHART OF A LARGE JAPANESE COMPANY WITH MULTIPLE PRODUCT LINES

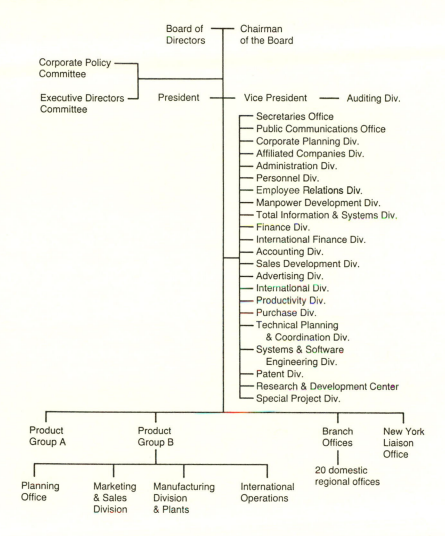

Source: Constructed by the author using the company's annual report.

FIGURE 5-4
MATRIX ORGANIZATION OF A LARGE JAPANESE COMPANY

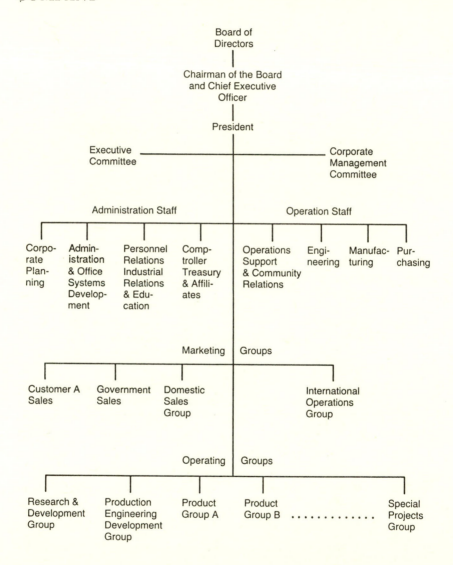

Source: Constructed by the author using the company's annual report.

Another large company has an employment size of 35,000. Its organizational structure is grouped neatly into four segments: administration staff, operation staff, marketing groups, and operating groups. The organization chart, which is characterized as a matrix organization, is presented in Figure 5-4.

This company also maintains two supreme decision-making committees: the Executive Committee and the Corporate Management Committee. The Executive Committee (*Keiei Kaigi*) is headed by the corporate chairman and handles long-term strategic planning. The Corporate Management Committee — that is equivalent to the Council of Managing Directors, Jomukai — is headed by the corporate president and instrumental for Nemawashi to reconcile divergent opinions among the members regarding possible alternative solutions to current management problems. A consensus reached at the committee is formalized as a final decision through the Ringi process at the Board of Directors' meeting.

Tsurumi also observed an existence of two parallel committees at the top-management level in major Japanese corporations:

> As a buffer between *Jomukai* and *Ringi* procedure of operational decisions, a number of firms have a management committee that often consists of the same members as *Jomukai*. But this committee is clearly defined as a "discussion" group in which strategic decisions are freely evaluated. This seemingly redundant forum serves well in Japanese corporate culture to identify sensitive issues and diffuse oppositions, without committing anyone to a specific position.[6]

Another large company with 14,000 employees maintains seven product-based divisions, each of which is headed by a managing director. In addition, this firm retains three vice-presidents in charge of each of the following three areas: R & D, production and sales, and magnetic materials. The interviewee at this company stressed that there was no clear division of responsibilities among the management, meaning that responsibilities for all major decisions are shared among the groups of individuals concerned.

The remaining three companies have also organized their corporate structures similarly based on the multidivisional system. However, the interviewee at one of these firms mentioned that the company's organizational structure contained too many subdivisions.

Another large firm has been going through a major restructuring of its organization since the mid-1970s. Up to the early 1970s the company had experienced a phenomenal growth with essentially a single product line.

Then, it recorded net operating losses for the first time in its corporate history during the recession following the first oil shock of 1973-74. The company reassessed its corporate strategies and embarked upon a fundamental change in its corporate structure. It adopted a matrix system to coordinate three basic functions: R & D, production, and marketing. Each manufacturing facility was realigned to specialize in particular production. Then, three product-based divisions were created, and these were structured in a grid pattern with the three basic functions. In addition, in order to strengthen the headquarters functions and to coordinate its international activities, the company created the International Operations Headquarters in the late 1970s. Since the early 1980s, it has been making an attempt to integrate managerial functions on a worldwide basis. The U.S. manufacturing subsidiary, which was established originally with a strong initiative and under the direct control of the company's U.S. sales subsidiary, is now required to report its operating results and other business-related information to the related product-based group at the headquarters.

All of the large firms stated that their corporate structures were organized globally according to product lines, meaning that their overseas manufacturing plants were under direct supervision of their corporate product divisions. However, some companies have their own idiosyncracies in managing their overseas activities.

At the company with the organization chart presented in Figure 5-3, each Product Group Division has its own international operations division that handles both international trade and foreign direct investment activities of the product division. In addition, the company has the International Finance Division and the International Division at the administrative level. The former division came into being as a result of the company's increased capital commitments for its overseas activities. Specifically, the International Finance Division at this company is charged with the following three major functions: centralized control of foreign exchange transactions arising from the company's international trade activities, obtaining loans from overseas capital markets, and the temporary investments of excess funds. The International Division was created to handle international licensing and sales agreements as well as overseas contracts for large-scale projects. It is staffed with employees with legal and public relations expertise.

Another one of the largest two firms has an independent international operations group serving all of its product-based divisions, each of which is quite autonomous and has a strong voice in decision making with regard to the company's overseas manufacturing investments and operations. The International Operations Group consists of five segments: the International Sales Division I, the International Sales Division II, the China Business Division, the Overseas License and Business Support Division, and a group of overseas offices. The first three divisions administer mainly the corporation's export activities. The fourth division handles various legal matters associated with technology licensing agreements as well as foreign direct investments; it is subdivided into four sections based on geographical regions: North America, Europe, Latin America, and Southeast Asia. The fifth division is an assortment of the company's representative offices scattered around the world. Its primary function at the headquarters level is to maintain a communications linkage with these overseas representative offices for information processing and assisting of their sales and promotional activities.

In general, the majority of the large companies maintain their primary structural linkage with their U.S. manufacturing plants through the product-based divisions at their corporate headquarters in Japan. Some of these firms have transferred their corporate directors to their U.S. subsidiaries in order to strengthen the parent-subsidiary communications linkage at the top management level. Here, the international division in most cases plays a secondary role. Furthermore, management responsibilities with regard to the U.S. manufacturing and sales subsidiaries seem to be widely diffused both at the parent and subsidiary levels. Operationally this means a multiple communications link between the parent and the subsidiary. Although the current research did not survey the subsidiary side, there is some evidence to support this assumption of a multiple communications link.

In comparing management practices of nine Japanese-owned and six non-Japanese foreign-owned manufacturing subsidiaries in the United States, Kujawa observed that the board of directors of the Japanese-owned manufacturing subsidiaries were laden with parent-company nationals (PCNs). He noted, further, the extensive use of PCNs in general at the Japanese-owned subsidiaries:

> The Japanese firms used PCNs fairly extensively in both managerial and technical positions at the subsidiaries. Moreover, this finding was in contrast to the experiences at the other foreign-owned firms where the incidence of PCN-usage in management position was less than half that of the Japanese, and in non-managerial, technical positions was about one-tenth that of the

Japanese. . . . To conclude, the Japanese firms were found to use PCNs extensively and continuously — and were distinctive in this regard.[7]

Similar evidence of extensive use of PCNs at Japanese firms' subsidiaries in Southeast Asia was observed by Tsurumi and Yoshino. Tsurumi ascribes the reason for such extensive use of PCNs to the Japanese companies' idiosyncrasies of production process–related technologies and patterns of communications.[8] Yoshino argues that the extensive use of PCNs is due to the closed nature of Japanese organizations, which emphasize shared understanding among the employees, and that as a result the role of personal communications becomes critically important between the parent and the subsidiary abroad.[9]

It appears that the extensive use of PCNs in Japanese-owned overseas subsidiaries is the norm and that this may be related to the "groupism," in contrast to the Western "individualism," in a narrow sense. In extreme groupism, the individual identity succumbs to the group identity to a dangerous degree. Group members, consciously or unconsciously, practice exclusionism or cliquism. The majority of the Japanese tend to feel uncomfortable and become ineffective when they have to deal with people outside their own group. This tendency among the Japanese becomes pronounced especially in their dealing with non-Japanese (even with nonnative Japanese, for example, Nisie, Sansei, etc., in the United States) due partly to their embedded insular attitudes and their lost identity as individual human beings. The change in how human relations are structured in general is slow to come by, as aptly assessed by the interviewees for the current research (see Table 3-6 in Chapter 3), unless the people in question find it necessary and are willing to change.

The extensive use of PCNs in overseas subsidiaries may hinder multinationalization of the Japanese companies because the costs of maintaining expatriates tend to be higher than those of employing host-country nationals, the number of Japanese employees assignable to overseas ventures in a given firm are limited, and the host countries may object to such an extensive use of PCNs. Thus, it has become critically important for Japanese multinational companies to design appropriate organizational structures and communications linkages with various operating units at home and abroad. The multinationalization also requires these companies to develop employees equipped with intercultural communications skills.

From Organizational Fragmentation
to Coordination

A tendency of organizational fragmentation in a Japanese company was often cited as weakening management control, as Yoshino observed in 1968.

> *Jigyobusei*, or the independent divisional system, had received much attention during the boom years of the late 1950's and early 1960's. The success of this system in the United States was well publicized and stirred much interest among Japanese executives. Anxious to emulate this success, a number of firms rushed to adopt it without a careful prior examination of its applicability to Japanese needs. . . . In many cases, the American divisional system only worsened the very conditions in Japan it was meant to remedy; that is, it only contributed to the overlapping of authority and the duplication of functions, creating further overhead burdens and organizational fragmentation.[10]

Yoshino cites a few reasons for such organizational fragmentation with a narrow span of control assigned to each unit: (1) the top management has traditionally been reluctant to delegate authority to lower levels; (2) the very rapid postwar growth of most Japanese firms rendered a systematic approach to organizational development very difficult; (3) the importance of organizational planning and development, as a continuing process, is not always appreciated by top management — some executives believe that organizational structures per se make little difference, and others fear a possible weakening or destruction of their informal power structure; and (4) due to the lifetime employment and the seniority-based reward systems, personnel considerations, rather than the optimum division of tasks, frequently become the overriding criteria for the creation of new organizational units; for example, a new unit may be created just to give status recognition to managers.[11]

In addition to the proliferation of divisions and sections, there is another form of organizational fragmentation in Japanese corporations. Aside from the product-based divisions, the majority of the large and small firms interviewed opted for establishing a large number of domestic subsidiaries through spin-offs of their internal divisions or in order to diversify into new promising ventures. Yoshino also observed this proliferation of subsidiaries among major Japanese manufacturing firms and cited the following reasons:

1. The large firms found it advantageous to organize subsidiaries for the performance of labor-intensive operations because of a ubiquitous presence of a substantial wage scale disparity between large and small enterprises in Japan.
2. They established subsidiaries to separate unprofitable phases of their operations, as consolidation of financial statements was not required by Japanese commercial law.
3. Due to the wide diffusion of responsibilities prevailing in Japanese corporate culture, the creation of a separate corporation makes it easier to assign more clear-cut responsibilities.
4. There is the need for management to find suitable employment opportunities for retired personnel due to the traditional practice of lifetime employment.[12]

Among the companies interviewed for the current study, the most frequently cited reason for establishing separate corporate entities was related to the motivation of Japanese employees. For example, instead of divisional managers (*bucho*) or section chiefs (*kacho*), the employees assigned to a new entity will bear the title of corporate directors (*torishimariyaku*) and become strongly motivated to fulfill administrative responsibilities implied in the title. The new entity also gives the employees a sense of new direction and importance of the mission. Therefore, given the traditional decision-making process based on group participation and the strong emphasis on hierarchical relationships between seniors and juniors in Japan, the newly formed subsidiary can function flexibly and efficiently within its own corporate boundary detached from the internal politics and personal (emotional) ties within the parent company. Furthermore, as a result of establishing a number of subsidiaries, an important benefit accrues to the parent company. From the perspective of the corporate group as a whole, the parent can train and develop more employees equipped with management skills and business acumen.

The wage factor was also cited as a reason for establishing separate corporate entities. Although the wage differential between large and small enterprises in Japan has been shrinking,[13] the creation of a new subsidiary is considered instrumental in introducing a new wage structure for employees because company-based unions, rather than industry-based unions, are the norm among Japanese companies. One executive stated, "Since wages cannot be differentiated among employees working in different divisions within a corporate entity due to a strict labor union contract prevailing in Japan, forming a new entity would solve the problem of rigidity in the parent's wage structure."

Until recently, consolidated financial statements were neither required nor prepared by the vast majority of companies in Japan. Subsidiaries were often used by parent firms to conceal unprofitable operations. The impropriety of disclosure of financial information among some publicly-held corporations became a problem in the 1960s and the early 1970s. After lengthy deliberations at the Business Accounting Deliberating Council (Kigyokaikei-Shingikai), an advisory organ to the MOF, accounting for consolidation was put into practice, starting in the fiscal year ending March 1978. Although the equity method of accounting was not required at the time, it became mandatory beginning in the fiscal year ending March 1984 under the Securities and Exchange Law (Shokentorihikiho) administered by the MOF. Although these requirements are expected to affect parent-subsidiary relations as well as the mind-set of the top management of large firms, the actual effects remain to be seen.

The fragmentation in organizational structure (and the cross-divisional as well as parent-subsidiary communications that accompany it) should hinder the Japanese companies in developing integrated multinational operations. At some of the large firms interviewed, coordination of various units of operations and strategic planning have become important considerations for corporate survival and success.

The majority of the large firms interviewed had been making efforts to increase their competitive strengths by coordinating the activities of their subsidiaries and affiliates. Some of these companies have established a separate division (named as the Affiliated Companies Division or the Subsidiaries Office) to deal with this problem of coordination. Especially in the area of factory automation, these companies began to hold regular meetings between their product divisions at the headquarters and their manufacturing subsidiaries in order to set development strategies by combining technological know-how as well as human and financial resources of the member firms.

A corporate planning division at some of the large firms has also begun to assume an increased role in recent years. Instead of relying solely on planning activities at the level of each product division, these companies began to find it important to formulate strategic plans at the corporate level. Such a corporate-planning division is generally responsible for setting medium-range (three-year) to long-range (ten-year) plans and reports directly to the corporate president.

At one of the large corporations interviewed, the Corporate Planning Division consists of one board member, five assistant general managers from product-based divisions, and approximately 30 staff employees. The five assistant general managers are periodically replaced within two to three years in order to introduce fresh ideas to the planning division. The division's influence is strengthened by the involvement of the board member in the process of formulating corporate strategies. The division is charged with the responsibility of drafting a three-year plan as well as in planning and organizing corporate-wide efforts in launching new ventures that do not fit readily into any one of the existing product-based divisions. The Corporate Planning Division at this company also plays a vital role in resolving conflicts among the firm's U.S. subsidiaries, which were established separately and autonomously according to the respective product-based divisions at the headquarters. If any one of these subsidiaries does not perform as expected or causes serious business problems (such as poor customer services and imminent business failure), it will tarnish the entire corporate image to a certain degree. To spot and to deal effectively with such problems at the corporate level, the company holds a bimonthly meeting attended by the corporate president, the managers of the Corporate Planning Division, and the heads of the product-based divisions.

Another large company introduced a nine-year strategic plan in the late 1970s to achieve a targeted net annual sales figure by the end of the planning horizon. The plan is evaluated every three years and remedial operational policies are to be installed at each juncture. To be more specific, the company has currently identified the following three strategic areas to meet its nine-year goal: improvement of profitability through corporatewide measures to cut costs and by increasing asset turnover ratios; strengthening of R & D activities in basic and applied research to expand product lines and to encourage synergies among various technologies accumulated; effective utilization of the company's international network and expansion of its overseas operations in sales and manufacturing as well as in information-gathering activities abroad. Clearly, this company sees its international activities in both sales and manufacturing as a key element in achieving the corporate goal. In general, the three areas of management attention cited are equally shared by the other large firms as well.

All the large corporations interviewed have been intensifying their R & D strategies to stay competitive in their markets. Despite the common belief that Japan has surpassed the United States in terms of production-process technologies in some areas, these companies hold the general consensus that the basic research capability of Japanese firms is far behind that of U.S. firms. As targeted in the nine-year plan of the company cited earlier, the other large firms have also been restructuring their research-related activities in recent years by expanding their existing laboratories or creating new central research laboratories and through collaborative research projects with domestic and foreign companies.

Overseas manufacturing operations require more coordinating efforts at the headquarters level than do marketing activities abroad. Furthermore, if a company opts for an intrafirm international division of labor among its manufacturing plants at home and abroad in order to preserve scale economies to a certain degree, coordinated planning and implementation become doubly important. The following section reviews the structural linkage between the parent and the U.S. subsidiaries of the large companies and examines the concept of the regional headquarters adopted by some of these large Japanese companies.

Development of Regional Headquarters

In eight of the nine large companies interviewed, the structural linkage between the home office and the U.S. subsidiary is normally maintained through the relevant product-based division at the headquarters with participation in varying degrees of such other functional divisions as the international division, the corporate planning office, the subsidiaries office, and the finance and accounting departments. Although the success of the U.S. subsidiary is viewed as a shared responsibility of several divisions, the core linkage with the U.S. manufacturing plant is generally maintained through the product-based division at the home office and the U.S. subsidiary as depicted in Figure 5-5.

As the importance and the complexity of the manufacturing and sales activities in the United States increases through addition of product lines and expansion of manufacturing operations at more than one plant, some of the large firms have gradually been transforming their main U.S. subsidiaries into their regional headquarters. One of these companies plans, for example, to restructure its U.S. and Mexican subsidiaries as depicted in Figure 5-6.

The parent company owns 100 percent ownership interests in the first-tier subsidiary in the United States as a regional headquarters and in the Mexican subsidiary. The U.S. subsidiary then owns 100 percent ownership interests in three product-based subsidiaries: Subsidiary A, B, and C. Each of these second-tier subsidiaries operates manufacturing plants and sales offices. The regional headquarters office coordinates various activities performed at all of the U.S. and Mexican subsidiaries. It also prepares statements reporting the consolidated results of operations in the region and feeds the information back to the parent company in Japan.

In this transitional period of creating the regional headquarters, however, the company has been plagued with several administrative problems due to difficulty in finding proper personnel capable of administrating the regional headquarters office. For example, a Japanese director who was dispatched to the U.S. office in the past has proved to be ineffective in the new environment because of his advanced age and his inability to communicate well in English with the U.S. managers. One of the company's current objectives, therefore, is to develop a cadre of young employees capable of handling international activities.

At another progressive company, a drastic measure was taken to improve the operational efficiency of its U.S. subsidiary. This company detached its U.S. subsidiary from the home office and gave the

FIGURE 5-5
TRIANGULAR LINKAGE FOR MANAGING A U.S. MANUFACTURING PLANT

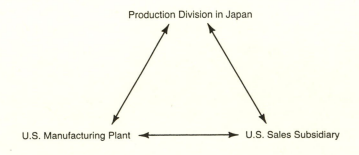

Source: Constructed by the author.

FIGURE 5-6
THE PARENT-SUBSIDIARY LINKAGE BASED ON THE
REGIONAL HEADQUARTERS IN THE UNITED STATES

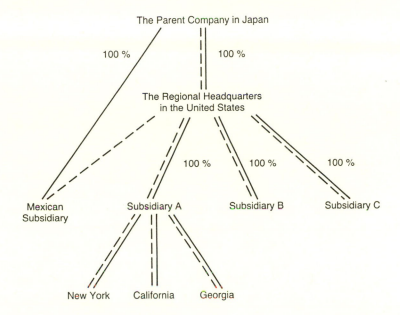

Note: Solid lines show ownership links, and dashed lines indicate operational reporting and control links.

Source: Constructed by the author.

subsidiary complete management authority over sales and manufacturing operations. To do this, it hired a young and able U.S. executive from a large U.S. firm and placed him as president and chief executive officer of the subsidiary. During his tenure in the major part of the 1970s, the subsidiary became a strong, autonomous company and enhanced its corporate image as a successful U.S. enterprise. However, as a result of the successful Americanization of its U.S. subsidiary, the communication gap between the parent and the subsidiary widened to the extent that the management on the Japanese side became wary of basic differences in management philosophy, especially in the areas of short-term versus long-term profitability strategies and human relations management style.

The conflict led to the resignation of the U.S. executive and a comprehensive restructuring of the company's U.S. operations. A Japanese executive with many years of business experience in the United States is now in charge of the U.S. operations. The headquarters office in New York handles such administrative functions as finance, personnel, public relations, and other general affairs. It oversees production and marketing activities performed by a group of its wholly owned subsidiaries in the United States. Consequently, the communications linkage between the Japanese parent and the group of U.S. subsidiaries in this corporation was restored again in recent years.

As the experiences of the companies cited here indicate, it may not be easy to develop a regional headquarters office that can effectively coordinate the corporate activities on a regional basis and at the same time maintain a close linkage with the parent. The major difficulty for the Japanese companies is in finding and developing managers capable of bridging the two distinctive cultures of Japan and the United States. Despite this difficulty, the development of the regional headquarters in the United States appears necessary because of the following reasons:

1. The size and the geographical spread of the U.S. market warrants coordination of marketing and manufacturing activities on a regional basis.
2. The extensive use of PCNs in each operating unit in the United States can be reduced by maintaining a limited number of able and key PCNs at the regional headquarters.
3. Conflicts of interests among several manufacturing subsidiaries, which might be linked operationally to the relevant product-based divisions at the parent company, can be arbitrated effectively and efficiently by the regional headquarters with appropriate authority and cooperation from the top management of the home office.

THE CONTROL SYSTEM

As reviewed in Chapter 3, a control system encompasses a whole range of administrative issues such as strategic planning, selection of corporate structure, allocation of corporate resources among various units, and the degree to which decision-making power and authority should be delegated to various organizational units. The main concern of this section is limited to how the parent companies at the headquarters level in Japan control their manufacturing operations in the United States. Topics particularly relevant in this regard can be addressed in the following questions:

1. What types of corporate decisions are made locally at the subsidiary in the United States, at the headquarters in Japan, or jointly?
2. What kinds of communication methods are being used currently to facilitate information flows between the parent and the subsidiary?
3. Who, or which divisions at the home office, are responsible for monitoring the subsidiary's operations, and what kinds of methods are being used to evaluate the subsidiary's performance?

An effective control system should provide useful and accurate information to the corporate management on a timely basis so that new policies can be formulated to guide future courses of actions in order to improve the market position or the profitability of the corporation. To answer the preceding questions, this section is divided into three subsections: locus of policy formulation, communication methods, and evaluation of subsidiary performance.

Locus of Policy Formulation

With regard to overall operating policies, ten out of the 15 firms stated that their U.S. manufacturing operations were managed jointly by their corporate headquarters and the U.S. subsidiaries. The remaining five companies reported that their U.S. manufacturing operations were permitted a substantial degree of local autonomy. These five companies with decentralized U.S. subsidiaries consist of one large and four small firms. The large firm owns several newly acquired manufacturing subsidiaries that continue to operate under the former U.S. management plus one Japanese managing director transferred from the home office. At the current stage, most of the policy decisions relating to the U.S. subsidiary are made at the local level.

Three of the four small firms, which stated that their U.S. manufacturing subsidiaries were given a substantial degree of local autonomy, have their Japanese personnel in charge of the local units. One other small firm does not exercise any management control over its U.S. manufacturing subsidiary from the home office, nor does it maintain any full-time Japanese management at the subsidiary. The investment was undertaken by this company and its sister company in Japan, which jointly account for 65 percent of the ownership interest in the U.S. manufacturing subsidiary, with the remaining ownership shares in the hands of the U.S. management. The Japanese side is a provider of venture capital and imports approximately 35 percent of products manufactured at the U.S. subsidiary. Japanese members of the Board of Directors of this startup manufacturing venture attend the board meeting held every three months at the U.S. subsidiary. In this case and the case of one large firm mentioned earlier, the investments were part of their strategies to diversify into new lines of products developed at the U.S. side.

In order to investigate further the locus of policy formulation and the degree of control exercised by the 15 Japanese firms, these companies were asked to indicate where their policies for 16 specific policy items would be determined. These 16 items cover five areas of basic policies: sales, production, purchasing, finance, and labor. The actual responses from the 15 companies are coded on a three-point scale ranging from centralization (policy formulation at the headquarters level) to decentralization (policy formulation at the subsidiary level). Table 5-1 summarizes these responses. Personal interviews probed further the reasons for particular responses.

Indeed, the two (one large and one small) companies mentioned earlier have a very high degree of decentralization in their control systems. Their home offices delegate to their subsidiaries the management authority on all major policy decisions, except for such areas as financing of a long-term nature, monitoring of new product development, and transferring of certain Japanese personnel to the U.S. operations. The following discussions on locus of policy formulation, therefore, focus on the 13 firms other than these 2. The five major policy areas enumerated above are covered in order.

All 13 firms have their own sales subsidiaries in the United States. These sales subsidiaries were established to sell products imported from their parent companies and to provide technical services to their U.S. customers. Marketing policies are determined mainly at these sales subsidiaries, with some involvement of the home office in the case of three large and two small companies.

There are several variations in the methods of distributing products depending on the products and the size of the market in a particular area within the United States. In some cases, products are sold to the end users through sales representatives or sales agents. In other cases, they are distributed directly, or indirectly through distributors, to retailers.

TABLE 5-1
LOCUS OF POLICY FORMULATION

	Large Firms		Small Firms	
	Average Scores	*n.a.**	*Average Scores*	*n.a.**
Sales				
Marketing strategy	1.33	0	1.33	0
Pricing of products	1.67	0	1.33	0
Production				
Selection of products	2.11	0	1.83	0
Product development (R & D)	2.56	0	2.00	0
Product modification	1.56	0	1.33	0
Selection of process technology	1.78	0	1.83	0
Production volume	1.56	0	1.17	0
Purchasing				
Procurement of materials	1.22	0	1.17	0
Intercompany transfer prices	1.89	0	2.50	0
Finance				
Long-term financing	2.11	0	1.80	1
Short-term financing	1.67	0	1.17	1
Major capital expenditures	2.44	0	1.83	0
Dividend payout	2.17	3	1.00	5
Labor				
Transfer of Japanese employees	2.33	0	2.40	1
Management-level local personnel	1.33	0	1.17	0
Other local personnel	1.00	0	1.00	0
Total average	1.80		1.55	

*Indicates the number of firms that have not experienced the specific policy making.

Note: The average scores are based on a three-point scale: 3 = policy formulation at the headquarters level, 2 = joint policy formulation, and 1 = policy formulation at the subsidiary level.

Source: Compiled by the author.

In a majority of the 13 firms, more than 90 percent of the products manufactured or assembled in the United States are sold within the country (including Canada in some cases). At five companies (four large and one small), 5 to 30 percent of the products are shipped to Latin America and Europe.

Due to frequent — and sometimes volatile — exchange rate fluctuations coupled with legal considerations, product pricing is a difficult problem to deal with in international business. Pricing decisions also have to be based on an analysis of such factors as market position of the company's products, current and future expected demand for the products, and competitors' reactions. About half of the firms let the subsidiaries determine the sales prices. Two large companies with high export ratios use worldwide uniform pricing that is determined at their home office. The rest of the companies tend to prefer consultation and negotiations on selling prices between the home office and the subsidiary.

Aside from the obvious case of the home office's decision on selection of product lines for its newly established manufacturing subsidiary in the United States, the majority of the companies have switched to a joint process of policy formulation for subsequent selection of product lines. Here, it should be noted that the ultimate decision authority still rests with the home office and that the subsidiary's participation in the policy-making process is largely limited to the task of providing the home office with some local specific information such as estimates on demand, cost of production, and availability of resources.

With regard to policies on product development, the majority of the large firms determine their policies at the headquarters level, and the majority of the small firms opt for joint policy making involving both the home office and the subsidiary. This is consistent with the current research findings on the reasons for direct manufacturing investments in the United States reported in Chapter 4. Overall, the small companies attached the highest importance to "securing access to technology" as the reason for their investments. As noted, also in Chapter 4, four of the nine large firms have already established in recent years separate entities in the United States that specialize in product development. Therefore, it appears they are developing some sort of a joint policy-making apparatus for R & D strategies between their home office and their R & D subsidiaries in the United States.

Product modification is made at the local level with authorization from the home office for major modifications in the case of three large and four small companies, and jointly with product divisions at the headquarters level in the case of five large companies and one small firm. For selection of process technology, again the majority of the small firms delegate the policy-making authority to their U.S. subsidiaries, while the majority of the large firms make collaborative efforts. Thus, the headquarters of the large firms tend to get involved more closely in product modification and selection of process technology for their U.S. manufacturing plants than do the small companies. Since the large companies in general have strong and autonomous product-based divisions with adequate human resources, this difference in the locus of policy making between the large and the small firms seems to be justified.

The market success of the companies in high-technology industries is more and more dependent on the ability to respond quickly to the differentiated needs of customers. Thus, it has become critically important for the Japanese firms to develop close relations — in terms of technical services and product development — with their existing and potential customers at the local level. In this respect, the relationship between the home office and the U.S. manufacturing subsidiary is likely to undergo several changes centering around their product and process technology strategies.

In the same study cited earlier, Kujawa observed a significant difference in technology strategies between the U.S.-owned and Japanese-owned case-study companies. In the case of the U.S.-owned firms, the primary focus of their technology strategies was on development of new product-related technologies, responding to the distinct needs of their customers in the United States. On the other hand, the competitive edge of the Japanese-owned companies was based primarily on production process-related and/or institution-related (that is, management) technologies that had been transferred from their parent. However, Kujawa noted further that some of the Japanese investors began to utilize their U.S. presence for initiating or amplifying their capabilities to generate new products and thus were moving toward the integration of technology strategies between the parent and the U.S. subsidiaries.[14]

The current study confirms the general pattern of the Japanese firms' technology strategies observed by Kujawa. In the area of the development and complex application of highly sophisticated technologies, close contacts with customers and users of such applied technologies have become increasingly important. Without the actual presence of engineers and their constant communications with these customers within the market, success in developing technologies suitable for the customers' needs may not be great. Knowing this, it follows logically that the majority of the 15 Japanese companies rated as important the establishment of close relations with U.S. customers through their direct manufacturing investments in the United States, as reported in Chapter 4.

Although it is not clear whether there is some sort of master plan in technology strategies at the U.S. manufacturing plants of the Japanese companies interviewed, some progressive companies — as noted earlier — have already initiated a plan to expand their R & D activities in the United States by establishing research laboratories in the country. Technology strategies of the Japanese firms in the United States have begun just recently and are in a developmental stage. Before their U.S. subsidiaries can develop any significant technological breakthroughs, these companies have to retain and develop qualified engineers at the subsidiary level. It could be a time-consuming and painstaking process for the management at both the parent and the subsidiary.

Actual production volume and production schedules are controlled at the local level. However, due to export sales of finished products from the parent to the sales subsidiary, an overall plan of allocation of production volume between the headquarters plants and the U.S. manufacturing plants becomes necessary in some cases. A coordination procedure generally followed at one of the large firms is as follows: The sales subsidiary submits a demand analysis of the product in question for the next three to five months; the home office holds a production adjustment meeting at the product-based division in order to determine share of production volume between the home and the local plants; and then, based on the overall production schedule, the local plant prepares its operational plan and through facsimile on a daily basis feeds information on its actual production volume to the home office.

Materials used in production at the U.S. manufacturing plant are procured generally from local sources and from the parent in Japan. These materials can roughly be categorized into three groups according to the level of prior processing completed — raw materials, parts, and intermediate products (subassemblies) — in the ascending order of completion of prior processing. Generally, materials at the higher level of processing completed are procured more from Japan than from within the United States.

U.S. manufacturing plants of five of the large Japanese companies procure approximately 30 percent of their parts and intermediate products from their sister companies in Southeast Asia. The implication of this might be that at these companies the procurement policy for their U.S. plants is largely determined at the headquarters level and that these companies are implementing an integrated multiplant strategy on a global scale. However, these and the majority of the remaining firms stated that they delegated the policy-making authority on procurement strategies to their subsidiaries in the United States. Only two large companies and one small firm began to set up a joint process of policy making on procurement strategies, but with a limited level of integration.

Since maintenance of product quality is a major concern among the Japanese firms, a program of quality assurance is also extended to the local level. On this point, two large firms specifically comment that they request their U.S. manufacturing plants to send samples of materials procured locally to their headquarters for quality testing.

In the case of one large and four small firms, prices of materials to be shipped from the parent to the U.S. manufacturing plant are determined solely at the headquarters level, and in the case of the remaining firms, based on negotiations between the parent and the subsidiary. The current finding appears to support the result of the study conducted by Tang, Walter, and Raymond. Based on their questionnaire survey of 85 U.S. and 42 Japanese companies on international transfer pricing decisions, they noted that

> the process of determining transfer pricing policies was primarily a centralized function handled by executives of the parent companies. Relatively speaking, the policy-formulating process among Japanese companies is more decentralized than that of the American firms. . . . Policy disagreements are settled primarily by parent company executives in American firms, whereas Japanese firms dissolve such disagreements mainly through negotiation.[15]

In the current study, a majority of the firms interviewed are aware of the sensitive issue of transfer pricing. Among Japanese companies doing business in the United States, the issue became known in the late 1970s when the U.S. Internal Revenue Service (IRS) alleged that the U.S. subsidiaries of major Japanese automobile manufacturers had underpaid federal corporate income tax by raising transfer prices of the products shipped from their parent companies in Japan. The IRS adjusted the tax liabilities of these companies under Section 482 of the Internal Revenue Code. Although a tax treaty between the United States and Japan attempts to avoid double taxation, such reallocation of taxable income between the parent and the subsidiary would result in double taxation for the related parties because administrative procedures to adjust conflicting positions between the tax authorities of the two countries have not been worked out.

Recently the National Tax Administration Agency (Kokuzeicho) in Japan requested the IRS in the United States to issue guidelines for its applications of the tax code. At the same time the MOF in Japan has begun a study of international transfer pricing practices of multinational corporations and their tax implications in an atttempt to create new tax rules, which could be introduced in the fiscal year 1985 at the earliest. [16] Therefore, as in the case of U.S. multinationals, international transfer pricing policies of Japanese companies will likely be more centralized in the future.

Policy on long-term financing is generally determined jointly, but that on short-term financing is determined more at the local level. In some cases, the parent company directs its U.S. subsidiary from which banks the subsidiary can borrow. Such directive is intended to maintain a balanced relationship with the banks with which the company normally deals.

Robbins and Stobaugh postulate three phases in the evolution of the financial system and control of a multinational company.[17] At the first stage in the company's overseas expansion, the enterprise tends to ignore the potential benefit to be gained through centralizing the function of international financial management due to the small size of foreign operations relative to its domestic operations as well as in absolute terms. At this stage, "the minuscule staff has neither the time to manage closely the financial problems of the foreign subsidiaries nor the experience to issue decision rules to the subsidiaries."[18] Consequently, the financial activities of the foreign operations are managed independently at the subsidiary level.

As the relative importance of the foreign business grows, the company enters the second phase, where "the central staff makes most financial decisions of major importance and issues frequent orders to subsidiaries"[19] in order to optimize benefits from the intercompany finanical links. As the foreign operations grow further in size and number of subsidiaries, complexity of various transactions forces the parent to delegate more authority to the subsidiaries, using a rule book specifying such items as "the limits of local borrowing, standard terms of payment on intercompany accounts, and standard rates for management fees."[20] At this third phase of development, the company creates regional financial headquarters.

Financial activities have become sophisticated at some of the large Japanese companies interviewed. As noted earlier in this chapter, these firms have established an international finance division that regularly scans the international capital market and provides necessary capital to overseas subsidiaries as the needs arise. The majority of the large Japanese firms have accumulated experiences in financial transactions at their U.S. sales subsidiaries (eight of the nine large companies established their U.S. sales subsidiaries by the mid-1960s and another large firm in 1970), and some of these companies have been utilizing their main U.S. offices as regional headquarters. According to the evolutionary pattern of the financial system and control postulated by Robbins and Stobaugh, these large Japanese firms seem to be in transition from the second phase to the third phase. At this juncture, however, none of these Japanese firms seem to have resorted yet to the "rule book" approach for delegating authority, in contrast to the findings of Robbins and Stobaugh in their study of financial policies of U.S. multinational enterprises.

For major capital expenditures at the U.S. manufacturing plants, a majority of the firms currently require their subsidiaries to submit their acquisition plans to the headquarters semiannually for approval. It appears that most of the large and small parent firms exercise tighter control and supervision in the area of finance.

Three large and four small companies have not received dividends from their U.S. subsidiaries yet. One of the small firms has a specific policy to reinvest locally all the profits earned at the subsidiary level. The other firms, which have already received dividends from their U.S. subsidiaries, normally determine the dividend policy jointly with formal approval at the board of directors' meeting of the subsidiary. Since these parent companies own 100 percent of the voting shares in their subsidiaries, their home office seems to have a strong say in determining the amount and timing of dividend distribution.

Generally, the firms interviewed transfer their Japanese employees (directors, general managers, or staff employees) to their U.S. subsidiaries for the period ranging from three to five years. The transfer period is normally longer for those in administrative functions than those engaged in engineering duties. Selection of these transferees is made by the personnel department of the home office after consultation with appropriate divisional heads, from whose divisions the transferees are chosen. In the majority of the companies, the selection is made with due consideration of particular needs of and requests from, their U.S. subsidiaries. Therefore, the often-cited Japanese practice of shifting unwanted or redundant employees at the parent company to its subsidiaries does not seem to be used in the case of the Japanese firms with respect to their U.S. subsidiaries.[21]

Personnel policy on local employees (hiring and firing) is delegated to the local management to a significant degree at all the companies interviewed. However, at three large companies and one small firm, the subsidiary must seek formal approval from the home office when local individuals are to be hired or promoted to the top- and middle-management jobs.

The current study noted that in the case of acquisitions and ventures with U.S. entrepreneurs, the Japanese parent has delegated substantial autonomy to its U.S. subsidiary. In the case of the companies with startup and wholly owned subsidiaries, there are frequent consultation and negotiations between the parent and the subsidiary in several key policy areas, notably in selection of products, product development, intercompany transfer prices, long-term financing (including major capital expenditures), and transfer of Japanese employees from the home office to the subsidiary. However, marketing policies are mainly made at the local sales subsidiary level. Personnel policies except for Japanese transferees are also highly decentralized.

With regard to the latter point, in his study of Japanese-owned manufacturing subsidiaries in the United States, Kujawa observed that

> significantly, at every company, the chief personnel officer was a U.S. national. Moreover, at those firms that had a personnel staff, there were no Japanese nationals assigned to personnel. At six of the nine case-study companies, the chief personnel officer reported to a Japanese national. It appears quite evident the Japanese view personnel as one area best administered by local staff.[22]

The current study confirms his finding from the parent company's perspective as well. However, it should be noted that some companies are concerned about management-employee relations at the subsidiary level and monitor the results of the effectiveness of personnel management through reports furnished by the subsidiaries. This point will be discussed later.

Communication Methods

An efficient communications channel between the home office in Japan and the U.S. subsidiary is difficult to achieve due to the geographical distance and the difference in language. Five communication methods were rated by the 15 companies interviewed, using a four-point scale ranging from "very important" to "not important." Table 5-2 summarizes their responses in the descending order of importance perceived by the large companies (the order slightly differs in the case of the small firms). In general, the majority of the large companies utilize all the five methods of communication. The small firms tend to rely on written reports from the subsidiary.

In 13 of the 15 companies, management conferences are held once or twice per year. These firms generally convene a meeting of management-level personnel of both the home office and all their major overseas subsidiaries at their corporate headquarters in Japan. Typically such a meeting is attended by the top management consisting mostly or only of

TABLE 5-2
RELATIVE IMPORTANCE OF FIVE
COMMUNICATION METHODS

	Large Firms		Small Firms	
Communication Method	Average Scores	n.a.*	Average Scores	n.a.*
Regular conferences of management personnel at the headquarters or at the subsidiary	3.44	0	3.25	2
Written reports on a regular basis from the subsidiary to the home office	3.33	0	3.67	0
Frequent communications via telephone, telex, and/or facsimile	2.88	1	3.25	2
Training and indoctrination (as to corporate philosophy) of key Japanese personnel at the home office prior to task assignment and transfer to the subsidiary	2.86	2	2.33	3
Personal visits by decision-making authorities to the subsidiary whenever problems arise	2.78	0	2.75	2

*Indicates the number of firms that do not normally utilize the particular communication method.

Note: The average scores are based on a four-point scale: 4 = very important, 3 = important, 2 = less important, and 1 = not important.

Source: Compiled by the author.

Japanese nationals. Cultural and language barriers make it difficult for the majority of the Japanese executives and managers to interact with their U.S. counterparts at formal corporate meetings.

In addition to top-management meetings, some firms hold meetings of middle-level management in engineering, product planning, marketing, and accounting on a more frequent basis. One large firm started an international zero-defect meeting in Japan in the early 1980s in which its employees from the headquarters and overseas manufacturing plants present their experiences and practical solutions on quality control problems.

All the companies require regular written reports from their subsidiaries, and the majority of them have U.S. accounting firms audit annual financial statements of their subsidiaries. Specificity and frequency of written reports seem to vary according to the size and importance of the subsidiary and the company's experience in overseas business operations. In general, the large companies require their subsidiaries to submit more detailed and frequent reports than do the small companies.

The large firms generally require their subsidiaries to submit semiannual financial statements with pro forma statements of budgets as well as detailed monthly reports. In addition, one large firm requires weekly flash reports regarding manufacturing operations. One other large firm requires its U.S. subsidiary to submit a medium-range (three-year) corporate plan, which is reevaluated and reported to the parent by the subsidiary every year.

The monthly reports generally cover the following items, with differing degree of minuteness:

1. Financial reports, including a balance sheet and an income statement (frequently only the latter statement is required for monthly reporting purposes), cash flow analysis, analysis of budget variances, inventory turnover, and analysis of accounts receivable.
2. Production reports, including volume of actual production, analysis of productivity and production costs, and comments on quality control and general conditions of plant operations.
3. Personnel reports, including number and allocation of employees among various divisions at the subsidiary, employee turnover ratios, and absenteeism.
4. Business reports, including analyses of U.S. economy and industries (including competitors' activities in some cases), and operational plans on future sales, production, and management.

In addition to requiring the preceding monthly reports, two large firms call upon their subsidiaries to furnish semiannual or monthly reports on their R & D activities and plans.

Although preparation of financial statements on a semiannual basis instead of a quarterly basis is a norm in Japan, one large firm has been considering the possibility of preparing quarterly statements as practiced among large U.S. corporations. The interviewee at this company commented that in order for this type of idea to be accepted by the top management, the importance of the idea had to be communicated repeatedly to the corporate president until he began to believe the idea as his own. In contrast, another large company has already been requesting its main U.S. subsidiary to submit quarterly financial statements on a consolidated basis, combining financial positions and results of operations of all its U.S. subsidiaries.

Facsimiles are widely used for communications to and from the subsidiary. Frequent communications between the parent and the subsidiary, however, do not necessarily mean an effective coordination of corporate activities. In some cases, delegation of decision-making authority to the subsidiary's management is not well articulated, and thus frequent consultation and communications are required. As Yoshino observes:

> Because tasks are defined ambiguously, the manager of a subsidiary must have an intuitive understanding of which types of decision can be made by him and which must be referred to the parent company. . . . A new manager of a foreign subsidiary is often told by his superiors prior to his departure that he will have total freedom of action in managing the subsidiary. The statement is made with full understanding on the part of everyone that no major decisions will be made without appropriate consultation with the parent company.[23]

In recent years, the top management of major Japanese corporations are increasingly interested in computer-assisted decision making at their corporate headquarters.[24] This fervor in computerization and quick decision making on the part of top management at the home office seems certain to be extended to cover the area of managing overseas subsidiaries in the near future. One of the large firms interviewed has been trying to install a comprehensive computer and telecommunications system linking its overseas subsidiaries with the headquarters.

Some of the large companies have in-house training programs. One large firm has, for example, a program at the level of its product-based divisions for foreign managers. These foreign managers can visit the company's headquarters plants in Japan to receive first-hand experiences in manufacturing operations. At the corporate level, this company has recently added a new training course to develop executives for overseas assignments. At another large firm, employees to be transferred to its overseas subsidiaries must go through an intensive training for approximately half a year at the home office. They spend about six months at the international division and the other related departments, and then complete plant tours and lectures on corporate philosophy and other subjects for one week.

Personal visits are not considered particularly effective if they are made only at the time when problems arise at the subsidiary level. Instead, the top or the middle managers of the corporate headquarters in some of the companies visit their U.S. subsidiaries on a regular basis. At one large company, for example, a general manager of the corporate planning division visits overseas subsidiaries every three months. At another large company, the corporate executive visits the U.S. subsidiaries almost every month.

Evaluation of Subsidiary Performance

Seven large and two small firms apply basically the same performance evaluation methods to their U.S. manufacturing subsidiaries as used for their other manufacturing operations. However, two large and four small companies use different evaluation methods for their U.S. manufacturing plants. In these latter cases, two firms reason that the unique business environment in the United States requires different evaluation methods. One of these two is a large company that acquired 100 percent ownership interest in an existing U.S. firm. This subsidiary is being operated quite autonomously and the parent seems to be in the learning stage to determine a proper mix of evaluation practices at the headquarters as well as at the subsidiary level. Another is a small firm that started its manufacturing venture in the United States with a primary objective of developing engineering personnel at the subsidiary level. This company seems to be pursuing management practices at its U.S. subsidiary different from those at the home office.

The other four (one large and three small) firms justify the use of different methods by claiming that the activity of their U.S. plants is different. The large company applies different evaluation methods to its acquired plant and startup plant, both of which are wholly owned subsidiaries but differ in managerial settings. The primary operations at the plants of two of the three small firms are service oriented rather than manufacturing oriented. Another small firm uses a different evaluation method because its capital participation in the U.S. manufacturing operation is more like a portfolio investment rather than a direct investment.

All 15 companies were requested to indicate the relative importance of eight possible measures to evaluate the performance of their U.S. manufacturing subsidiaries, using a four-point scale ranging from "very important" to "not important." In addition, they were asked to specify any other performance evaluation methods being used. Table 5-3 summarizes the relative importance of these evaluation measures perceived by the nine large and the six small firms. The table lists the eight measures in the order of importance to the large firms.

The majority of the firms — large and small — use local profits as the primary measure to evaluate their subsidiaries. Relating to local profit, two other profitability measures are also used: contribution to consolidated profit and return on investment. Six of the nine large companies and three of the six small firms consider their subsidiaries'

TABLE 5-3
RELATIVE IMPORTANCE OF PERFORMANCE EVALUATION MEASURES

	Large Firms		Small Firms	
Performance Evaluation Measure	Average Scores	n.a.*	Average Scores	n.a.*
Local profit	3.63	1	4.00	1
Contribution to consolidated profit	3.56	0	3.00	1
Budget variance	3.44	0	3.00	2
Market share	3.43	2	3.50	0
Return on investment	3.00	1	3.40	1
Productivity	3.00	2	2.75	2
Employee turnover (low)	2.57	2	2.80	1
Cash flows to parent	1.86	2	1.60	1

*Indicates the number of companies that do not use the particular measure of performance evaluation.

Note: The average scores are based on a four-point scale: 4 = very important, 3 = important, 2 = less important, and 1 = not important.

Source: Compiled by the author.

contributions to their consolidated profits as a "very important" measure. This may imply that their local operations have a significant effect on their overall operating results. Return on investment is preferred by one large firm and one small company, whose investments can be characterized more as portfolio than as direct investments.

Market share receives close attention also. Because it is basically monitored at the sales subsidiaries with reference to sales volume and based on data provided by U.S. market research firms, the majority of the large firms considered the measure as having a secondary importance for their U.S. manufacturing plants. Some large firms also use in-house statistics collected through customer surveys on product acceptance and corporate image.

Budget variances are considered as a "very important" evaluation measure by five of the nine large firms and one of the six small companies. Robbins and Stobaugh's study of the performance evaluation of foreign subsidiaries of U.S. multinationals also noted that the medium and large enterprises considered the budget as the most important tool for evaluating performance:

> Although the budget is a tool employed by practically all enterprises in the evaluation of overseas subsidiaries, it assumes special significance in the large enterprises. In such firms, the budget is a major yardstick against which subsidiary operations may be gauged. In these relatively sophisticated systems the managements use a number of supporting measures whose current changes help throw light on the subsidiaries' performance.[25]

The current study also revealed that in comparison to the smaller firms the large Japanese firms tended to view the budget as a major evaluation measure.

Productivity and employee turnover are also used as evaluation measures and considered "very important" by some firms. These firms are generally concerned with the high employee turnover at their U.S. subsidiaries. Some efforts to improve the situation have been tried at the subsidiary level. For example, the subsidiary of one large firm initiated a companywide program of holding sporting events, parties, and quality control circle activities on a regular basis in an attempt to create an atmosphere of "one corporate family." Another large firm, which had experienced a high employee turnover and low productivity at its California plant, sent a group of Japanese training personnel to its new plant in Georgia to create a better working environment and to improve management-labor relations.

The literature on performance evaluation of overseas subsidiaries is not abundant. In their study of performance evaluation techniques employed by U.S. multinationals based on 17 personal and 16 telephone interviews, Morsicato and Radebaugh concluded that

the U.S. dollar financial measures employed, in order of popularity, include profit, return on investment, and budgets, whereas the local-currency measures include budget and profit. Return on investment in local currency is not a popularly used measure. . . . A majority of corporations use the same basic technique to evaluate subsidiary performance as they used to evaluate manager performance. Likewise, a majority of firms apply the same performance evaluation domestically as they do abroad.[26]

In general, the Japanese companies interviewed appear to use a variety of measures of importance to them to evaluate their subsidiaries' performance. They also tend to apply the same home-grown evaluation techniques to their U.S. subsidiaries. The current study also noted that the majority of the firms considered the market share as a "very important" measure. It is a direct measure against the competitors in the market and cannot be used as a yardstick on a short-term basis, say as a quarterly performance evaluation. This implies that they rely on long-term market strategies and, thus, evaluate their subsidiaries accordingly. In addition, some of these companies use such nonfinancial measures as productivity and employee turnover, which may be used to evaluate the effectiveness of the local management on employee relations.

6 CHANGES IN GOVERNMENT-BUSINESS RELATIONS

The preceding two chapters investigated the investment decision-making processes and control systems of the 15 Japanese companies. This chapter examines government-business relations (macro-micro interactions) with respect to Japan's direct manufacturing investments in the United States.

Interactions between the macro-level actors and the micro-level actors are difficult to analyze, for they are interwoven in a complicated way and vary depending on the specific issues involved and according to changes in time and environment. The current chapter attempts to find an evolving pattern of the macro-micro interactions that may explain the rapid increase in Japan's direct manufacturing investments in the United States since the early 1970s. Identification of such a pattern would also be instrumental in predicting possible future directions of Japan's overseas direct manufacturing investments in general.

This chapter shows that there have been two major currents working to trigger Japan's direct manufacturing investments in the United States. One, which is the politically-oriented current, relates to Japan's drive for export-led economic growth that continued with vigor for more than two decades after the end of World War II. As a result of Japan's success in attaining trade surpluses as well as its phenomenal economic development, political pressures from her trading partners to liberalize her restrictive trade and investment practices began to increase in the 1960s. Faced with these pressures, the Japanese government undertook trade and capital liberalization measures in several stages.

Another current, which is enterprise-oriented, is characterized by private initiatives of Japanese companies and business leaders. As these firms have increased their international competitiveness and accumulated capital, technologies, and management know-how at a rapid pace during the postwar reconstruction and development period, they began to pursue their own international business strategies. Leading companies have been successfully and vigorously restructuring their business operations in order to cope with increased competition at home and abroad. As will be noted later in this chapter, the business leaders in Japan began to involve themselves more and more actively with private diplomacy in order to help solve the bilateral economic conflicts between Japan and her main trading partners, especially the United States.

The first current seems to have worked as a pull factor and the second as a push factor for the rapid increase in Japan's direct manufacturing investments in the United States in recent years. The late 1960s can be viewed as a turning point in Japan's economic management in several respects, for example, the necessity to reexamine the earlier policy of export-led economic growth and a gradual shift from the state-guided market system to the private-sector-led market system.

The chapter is divided into four major sections: relaxation of foreign exchange controls, MITI's new direction, private initiatives, and Japan's direct manufacturing investment. The first section recounts the important historical development of changes in the government controls on foreign exchange and international transactions of private business, which explains the underlying reason at the macro level for the rapid increase in Japan's foreign direct investment since the early 1970s. The next two sections examine the change in the pattern of macro-micro interactions in recent years. Finally, the fourth section analyzes the current and future prospects of Japan's direct manufacturing investment in the United States in light of the ongoing changes in government-business relations.

RELAXATION OF FOREIGN EXCHANGE CONTROLS

This section examines the historical development of changes in the Japanese governmental policy on foreign exchange controls. These changes have had a direct effect on the freedom of Japanese companies' decisions to undertake their direct investments abroad.

For approximately 30 years until the Japanese Diet (legislative assembly) enacted a revision in 1979, two basic laws governed foreign exchange transactions: the Foreign Exchange and Foreign Trade Control Law of 1949 and the Foreign Capital Law of 1950. The former was intended to control international transactions in general — for example, exports and imports, international trade in services, and various other international monetary transactions. The latter was to control Japan's importation of foreign capital and technologies. These two laws were based on the principle of "prohibition" of international transactions. However, for practical applications of the laws, various government ordinances (*seirei*) and ministerial ordinances (*shorei*) permitted certain transactions, which were deemed necessary for Japan's economic development, through exemptions or by subjecting them to a license system (*kyokasei*).[1]

The revision of the two laws became effective on December 1, 1980. The Foreign Capital Law of 1950 was abolished, and the basic principle governing international transactions was altered from "prohibition" to "freedom." Although the change in the basic principle was codified as a new legal ground through this revision of the Foreign Exchange and Foreign Trade Control Law in 1979, the governmental control over foreign exchange transactions had been gradually relaxed at the administrative level through several revisions in government and ministerial ordinances in order to respond to internal and external pressures. These pressures can be analyzed from two perspectives. One is Japan's export-led growth, and the other is trade and capital liberalization. Thus, the history of gradual development and relaxation of foreign exchange controls under these two pressures is examined in the following four subsections: origin of strict controls over foreign exchange, export-led growth, trade and capital liberalization, and the new law on foreign exchange and foreign trade.

Origin of Strict Controls over Foreign Exchange

During the postwar years of economic reconstruction and development, Japan had to overcome several internal constraints. Among these constraints, the most important were scarcity of natural resources, scarcity of capital and foreign exchange, scarcity of industrial technologies, and surplus of population. In order to pay for imports of essential raw materials for domestic production, Japan had to become able to export high value–added products. Since capital and foreign exchange were scarce and had to be directed to expansion of domestic production and establishment of a strong international marketing network, some form of an effective system of resource allocation had to be devised. In addition, industrial technologies had to be introduced from the advanced countries in order to modernize Japan's production base.

Although the traditional economic theory of comparative advantage might have justified specialization in labor-intensive industries because of the surplus of population, economic policy makers (especially MITI officials in concert with private business leaders) in Japan opted for establishment of capital- and technology-intensive industries to catch up with the advanced industrial countries. Selection of products and industries for development was based on the following conditions: the products chosen were those for which the income elasticity of demand in the world as a whole was judged to be high and the industries chosen were those in which a rapid technical progress was expected to increase productivity and, thus, steeply to reduce manufacturing costs.[2]

Since ample studies are available showing how the strategies of Japan's high economic growth in the postwar years were implemented in conjunction with her industrial policies, they are not repeated here.[3] However, it should be noted for the purpose of the current study that the selection criteria stated above were closely associated with the expected positive effect to be derived from these industries upon Japan's terms of trade and competitive position in international markets.

During the early postwar years, scarcity of foreign exchange and the attendant problem in Japan's balance of payments required serious attention of policy makers. In order to solve these problems, two systems were devised: a foreign exchange budget system and a centralized allocation system of foreign exchange. The latter system prohibited exporters from using foreign exchange earned through their export sales but, instead, required them to turn the foreign exchange over to a government account for its centralized allocation.[4]

In 1949, the Supreme Commander for the Allied Powers (SCAP) transferred its responsibility over foreign exchange controls to the Japanese government. With encouragement of SCAP, the Japanese government then enacted the Foreign Exchange and Foreign Trade Control Law of 1949. In the early 1950s, MITI was empowered with authority to enact and supervise the foreign exchange budget and to supervise all imports of technology and all joint ventures of Japanese firms with foreign entities. As Johnson notes, "When these changes were made, MITI came to possess weapons of industrial management and control that rivaled anything its predecessors had ever known during the prewar and wartime periods."[5]

Export-Led Growth

The importance of international trade, especially exports, for the economic development of Japan has been well recognized by both the government and private business leaders in Japan. As Allen observes, two basic reasons explain this: (1) Japan's dependence on imported raw materials, fuel, and food and (2) the stabilizing effect of trade during periods of domestic recession.[6]

Table 6-1 shows Japan's total merchandise trade as well as Japan's bilateral trade with the United States for the period of 1955 through 1982. Japan's total exports exceeded her total imports for the first time in 1965,

TABLE 6-1
JAPAN'S MERCHANDISE TRADE, 1955–82: TOTAL VERSUS JAPAN–U.S. BILATERAL TRADE
(In Millions of U.S. Dollars)

	Total			Japan-U.S.		
	Exports	*Imports*	*Balance*	*Exports*	*Imports*	*Balance*
1955	2,011	2,471	–460	456	774	–318
1960	4,055	4,491	–436	1,102	1,554	–452
1965	8,452	8,169	283	2,479	2,366	113
1970	19,318	18,881	437	5,940	5,560	380
1971	24,019	19,712	4,307	7,495	4,978	2,517
1972	28,591	23,471	5,120	8,848	5,852	2,996
1973	36,930	38,314	–1,384	9,449	9,270	179
1974	55,536	62,110	–6,574	12,799	12,682	117
1975	55,753	57,863	–2,110	11,149	11,608	–459
1976	67,226	64,799	2,427	15,690	11,809	3,881
1977	80,495	70,809	9,686	19,717	12,396	7,321
1978	97,543	79,343	18,200	24,915	14,790	10,125
1979	103,032	110,672	–7,640	26,403	20,431	5,972
1980	129,807	140,528	–10,721	31,367	24,408	6,959
1981	152,030	143,290	8,740	38,609	25,297	13,312
1982	138,831	131,931	6,900	36,330	24,179	12,151

Source: Compiled from *Japan and the United States: Challenges and Opportunities,* ed. William J. Barnds, Council on Foreign Relations Book (New York: New York University Press, 1979) and *Japan 1983: An International Comparison* (Tokyo: Keizai Koho Center, 1983).

posting a trade surplus of $283 million. From then until the first oil shock of 1973–74, Japan's trade surplus grew steadily.

From 1973 to 1975, Japan's trade balance recorded deficits due mainly to the oil shock. Japan's vulnerability, due to her dependence on foreign sources for energy supply and other essential raw materials, was once again recognized. After three years of overall deficit in merchandise trade, Japan's trade surplus was restored in 1976 and continued for three years. By 1978, Japan recorded a huge trade surplus of $18 billion. Then the second oil shock of 1979 raised her import bills again, and Japan as a result recorded trade deficits in 1979 and 1980.

Japan's bilateral trade with the United States also posted a surplus in favor of Japan in 1965. As her trade surplus continued to grow since the late 1960s, the economic issue began to evolve into a serious political tension between the two countries. U.S. industries, first in textiles and then in steel, electronics, and automobiles, began to ask the U.S. federal government for protection from the Japanese competition. (Appendix E shows a chronology of Japan-U.S. trade frictions.)

Japan's phenomenal export-led growth was sustained by her structural adjustment toward capital- and technology-intensive industries. Table 6-2 shows a transformation in the structure of Japan's exports during the period of 1955 through 1980. It presents clearly that Japan's major export items were shifted from textiles, 37.2 percent of Japan's total exports in 1955 and 4.9 percent in 1980, to machinery and equipment, 12.4 percent of Japan's total exports in 1955 and 62.8 percent in 1980.

In the same table, the overall expansion of exports during the period is measured by indices with the base year of 1965. Japan's total exports in 1955 amounted to only 24 percent of those in 1965. However, they expanded to 15 times the 1965 level in 1980.

The share of mineral fuels in Japan's total imports has increased tremendously since the mid-1970s due to oil price increases. Table 6-2 shows that it expanded from 11.7 percent in 1955 to 49.8 percent in 1980 after the oil shock of 1979.

The period of the late 1960s to the early 1970s brought forth a turning point in Japan's bilateral relations with the United States and her domestic and foreign economic policies, a turning point signified by a shift in U.S. foreign economic policies. As bilateral trade negotiations on textiles came to a political deadlock in the late 1960s and domestic as well as international economic and political problems — such as those caused by the U.S. involvement in the Vietnam War — mounted in the United

TABLE 6-2
THE STRUCTURE OF JAPAN'S EXPORTS AND IMPORTS, 1955–80
(In Percentage of Total Value)

Exports	1955	1960	1965	1970	1975	1980
Foodstuffs	6.3	6.3	4.1	3.4	1.4	1.2
Textiles	37.2	30.4	18.7	12.5	6.7	4.9
Chemicals	5.1	4.5	6.5	6.4	7.0	5.2
Metals	19.2	14.0	20.3	19.7	22.5	16.4
Machinery & Equipment	12.4	25.5	35.2	46.3	53.8	62.8
Other	19.8	19.3	15.2	11.7	8.6	9.5
Total	100.0	100.0	100.0	100.0	100.0	100.0
Index* (1965 = 100)	24	48	100	229	660	1,536

Imports	1955	1960	1965	1970	1975	1980
Foodstuffs	25.3	12.2	18.0	13.5	15.2	10.4
Textile Materials	23.7	17.0	10.4	5.1	2.6	1.7
Metal Ores	7.5	15.0	12.5	14.3	7.6	6.0
Other Raw Materials	19.9	17.2	16.6	16.0	9.9	9.2
Mineral Fuels	11.7	16.5	19.9	20.7	44.3	49.8
Chemicals	4.5	5.9	5.0	5.3	3.6	4.4
Machinery & Equipment	5.3	9.7	9.3	12.2	7.4	7.0
Other	2.1	6.5	8.3	12.9	9.4	11.5
Total	100.0	100.0	100.0	100.0	100.0	100.0
Index* (1965 = 100)	30	55	100	231	708	1,720

*Index was computed by dividing total exports (or imports) in each year by total exports (or imports) in 1965.

Source: Compiled from *Japan and the United States: Challenges and Opportunities,* ed. William J. Barnds, Council on Foreign Relations Book (New York: New York University Press, 1979) and *Japan 1983: An International Comparison* (Tokyo: Keizai Koho Center, 1983).

States, the Nixon administration made two major policy changes in 1971, both of which surprised the Japanese government. In July, the Nixon administration suddenly announced its basic shift in U.S. policy toward the People's Republic of China without any prior notice to Japan, a long-time ally of the United States in the region of East Asia. Then, it suspended convertibility of the U.S. dollar into gold, which eventually led to a nullification of the postwar international monetary agreement based on the fixed exchange rate system (the Bretton Woods Agreement of 1944), and imposed a 10 percent import surcharge — actions that soon caused a drastic revaluation of the Japanese yen.[7]

The so-called Nixon shocks signified a newly emerging pattern of U.S.-Japan relations, a change from a postwar paternal relationship to an equal-competitive relationship. Japan had to search for a new policy response to this changed pattern in the bilateral relations. As Destler and others observe, "The fact that broader international economic and political relationships were changing in the early seventies fed fears in Japan that the United States might be moving to abandon the alliance entirely or at least to reduce it to a formal shell without substance."[8]

Trade and Capital Liberalization

Japan's rapid economic development during the first two decades after the end of World War II was supported directly and indirectly by the postwar U.S. foreign policies. Again, as Destler and others observe:

> The general thrust of U.S. policy was to encourage Japanese economic expansion. The predominant official American view was that a full-employment economy in Japan depended on trade and that Japanese democracy, in turn, depended on a healthy economy. It was also important that Western markets be open to Japanese trade so that Japan would not have to turn toward the communist countries. Furthermore, it was believed, if special barriers were erected against Japan and Japan were treated like an outcast, hostile forces might once again become dominant there. Thus during the 1950s and well into the 1960s the attitudes of American and Japanese officials on free trade for Japan were basically parallel, stressing (except on special products) nondiscriminatory treatment of Japanese exports and not expecting Japanese reciprocity on imports.[9]

Thus, with strong encouragement from the United States, Japan was gradually drawn into the international community throughout the postwar years. She became a member of the IMF in 1952, and she was then admitted to the General Agreement on Tariffs and Trade (GATT) in 1955. As the free trade movement became a strong current among the industrialized countries in the early 1960s, Japan began to receive political pressures from her trading partners. The Japanese government abandoned foreign exchange controls over current transactions in accordance with Article VIII of the IMF agreement and adopted Article XI status of GATT, which required the elimination of quantitative restrictions on imports and the modification of her subsidies to exports.[10]

In 1964, Japan joined the OECD as the first Asian nation admitted to membership. The admittance meant that Japan had to adhere to the OECD's code of capital liberalization. In the same year, MITI relinquished its control over the foreign exchange budget system.[11]

Reflecting the general trend toward internationalization of the Japanese economy, MITI issued a paper on basic directions for future policy in 1969. The following quotation describes clearly the basic thought on trade and capital liberalization developing in Japan in the late 1960s:

> We now need to push strongly the expansion of the Japanese economy in the international market. With the enlarged size of the economy, the favourable balance of payments and other recent developments, policy questions have been raised recently as to the removal of remaining import restrictions, the liberalization of international capital transactions and the promotion of economic cooperation with the developing countries. We are now approaching the stage where we need to promote our economy's internationalization by opening the door wider to our trading partners, by promoting capital liberalization while overcoming various difficulties, and by actively advancing abroad. Such a positive policy is a must in order not only to develop and secure the markets and resources necessary for the future development of Japan's economy but also to request other nations to hold to the principle of free trade. At the same time, we must strengthen the competitiveness of smaller firms, not to mention that of large enterprises, so that they can survive in the internationalized economy. The improvement of the industrial structure in every sector is thus required for the smoother development of economic internationalization without sacrificing the independence of Japanese industry.[12]

As Japan's commitment to trade and capital liberalization became a national agenda in the 1960s, Japanese industries accelerated rationalization and modernization of their business practices. Some Japanese business leaders began to realize that the Japanese companies had to internationalize in order to avoid isolation from the international community.

In June 1971, Japan removed most of the restrictive policies on overseas investments. Prior to June 1971, every case of outward investment and each increase of capital had to be approved individually by the MOF in consultation with other appropriate ministries, especially MITI. Presumably, the criterion for such approval had been based on one of two major conditions, that is, promotion of exports from Japan or development and securing of natural resources overseas. The practice of such individual screening was changed to a system of automatic approval by the Bank of Japan (BOJ) in 1971.[13]

Furthermore, effective in May 1972, the centralized control system on foreign exchange was deleted from the government ordinance.[14] As noted earlier, one other strict control measure — the foreign exchange budget system — was abolished in 1964. Thus, by the early 1970s MITI lost both of its two powerful tools for guidance and control over Japanese industries.

In addition to the positive effect of Japan's trade surplus on foreign exchange reserves, another macroeconomic pressure, which also hastened the changes in the basic governmental policy toward Japan's

TABLE 6-3
JAPAN'S PRIVATE CAPITAL TRANSACTIONS, 1956–72
(In Millions of U.S. Dollars)

	Inflow				Outflow			
Year	Direct Invest-ment	Other Private Long-term Capital	Other Private Short-term Capital	Total Inflow	Direct Invest-ment	Other Private Long-term Capital	Other Pirvate Short-term Capital	Total Outflow
1956	16	–2	51	65	27	49	–8	68
1957	30	14	73	117	33	21	–5	49
1958	12	73	–11	74	27	17	7	51
1959	19	80	–54	45	48	70	7	125
1960	59	166	36	261	93	173	15	281
1961	59	166	36	261	93	173	15	281
1962	58	381	96	535	77	214	–11	280
1963	102	641	99	842	122	114	–8	228
1964	109	432	224	765	57	342	–8	391
1965	45	8	–66	–13	77	258	–4	331
1966	30	–160	–49	–179	105	425	29	559
1967	45	10	520	575	123	498	16	637
1968	76	721	191	988	220	636	1	857
1969	72	1,335	247	1,654	206	716	71	993
1970	94	433	692	1,219	355	916	24	1,295
1971	210	1,041	2,423	3,674	360	994	24	1,378
1972	168	465	1,872	2,505	723	882	–40	1,565
Total	1,204	5,804	6,380	13,388	2,746	6,498	125	9,369

Note: For 1971 and 1972, statistical figures expressed in terms of Special Drawing Rights (SDRs) were converted to the U.S. dollar basis by the current author. Conversion rates (U.S. dollar per SDR) were obtained from *Balance of Payments Yearbook,* vol. 27 (1976).

Source: Compiled from *Balance of Payments Yearbook,* vol. 13 (June 1962), vol. 17 (October 1965), vol. 21 (December 1969), and vol. 27 (December 1976), International Monetary Fund.

foreign direct investment, had been developing since the late 1960s — this was a massive inflow of foreign capital in the form of long-term and short-term investments. Table 6-3 shows Japan's private capital transactions from 1956 to 1972.

Inflow of foreign capital into Japan, especially in a form other than direct investments, began to increase by a significant amount in 1969. The cumulative total of capital inflow for the 1956–72 period amounted to $13.4 billion, whereas the cumulative total of capital outlow for the same period was only $9.4 billion. This unbalanced net capital flow must also have affected the upward adjustment of the value of the Japanese yen as well as the Japanese government's attitude toward foreign direct investments in the 1970s.

The New Law on Foreign Exchange and Foreign Trade

Although the Japanese government's administrative control over foreign exchange transactions was greatly relaxed by the early 1970s, the original statutes prohibiting international transactions in principle were unchanged until 1979. Following Japan's accord with her trading partners at the conclusion of the Tokyo Round of Multilateral Trade Negotiations in 1978, a revision of the original statutes was finally made in 1979.

The new Law on Foreign Exchange and Foreign Trade Control, which became effective in 1980, subscribes to the basic principle of "freedom" in international transactions. However, the government retains its authority to intervene in such transactions in case of emergency situations. An emergency measure will be applied if a transaction is deemed to cause one of the following events: (1) difficulty in maintaining an equilibrium in the nation's international balance of payments, (2) a radical fluctuation in the rate of foreign exchange, or (3) an adverse effect on the nation's financial and capital markets.[15]

There is no detailed elaboration on when such an emergency measure might be exercised. However, because the basic objective of the new law is intended to give a greater freedom in international transactions and because many factors and policies affect the foreign exchange rate as well as the balance of payments, one would expect such emergency measures to be used sparingly and cautiously.

With regard to overseas direct investments, administrative procedures are currently based on an application system. Under the system, an investor files an application, which details the nature and the date of his direct investment, with the MOF through the BOJ within two months prior to the expected date of the investment. During the next 20 days following the date of the application, MOF evaluates the nature of the investment. If the investment is deemed to create an adverse effect on the domestic and international order, MOF can alter or rescind the original application. In practice, however, BOJ accepts an application for overseas direct investment automatically and shortens the 20-day evaluation period as long as the investment does not fall into any one of the following categories: (1) investments in such industries as fishery, textiles, banking and stockbrokerage, arms (weapons), narcotics, and so on; (2) investments in South Africa and Namibia; or (3) investments by banks and strockbrokerage firms.[16]

Therefore, Japan's direct manufacturing investments in the United States do not seem to be unduly constrained by the macro-level actors. Furthermore, given various trade frictions with the United States, the Japanese government may be pleased to see Japanese companies investing in U.S. manufacturing. As one government official stated, "A decision to invest or not depends entirely on each company's internal constraints."[17]

MITI'S NEW DIRECTION

At the macro level, structure also follows changes in strategies. This section examines MITI's major structural change in the 1970s in response to its newly defined mission and direction. The focus here, however, is to find a new pattern in MITI's relationship with private business enterprises in Japan and its effect on the decision-making process at the level of the firm. This section is divided into four subsections: new missions, structural reform, the process of policy making, and linkages with industries.

New Missions

MITI's search for a new direction in the late 1960s was precipitated by domestic and international constraints on the continuation of its established policies and practices. On the domestic side, Japan's rapid economic growth, which had been largely based on heavy and chemical industries in the 1950s and 1960s, brought about social problems such as industrial pollution and overconcentration of the Japanese populace in a few major cities.

An increasing number of cases regarding the dire effect of pollution were reported in the 1960s and 1970s, for example, victims of mercury poisoning of the waters around Minamata village in Kumamoto prefecture, cadmium poisoning in Toyama prefecture and other locations, asthma in the big petrochemical complexes at Yokkaichi and Tokuyama, and air pollution in all major cities.[18] Increased public protests on environmental damages caused by the high-powered economic growth policies forced the government to pay due attention to the long-neglected aspect of public welfare.

On the international side, Japan began to experience economic conflicts with her trading partners, especially in her bilateral relations with the United States. As Japan's trade surplus grew and her gross national product became the second largest in the noncommunist world in the late 1960s, the impact of the Japanese economy and her industrial policies on the international economic system began to be no longer neglected. Some Japanese government officials and business leaders began to realize that Japan had to internationalize her economy and enterprises through step-up liberalization of international capital transactions.

Recognizing this transitional period for the Japanese economy and society, Amaya, a MITI official, wrote a paper in 1969 that proposed and urged a new policy direction to be pursued by the ministry. After deliberations at the Industrial Structure Council, MITI issued a new industrial policy largely based on Amaya's vision in 1971. The new policy emphasized that "MITI would try to phase out industries that contributed to overcrowding and pollution and replace them with high-technology, smokeless industries ranking very high on the value-added scale."[19] This shift in policy direction prompted the adjustment of MITI's organizational structure.

Structural Reform

In 1973, MITI underwent its first major structural reform since 1952, reflecting its new policy direction. Figure 6-1 shows the basic structure of MITI's new organization. (Appendix F details the changes from the old to the new organizational structure.) The structural reform was intended to strengthen the following seven major areas of policy making and administration:

1. Formulation and implementation of comprehensive foreign economic policies: Policies will be aimed at development and enhancement of economic cooperation with other nations. The International Trade Policy Bureau will be charged with formulation of comprehensive international trade policies, encompassing such matters as exports, imports, and economic cooperation. The International Trade Administration Bureau will be charged with efficient implementation and administration of such policies as formulated at the International Trade Policy Bureau.

2. Strengthening the policy making and administrative functions with respect to industrial policies and enhancing the policy coordination of these industrial policies in conjunction with improvement of distribution systems and consumer protection: Industrial administration will be based on the primary objective of enhancement of public welfare. The Industrial Policy Bureau will be charged with comprehensive planning of industrial structure, industrial organization, corporate behavior, distribution systems, and consumer protection.

3. Coordination of policies on industrial location and environmental protection: The Industrial Location and Environmental Protection Bureau will be charged with formulation and administration of integrative policies.

4. Restructuring of vertical bureaus: Three existing bureaus — the Heavy Industry Bureau, the Chemical Industry Bureau, and the Textile and Sundries Bureau — will be restructured to form three new bureaus to reflect the commonality and position of each industrial sector in the economy. The new bureaus are the Basic Industries Bureau (including such industries as steel, chemical products, and nonferrous metals), the Machinery and Information Industries Bureau (including such industries as machinery, automobiles, aircraft, electronics, electrical machinery, and data processing), and the Consumer Goods Industries Bureau (including such industries as textiles, sundries, paper, ceramics, and construction materials).

5. Promotion of comprehensive policies on natural resources and energy sources: The Agency of Natural Resources and Energy will be established by combining two existing bureaus, the Mine and Coal Bureau and the Public Utilities Bureau.

6. Advancement of staff functions to deal with critical administrative matters: A new vice-ministerial position will be created to strengthen the staff functions to respond timely and flexibly to rapid changes in economic and social environments at home and abroad as well as to cope with the expanded administrative objectives of MITI and the complexity of administrative affairs.

7. Enhancement of technical staff and administrative functions with respect to patents: In order to cope with the increasing number of patent applications and the rapid development of international patent systems, the Patent Office will improve and rationalize the system of examination, registration, and administration pertaining to industrial property — for example, patent utility models, designs, and trademarks.[20]

As can readily be observed from Figure 6-1, the organizational structure of MITI is based on a matrix system. It consists of "horizontal" bureaus and "vertical" bureaus. The horizontal bureaus focus their attention on cross-sector activities and are thus mainly concerned with macroeconomic policies (international trade policy, industrial policy, and environmental protection and safety) or administrative matters (international administration). The vertical bureaus are designed to be industry-specific. There are three vertical bureaus: the Basic Industries Bureau, the Machinery and Information Industries Bureau, and the Consumer Goods Industries Bureau. Each bureau has several divisions dealing with specific products, and there is a continuing flow of information among these bureaus and various trade associations. This point will be examined later.

The Process of Policy Making

The process of policy making within the ministry depends on particular issues and topics. The nature of an issue determines who and at what level in the organization (for example, the section-chief level, the bureau-chief level, or other levels) will be in charge of the final decision. In some cases, a discussion leader for resolving a certain problem is selected according to his personal commitment to, and known knowledge of, the matter. Each policy decision has to be reached on the principle of consensus, which means a unanimous agreement or, in some cases, an implicit agreement with abstentions from voting.[21]

FIGURE 6-1
ORGANIZATIONAL STRUCTURE OF MITI
(New in 1973)

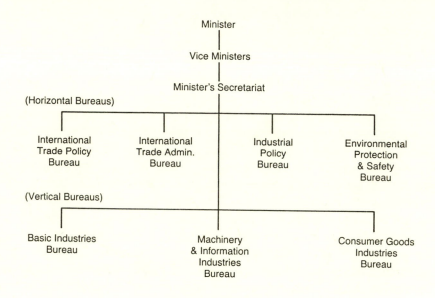

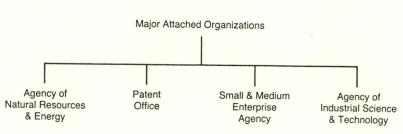

Source: Constructed by the author.

Three kinds of meetings are regularly scheduled: the ministerial meeting (*shogi*), the section-chief meeting (*shomukacho-kaigi*), and the laws and regulations examiners' meeting (*horeishinsaiin-kaigi*). The ministerial meeting is held once a week and attended by the highest officials in the ministry. The section-chief meeting is held twice a week and attended by the highest-ranking section chiefs from each bureau. The laws and regulations examiners' meeting is also held twice a week by the subordinates of the section chiefs.[22]

Aside from the regularly scheduled meetings, extensive communications are carried out among divisions of various bureaus through informal meetings. A trade dispute with the United States over Japan's exports of automobiles, for example, kept three divisions of the ministry busy: the Americas-Oceania Division of the International Trade Policy Bureau, the Export Division of the International Trade Administration Bureau, and the International Business Affairs Division of the Industrial Policy Bureau.[23] In this case, the main problem was how to allocate among the Japanese automobile manufacturers the quantity restriction to be imposed. Prior consultation with the industry would possibly infringe on the Japanese Anti-Monopoly Law. After deliberations on several alternative allocation methods, taking into account their possible administrative problems and reactions from the automobile industry, MITI formed its final policy.[24]

According to Frank and Hirono, a legal justification for export restraints is provided by the Export-Import Transaction Law and the Export Trade Control Ordinance. The original intent of the law was to reduce excessive competition among Japanese exporters and to encourage their cooperation in the long-run development of export markets. However, export controls have been used as a means to enforce "orderly marketing" and to enforce mostly the Japan-U.S. bilateral voluntary export control agreements.[25] The law was enacted in 1952, subsequently revised in 1965, and is still existent.[26]

When a particular problem involves several ministries, a final decision is difficult to reach because of strong parochial sentiments at each ministry. There has, for example, been a feud between MITI and the Ministry of Posts and Telecommunications (MPT) over the issue of the range of administrative control on the telecommunications industry. Regarding the issue of a copyrights law for computer software, MITI has to resolve an interministry conflict with the Agency for Cultural Affairs in addition to its disagreement with the U.S. government representing the interest of the U.S. computer industry.[27]

To formulate macro-level policies, the horizontal bureaus obtain essential information from the vertical bureaus. The Industrial Policy Bureau, for example, draws up a draft proposal of basic policies and measures regarding the future course of Japan's industrial structure based on information collected mainly from the vertical bureaus. The draft proposal is then presented to the Industrial Structure Council for its deliberations.

The Industrial Structure Council is composed of 20 commissions with approximately 300 individuals who are selected by MITI from a pool of experts in respective fields. These individual members of the Council represent a wide spectrum of professions and interest groups, including leaders of the industrial circles concerned, leaders from financial institutions, educators, mass media reporters, consumers, and workers. The role of the council can be viewed from two angles: It legitimatizes the bureaucratic policy making, and it has a positive effect on resolving and adjusting conflicts of interests among various groups.[28]

The U.S. government has criticized MITI's policies on structural adjustment of the Japanese economy as "picking winners." A MITI official interviewed responds to such a criticism as follows: MITI does not try to change the general trend of the Japanese economy that has been restructuring upward based on the market mechanism. It simply encourages the initiatives of the private industries.

In early 1984, the U.S. government requested Japan to permit U.S. businesspeople to attend the Industrial Structure Council's meetings. According to the MITI official interviewed in August 1984, "MITI rejects the idea, since it is an interference with Japan's domestic policy. Does the U.S. government admit the Japanese in the National Security Council? Certainly it will not." He expressed another worry, fearing that U.S. participation in the decision-making process of the council would lead to more confusion and that the North Americans might act on incomplete information and misunderstandings.

In September 1984, however, MITI started regular dialogues with U.S. companies that were member firms of the American Chamber of Commerce in Japan (ACCJ).[29] In late October 1984, in an attempt to alleviate foreign criticism, MITI invited four business representatives of U.S., U.K., French, and West German chambers of commerce in Japan as "guest participants" in a joint meeting of the Industrial Structure Council and the Industrial Technology Council.[30] How far the current development will continue and what effect the participation of foreign businesspeople will have on MITI's policy making remain to be seen.

However, it is clear that MITI now has to deal with multifaceted problems with domestic and international ramifications far more than in the past.

Linkage with Industries

As readily observed from its organizational structure, at its vertically structured bureaus MITI maintains a direct channel of communication with private industries through various trade (industry) associations. The nature of this linkage, which generates suspicion — the alleged government-business conspiracy in Japan — among U.S. businesspeople and government officials, was explained as follows by one of the large firms interviewed: Various trade associations were created under the guidance of MITI in the early postwar years.[31] The ministry has been gathering statistical data and other information on the Japanese industries through these trade associations to form its policy guidelines. When an issue arises affecting a certain industry, the trade association of the industry creates a forum for exchange of opinions among its member firms. Then, the trade association summarizes and submits its policy recommendations to MITI for the latter's policy consideration.

The U.S. government and businesspeople tend to believe that such forums might be used for collusive purposes, for example, cartels affecting prices and production volume. However, according to the interviewee, this is not the case. Individual member companies of the trade association do not resort to such practices as a result of the meetings at the association. On the contrary, these firms compete fiercely against each other in the market place. In general, interfirm competition is quite keen among the Japanese corporations, and winning such a competition is truly the first priority of every firm.

The relations MITI maintains with the Japanese business enterprises and its role in the Japanese economy have changed during the past two decades. Thus MITI no longer has direct control measures, such as the foreign exchange budget and allocation, to influence business decisions at the level of the firm. Because MITI, with its elite bureaucrats, has a strong capability in gathering information on domestic and international economic and business-related matters, it acts as a provider of such information.

According to a MITI official, there are two ways of getting MITI's policies across to Japanese industries. One is intensive communications between MITI's staff from the vertical bureaus and representatives of trade associations, who are executives of leading Japanese firms. Another is through annual publication of MITI's long-term vision of the industrial structure, which has been issued every year since 1974. Some may see a resemblance between MITI and a business consulting firm, but the major difference is that MITI does not target its policy for the benefit of any particular private business enterprise.

Among the 15 companies interviewed, there were various opinions regarding the ministry. One large firm expressed its confidence in MITI, citing the ability of the elite career bureaucrats who could comprehend quickly and accurately problems and opportunities for Japan and her relations with the international community. Although this company believes MITI's administrative guidance of Japan's growth industries unnecessary, it supports the role of government in solving problems of such structurally depressed industries as aluminum and dealing with pollution problems, which cannot be corrected without some form of governmental intervention in the market economy.

Another large firm had an opinion that administrative guidance should be used only to foster free and fair competition among market participants and, in some cases, to reach a compromise solution to Japan's trade disputes with her trading partners. The company cited an example of MITI's role as an arbitrator. It occurred when several Japanese companies were competing against each other in marketing typewriters in Europe. The price competition among the firms became fierce, and finally a dumping charge was filed against them. In this case, MITI had to set a floor price to resolve the matter. The company found it a fair solution to the problem of "excess" competition among the Japanese companies.[32]

In general, there seems to exist a strong sense of trust between MITI and Japanese business. According to the MITI official interviewed, for example, the mere moral support of MITI — which could have been a negligible subsidy in the past — on a certain project of a particular firm may be able to persuade the company's board members to carry out the project with vigor.

The link MITI maintains with private firms is a delicate one. As Kobayashi observed, the government-business relationship in Japan is "mutual dependence for convenience" rather than one of outright control by one group over the other.[33]

PRIVATE INITIATIVES

An analysis of the linkage between the macro actors and the micro actors is not complete without examining such meso-level actors as Keidanren and the emerging pattern of private initiatives in domestic and international affairs in Japan. A rapid economic growth and a structural adjustment of the Japanese economy in the past seem to have altered industrial organization and the government-business relationship in Japan. To report the findings of the current research, this section is divided into the following three subsections: current activities at Keidanren, private-level diplomacy, and a new pattern of industrial organization.

Current Activities at Keidanren

Keidanren, which was founded in 1946, has been providing a gathering ground for big business in Japan. Its membership is composed of trade associations and corporations, which numbered 110 and 812, respectively, as of August 1982.[34] Keidanren also conducts independent research studies on practical problems facing Japanese industries.

Among the issues being dealt with in recent years, according to a professional staff member at Keidanren, the most significant have been the unitary tax system in certain states of the United States (discussed in Chapter 4), the European Community's proposal on disclosure of corporate information to and consultation with employee representatives (the so-called Vredeling proposal), and a medium- to long-term vision for the Japanese industries and economy in light of changes in current and future business and economic environments. Regarding the last item, Keidanren's professional staff has been studying the member firms from 30 different industries. The study encompasses three major areas: information industries, internationalization of the Japanese economy, and technology development.

The research director interviewed at Keidanren contends that it is not possible for the government to change Japan's industrial structure. He argues further that the Japanese companies in general oppose MITI's administrative guidance and that a proper role of the government during the current economic transition should be, not to retain some old laws that restrict the freedom of private business activities, but to encourage the initiative of private industries.

As anti-big business sentiments grew in Japan in the 1970s due mainly to industrial pollution and the alleged cartels among some large firms in holding up consumer goods for price hikes during and after the first oil shock, Keidanren as well as MITI became targets of public protests.[35] During the 1970s, Japan's economic conflicts with her trading partners also accelerated.

In an attempt to rebuild the image of big business and to increase public understandings of the Japanese economy and the role of private business in society, Keidanren established the Japan Institute for Social and Economic Affairs (Keizai Koho Center) in 1978, which engages in public relations activities, both domestic and international. Keidanren believes that such private-level public relations activities are an important means to eliminate misunderstandings in the minds of Japan's trading partners, as illustrated in its following statement:

> International conflicts frequently stem from the "information gap," "communication gap" and "perception gap." The Center finds it imperative to avoid international conflicts by bridging these gaps. In cooperation with both governmental and private circles, the Center has so far been engaged in overseas public affairs activities as well as engaging in new undertakings and projects of its own from the standpoint of the overall business community.[36]

In promoting Japanese-U.S. relations, Keidanren has been supporting the Japan-U.S. Businessmen's Conference, which will be discussed later. It has also been holding an annual conference with its U.S. counterpart organization, the Business Roundtable,[37] since 1980.

In addition to Keidanren, there are three other nationwide economic organizations in Japan, having different members (overlaps in membership in some cases) and serving different purposes. These are (1) the Japan Committee for Economic Development (Keizai Doyukai), consisting of individual members who are business executives and focusing its attention mainly on broad economic issues; (2) the Japan Federation of Employers' Associations (Nikkeiren), dealing with management-labor issues; and (3) the Japan Chamber of Commerce and Industry (Nissho), dealing with regional economic problems, including those pertaining to small- and medium-sized corporations.[38]

According to the interviewee at Keidanren, representatives from these four economic organizations plus politicians from the Liberal Democratic Party hold a monthly meeting to discuss selected current economic problems. The meeting does not produce a consensus of opinions in general because of the diversified interests represented by the participants.

Among the Japanese companies interviewed, one large firm commented that no real or tangible results could be expected from salon organizations such as Keidanren. Another large company stated that the Keizai Koho Center could be instrumental in public relations overseas, and that the current concern of Keidanren seemed to be mainly on the structural problems of the Japanese basic industries. One other large company commented that the Japanese firms lacked consensus on Keidanren's campaign against the unitary tax in the United States and even on the tax itself.

Judging from these comments and the current activities described earlier, it seems that the ability of Keidanren to build consensus in the Japanese business community has been declining. One probable reason for this might be that the world of Japan's big business (*Zaikai*) has become pluralistic as a result of development of many successful business enterprises.[39] Thus, instead of trying to form a unified opinion on a specific business matter, it seems that Keidanren is concerned more with macroeconomic issues such as the study cited earlier on a long-range vision of Japanese industries and economy.

Private-Level Diplomacy

The diplomatic relationship between Japan and the United States would certainly affect the pattern of bilateral economic transactions as well as the Japanese companies' decisions whether or not to invest in U.S. manufacturing operations. Parallel with the development of growing economic tensions between the United States and Japan since the 1960s, Japanese business leaders began to take an active role in mending and promoting bilateral relations. As political and economic bases and powers are widely diffused and heterogeneous throughout the United States, these Japanese business leaders initially tried to establish bilateral communications networks on a regional basis, for example, the Japan-U.S. California Association (1965), the Japan-U.S. Middle-West Association (1967), the Japan-U.S. Southern Association (1969), and the Japan-U.S. Southeast Association (1976).[40]

In the late 1960s, a significant development was underway in private diplomacy. A prominent Japanese business leader advanced a proposal at the Far East–America Council's meeting in 1969 to establish a new channel of communication between Japan and the United States at the private, rather than governmental, level. The traditional communications channel between Keidanren and the U.S. Chamber of Commerce was considered inadequate. The proposal was also communicated informally to some influential figures in the United States by another Japanese business leader and was well received by the U.S. government and business circles. The proposed channel of communication came into being in 1971 when the Japan-U.S. Economic Council was established in Tokyo and the Advisory Council on Japan-U.S. Economic Relations was established in Washington, D.C.[41]

Each of the two councils seems to function as a "gatekeeper" for the four-way communication channels among the two business communities and the governments in Japan and the United States. For example, as stated in Article III of the Charter of the Japan-U.S. Economic Council, one of the major objectives of the council is to make policy recommendations to the Japanese government concerning economic and other related matters of mutual interest to the two countries.[42] Thus, a new pattern of government-business relations seems to be developing between the two countries. Each business community seems to be trying to influence the macroeconomic policies of the country of its counterpart. The pattern of communications flow seems to be complex. However, at least one unified meeting place for the two councils exists, and that is the Japan-U.S. Businessmen's Conference.

The Japan-U.S. Businessmen's Conference was established in 1963 "with the encouragement of both governments in the United States and Japan to serve as a forum for regular consultations at the highest levels of business."[43] It has been holding an annual conference since its establishment. The Japan-U.S. Economic Council and the Advisory Council on Japan-U.S. Economic Relations have been sponsoring the Japan-U.S. Businessmen's Conference since the early 1970s. Thus, a shift from state-initiated to privately initiated interactions and discussion on bilateral economic issues has taken place. Furthermore, the interests of the two governments and the two business communities have become increasingly interlocked in recent years.

There is evidence of this convergence of government and business interests at the bilateral level. At the request of President Carter and Prime Minister Ohira, the Japan-U.S. Economic Relations Group, the so-called Wisemen's group, was created in 1979. The group consisted of eight distinguished private individuals from the two countries. It commissioned a study on five politically volatile economic issues developing between Japan and the United States: steel trade, automobiles, agricultural products, telecommunications equipment, and macroeconomic coordination.[44] Subsequent to the termination of the group's task in 1981, Secretary of State Haig and Foreign Minister Sonoda requested the Businessmen's Conference to follow up the group's task and to make policy recommendations to both nations. A joint study was carried out by the Advisory Council on Japan-U.S. Economic Relations and the Japan-U.S. Economic Council in three areas: trade laws and practices, trade in services, and agriculture. Subsequently, their policy recommendations and specific suggestions for implementation were submitted to both governments. To translate these recommendations into policy, the two councils held follow-up meetings with appropriate U.S. and Japanese governmental and private-sector representatives.[45]

Another state-initiated bilateral study group was created in May 1983. The two governments, at the request of President Reagan and Prime Minister Nakasone, established the U.S.-Japan Advisory Commission, the so-called New Wisemen's group. The commission, comprised of seven private citizens on each side, was charged with making a comprehensive review of the bilateral relationship, including its political, security, economic, and cultural dimensions.[46] (Appendix G lists the U.S. and Japanese members of this commission.)

Prior to the president's visit to Japan in 1983, the U.S.-Japan Advisory Commission prepared a report to President Reagan and Prime Minister Nakasone. The report reaffirmed the importance of the bilateral relationship by stressing the prospects for long-term cooperation based on a broad range of common interests. It also touched upon the issue of direct investment as follows:

> Direct investment which facilitates the flow of goods, capital, technical information and managerial skills between the two economies is important in strengthening the economic relationship. To this end, the United States and Japan must assure their foreign investors that direct foreign investments will be encouraged. Laws and practices limiting the free flow of investments, such as the unitary tax method applied by certain states in the United States and Japan's prior-notification requirements for foreign investors, are damaging.[47]

The commission also supported industry-to-industry discussions at the bilateral level that could be instrumental in resolving economic conflicts by providing policy recommendations for constructive governmental action. The Japan-U.S. Businessmen's Conference is the case in point.

Bilateral interactions have also begun to spill over further down to the grassroots level. The Communication Industries Association of Japan and the U.S. Telecommunications Suppliers' Association, for example, became complementary members of each other's organizations in 1984. The Electronic Industries Association of Japan also established a formal relation with the American Electronics Association to exchange information and to cooperate on bilateral trade issues. The Keizai Koho Center, a unit of Keidanren, now instructs Japanese companies on how to conduct public relations activities overseas. An increase in this type of private diplomacy is due to the realization on the Japanese side that private enterprises in the United States do not put much trust in government-initiated campaigns. According to the head researcher at the center, "To earn trust, you've got to establish some sort of private-level exchanges."[48]

One of the large Japanese firms interviewed has been active in such public relations activities in the United States. Prompted by its belief a few years ago that the Japanese government had not been responding positively to U.S. pressures based on the bilateral trade frictions, the company started to search for an effective apparatus for private-level public relations activities. It started distributing to U.S. schools videotapes showing the Japanese customs and lifestyles, on the belief that explaining the Japanese thinking process, which reflects Japan's traditional values, may reduce misunderstandings between the two cultures.

From the perspective of private-level diplomacy, its seems clear that cross-investments between the two countries, if conducted in good faith on both sides, would enhance mutual understandings and benefits. Such investments would also increase a chance of macro-level coordination of governmental economic policies.

A New Pattern of Industrial Organization

The traditional model of Japan's industrial organization assumes that a hierarchical link exists between large and small companies within each major industrial group. It also assumes that large firms control smaller ones and that at the apex MITI controls and coordinates the entire activities of the microeconomic actors. (This model is depicted in Figure 2-1 in Chapter 2.)

One implication of the traditional model is that Japan's industrial organization is monolithic and, thus, gives credence to the concept of Japan, Inc. The model had a certain merit in explaining the government-business relationship in Japan of the 1950s and 1960s, when MITI had powerful and direct measures — such as the foreign exchange budget system discussed earlier in this chapter — to influence private business decisions. However, the model seems to have lost this foundation. There are several reasons for this.

First, Japan's rapid industrial expansion in the 1950s and 1960s made it possible for some small and independent companies to grow without depending on any particular industrial group. Banks were eager to lend money to promising ventures initiated by such firms. Moreover, the continuing trend of structural adjustment of the industrial base in Japan seems to accelerate development of new ventures and new enterprises independent of existing industrial groups.

Second, small- and medium-sized companies have been diversifying their customers, resulting in their multiple relations with several firms associated with different industrial groups or with large independent enterprises. Such diversification of customers goes beyond the national boundary, as evidenced by those small companies interviewed that have invested in U.S. manufacturing and/or assembly operations.

Third, as noted earlier, MITI no longer has direct measures for intervening in market activities. Its role has been shifting away from direct control at the micro level to more macro-oriented, supportive, indirect policies.

Fourth, as noted in Chapter 4, both large and small Japanese companies have been pursuing their own business strategies independently. It was observed that these firms made their direct-investment decisions at the level of the firm without prior consultation with any of their group-member firms or macro-level actors.

The current finding supports Aoki's observation of an emerging structure of Japan's industrial organization. This new structure — a quasi-tree structure, according to Aoki — is based on interlocking, web-like business relations among Japanese firms of various size from different industrial groups. It is seen as a gradual transformation — since the early 1970s — from the traditional, hierarchical relationship among firms within each industrial group with MITI at the top. Thus, according to Aoki, this new structure is characterized by the following three aspects:

the role of government is, not to control industries directly, but to provide information and a forum for cooperative behavior as such needs arise; many multiple relations have developed among large and small companies, and they cut across the traditional demarcation between industrial groups; and initiatives for technological innovations have been diffused among firms of different size.[49]

Japanese companies have been faced with increased uncertainties due to significant changes in domestic and international business environments evolving since the early 1970s. On the one hand, protectionism against Japanese-made products has been mounting in the industrialized countries. On the other hand, competition from companies in newly industrialized countries has been increasing. While being caught in the middle of these two forces, they have experienced rising production costs at home, that is, increases in wages, cost of land, and energy prices. A steady supply of raw materials has become increasingly uncertain. At the same time, structural adjustment toward knowledge-intensive (high-technology) industries requires them to find some innovative approach in their R & D activities. In addition, through capital liberalization, foreign firms have begun to establish their business and manufacturing operations in Japan. All these factors seem to continue to realign further large and small companies in a complex way.

JAPAN'S DIRECT MANUFACTURING INVESTMENT

This section presents some hard data in relative terms on Japan's direct investment in the United States. It also reports various views and experiences on direct investment in U.S. manufacturing communciated to this researcher by those macro and micro actors interviewed in Japan. In conjunction with the other research findings reported earlier, these data and discussions provide some further insights into macro-micro interactions with respect to Japan's direct manufacturing investment in the United States.

Comparative Data

Japan's foreign direct investment is still at the early stage of expansion in comparison to the long history and large scale of U.S. foreign direct investment. Table 6-4 compares foreign direct investments

TABLE 6-4
ANNUAL CHANGES IN FOREIGN DIRECT INVESTMENTS, 1960–83: COMPARISON BETWEEN JAPAN AND THE UNITED STATES
(In Billions of U.S. Dollars)

	Japan			The United States		
	In Japan	*Abroad*	*Net*	*In the U.S.*	*Abroad*	*Net*
1960	.01	.08	−.07	.32	2.94	−2.62
1961	.06	.09	−.03	.31	2.65	−2.34
1962	.06	.08	−.02	.35	2.85	−2.50
1963	.10	.12	−.02	.23	3.48	−3.25
1964	.11	.06	.05	.32	3.79	−3.47
1965	.05	.08	−.03	.42	5.01	−4.59
1966	.03	.11	−.08	.43	5.40	−4.97
1967	.05	.12	−.07	.70	4.74	−4.04
1968	.08	.22	−.14	.81	5.38	−4.57
1969	.07	.21	−.14	1.26	5.73	−4.47
1970	.09	.36	−.27	1.46	7.59	−6.13
1971	.21	.36	−.15	.37	7.62	−7.25
1972	.17	.72	−.55	.95	7.75	−6.80
1973	−.04	1.90	−1.94	2.80	11.40	−8.60
1974	.20	1.88	−1.68	5.28	9.17	−3.89
1975	.23	1.77	−1.54	3.31	14.28	−10.97
1976	.11	1.99	−1.88	4.99	12.32	−7.33
1977	.03	1.64	−1.61	3.72	11.89	−8.17
1978	.00	2.37	−2.37	7.90	16.07	−8.17
1979	.24	2.90	−2.66	11.86	25.24	−13.38
1980	.28	2.39	−2.11	16.89	19.27	−2.38
1981	.19	4.91	−4.72	23.37	9.52	13.85
1982	.45	4.53	−4.08	14.92	−4.86	19.78
1983	.41	3.61	−3.20	11.31	4.93	6.38

Note: From the year 1971 on, statistical figures expressed in terms of Special Drawing Rights (SDRs) were converted to the U.S. dollar basis by the current author. Conversion rates (U.S. dollar per SDR) for the period 1971–76 were obtained from *Balance of Payments Yearbook*, vol. 28 (1977), and those for the period 1977–83 from *Balance of Payments Statistics*, vol. 35, no. 11 (November 1984). Prior to 1971 an SDR was defined to have the same value as a U.S. dollar's worth of gold.

Source: Compiled from *Balance of Payments Yearbook*, vol. 17 (October 1965 and January 1966), vol. 22 (April and September 1971), and vol. 28 (1977); *Balance of Payments Statistics*, vol. 35, part 2 (1984), and no. 11 (November 1984), International Monetary Fund.

recorded in Japan and in the United States for the period of 1960 through 1983.

Japan's outward direct investment amounted to more than one billion dollars for the first time in 1973 and then shot up to more than four billion dollars in 1981. These two surges in Japan's overseas direct investment seem to have coincided perfectly with, first, the Nixon shock of 1971 and the subsequent introduction of the system of flexible foreign exchanges in 1973 and, second, the revision of the Foreign Exchange and Foreign Trade Law in 1979, which became effective on December 1, 1980. The annual inflow of foreign direct investments in the United States recorded for the first time an amount in excess of one billion dollars each in 1969 and 1970. Then, especially from the year 1973 on, the annual inflow of such investments continued to grow, recording approximately 23 billion dollars in 1981. Interestingly, U.S. overseas direct investments continued to grow even with several devaluations of the U.S. dollar in the 1970s, although net annual outflow of long-term capital in the form of direct investments peaked at 13 billion dollars in 1979. Since 1981, there have been net inflows of direct investments in the United States.

According to the 1980 benchmark survey of foreign direct investment in the United States conducted by the U.S. Department of Commerce, nonbank U.S. affiliates of foreign direct investors had assets of $292 billion at the end of 1980, which accounted for about 9 percent of the total for all U.S. businesses.[50] The survey collected information on the country and industry of the ultimate beneficial owner (UBO) of each foreign direct investment in the United States. Before presenting some of the survey data, definitions of some key words used in the survey need to be explained. Foreign direct investment, for the purpose of the survey, is defined as follows:

> Foreign direct investment in the United States is the ownership or control, directly or indirectly, by one foreign person of 10 percent or more of the voting securities of an incorporated U.S. business enterprise or an equivalent interest in an unincorported U.S. business enterprise.[51]

Second, the UBO is defined as follows:

> The foreign parent is the first foreign person in an affiliate's ownership chain; the UBO is that person, proceeding up the affiliate's ownership chain beginning with and including the foreign parent, that is not owned more than

50 percent by another person. The country of the UBO may be the same as that of the foreign parent, a different foreign country, or the United States.[52]

Table 6-5 compares the total assets of nonbank U.S. affiliates at the end of 1980, focusing on manufacturing and wholesale-trade industries, among Japan and other major investing countries as UBOs. As can be observed from the table, the U.S. affiliates of UBOs in seven countries (Japan, the United Kingdom, Canada, the Netherlands, West Germany, France, and Switzerland) owned $247 billion, or 85 percent, of $292 billion worth of the total assets of nonbank U.S. affiliates.

TABLE 6-5
TOTAL ASSETS OF NONBANK U.S. AFFILIATES AS OF THE END OF 1980: COMPARISON AMONG JAPAN AND OTHER MAJOR INVESTING COUNTRIES
(In Millions of Dollars)

UBO	Total Amount	%	Manufacturing Amount	%	Wholesale Trade Amount	%	Other* Amount	%
Japan	27,626	9.4	3,885	4.8	18,724	37.4	5,017	3.1
U.K.	56,594	19.4	14,646	17.9	5,064	10.1	36,884	23.0
Canada	47,879	16.4	13,140	16.1	1,898	3.8	32,841	20.5
Netherlands	36,103	12.4	6,132	7.5	688	1.4	29,283	18.3
Germany	31,196	10.7	17,766	21.7	5,459	10.9	7,971	5.0
France	25,654	8.8	9,253	11.3	5,108	10.2	11,293	7.0
Switzerland	22,031	7.5	7,650	9.4	2,069	4.1	12,312	7.7
Subtotal	247,083	84.6	72,472	88.7	39,010	77.9	135,601	84.6
Others	44,950	15.4	9,212	11.3	11,058	22.1	24,680	15.4
Total	292,033	100.0	81,684	100.0	50,068	100.0	160,281	100.0

*Includes mining, petroleum, retail trade, finance, insurance, real estate, and other primary and service-related industries.

Source: Compiled from "Foreign Direct Investment in the United States: Highlights from the 1980 Benchmark Survey," by R. David Belli, *Survey of Current Business* (U.S. Department of Commerce, Bureau of Economic Analysis), October 1983, pp. 25–35, and *Foreign Direct Investment in the United States, 1980,* by U.S. Department of Commerce, Bureau of Economic Analysis (Washington, D.C.: U.S. Government Printing Office, 1983).

The affiliates with UBOs in Japan had $27.6 billion, or 9.4 percent of the total assets owned by nonbank U.S. affiliates. Here, Japan ranked fifth among the seven countries of UBOs, following the United Kingdom (19.4 percent), Canada (16.4 percent), the Netherlands (12.4 percent), and West Germany (10.7 percent). The affiliates in manufacturing industries with UBOs in Japan, however, accounted for $3.9 billion, or only 4.8 percent of the total assets owned by all U.S. manufacturing affiliates. Therefore, in comparison with UBOs in the other six countries, the Japanese presence in U.S. manufacturing was still quite small as of the end of 1980. However, UBOs in Japan have invested heavily in the wholesale-trade industry in the United States. Their U.S. affiliates owned $18.7 billion, or 37.4 percent of the total assets of all U.S. affiliates in the wholesale-trade industry. This indicates clearly the Japanese companies' strong historical orientation toward trade and sales activities in the United States.

As examined in Chapter 4 and earlier in this chapter, many factors triggered Japan's direct manufacturing investments in the United States. One of these factors is the system of floating exchange rates, which came into being in the early 1970s. Revaluation of the Japanese yen vis-à-vis the U.S. dollar has made local production in the United States feasible for some Japanese manufacturing companies.

Figure 6-2 depicts the relationship between changes in the exchange rate of the Japanese yen per U.S. dollar on a quarterly basis and the number of Japanese-affiliated U.S. manufacturing plants established per year for the period of 1971 through 1983. As can be observed from the pictogram, a clear symmetry exists between these two variables throughout the period. The number of establishments surged shortly after the exchange rate hit a trough (a weaker U.S. dollar and a stronger Japanese yen) in 1973, 1978, 1981, and 1983. The year 1983 saw the largest number of establishments (startups and acquisitions combined) of U.S. manufacturing plants by Japanese investors. Thus, it appears that the changes in the exchange rate have influenced the timing of Japanese direct manufacturing investments in the United States.

Japan's direct investment in U.S. manufacturing is a recent phenomenon. The majority of Japanese-owned U.S. manufacturing plants have been established since the early 1970s. Of 521 Japanese-affiliated manufacturing plants in operation or under construction as of the end of 1983, only 22 plants were established prior to 1971. Some of the large-scale manufacturing operations in automobile and electronics industries existing today were opened after 1980, the cut-off year for

FIGURE 6-2
RELATIONSHIP BETWEEN CHANGES IN EXCHANGE RATES AND THE NUMBER OF JAPANESE-AFFILIATED U.S. MANUFACTURING PLANTS ESTABLISHED PER YEAR, 1971–83

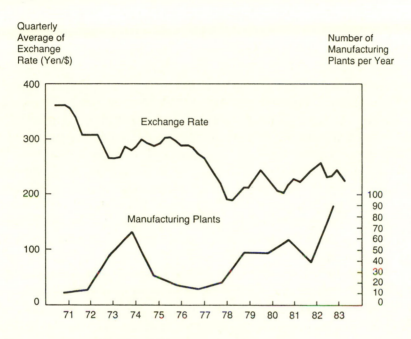

Note: The number of manufacturing plants established for each year is based on those plants in operation or under cosntruction at the end of 1983.

Source: For quarterly exchange rates, *IMF International Financial Statistics,* various volumes. For the number of Japanese-affiliated U.S. manufacturing plants, the census data published by the Japan Economic Institute of America, Washington, D.C., "Japan's Expanding Manufacturing Presence in the United States: A Profile," April 17, 1981, and "Japan's Expanding Manufacturing Presence: 1983 Update," April 13, 1984.

which the Commerce Department's survey was conducted. Judging from this trend and the other factors explained earlier, Japan's direct manufacturing investment in the United States will likely continue to expand in the future. The following sections present and discuss how MITI and private sectors in Japan perceive Japan's overseas manufacturing investments.

MITI's View on Japan's Direct Manufacturing Investment

According to a MITI official interviewed, the International Business Affairs Division of the Industrial Policy Bureau has been receiving numerous requests from industrialized countries to increase direct manufacturing investments of Japanese companies in their countries. MITI actually maintains a close channel of communication with such foreign governments' branch offices in Tokyo. This seems rather peculiar, since MITI cannot force Japanese companies to invest abroad, nor is it a participant in the board meetings of these private firms. However, the fact indicates a growing pressure on the Japanese government and especially private enterprises to produce and sell in foreign markets.

MITI officials generally contend that Japan's direct manufacturing investment overseas is in response to existing or expected future trade frictions. In recent years, Japanese firms in high-technology industries have also undertaken direct manufacturing investment in the United States and other countries. This development may contradict MITI's current industrial policy to restructure the Japanese economy toward one based on knowledge-intensive industries. A response to this issue by the MITI official interviewed is as follows.

There has not been a consensus reached within MITI regarding the effect of Japan's outward direct investment on the domestic economy and the industrial structure. Two conflicting views on this issue exist at the present time. One view favors and encourages Japan's outward direct investment. The scenario of this view is that the current structural adjustment will result in reduction of imports of raw materials and that, as a result, exports will keep exceeding imports, leading to a significant imbalance in the nation's balance of payments. Therefore, in order to alleviate current as well as future trade frictions with Japan's trading partners, outward direct investments should be encouraged.

The second view is rather pessimistic about the future of the Japanese economy. According to this view, Japan's current trade surplus is only a temporary phenomenon, and if Japanese firms continue to set up manufacturing plants abroad, Japan's domestic economic strength will be depleted. Those who hold this view are concerned that Japan lags far behind the United States in her ability to conduct basic research and to generate new technological breakthroughs.

The question as to which scenario will come true seems to depend on whether or not Japan can excel in basic research. Since MITI lost its long-cherished control measures on foreign exchange by the early 1970s, Japanese companies have been free to undertake overseas direct investments. The new Law on Foreign Trade and Foreign Exchange Control, which was enacted in 1979, guarantees freedom of decision on international transactions at the level of the firm, except for certain cases explained earlier. Furthermore, due to the two divisive views on the effect of outward direct investment and the persistent trade friction with the United States and other industrialized countries, MITI does not give any administrative guidance on this issue.

Views and Experiences of the Private Sector

A professional staff member interviewed at Keidanren believes that Japanese companies' direct manufacturing investments in the United States are necessary to reduce the bilateral trade friction. He shares the view generally held by the Japanese companies interviewed that local production has become an important means to sell in a large market such as in the United States. He does not accept the view of a possible adverse effect of outward direct investment on the Japanese economy, since he believes that Japanese private enterprises, large and small, have a strong resilience in adapting to changes and that they will continue to create new ventures and industries at home and abroad that will provide employment opportunities.

During this author's interviews with the 15 Japanese companies, each company was requested to estimate the effect of its direct manufacturing investment on its domestic operations in terms of production volume and employment size. Most of these firms have not experienced any adverse effect yet, because the industries they are in have been experiencing a rapid growth in recent years. Some of these industries have had, for example, an annual growth rate of more than 30 percent in the past five to ten years.

In terms of production volume and employment level, 14 out of the 15 companies have expanded their U.S. manufacturing operations since their initial undertakings of U.S. manufacturing activities. Only one small company has reduced the scale of its assembly operations. Yet all these firms have expanded the volume of their production at home during the same period. They have either increased or maintained at the same level the number of employees during the past few years.[53]

One large company states that it invested in overseas manufacturing operations in order to meet capacity shortfall in its domestic production units in the past. However, it currently faces a problem of overcapacity in Japan. Another large company has also run into the problem of overcapacity in its domestic production units and predicts that this, combined with the similar condition among the other Japanese firms in the same industry, would lead to a fierce competition in price cutting.

Asked about MITI's role and its industrial policy, one large firm comments that in high-technology industries MITI may have difficulty in keeping up with rapid developments and changes in business environments. One other large company states that Japan has now become the world center for electronics industries. These industries are characterized by rapid technological change and fierce competition. The company strongly believes that private enterprises would lose in such competition if they were merely following government industrial policies.

The future is uncertain. At the present time, however, both government and business leaders in Japan as well as in the United States seem to commit themselves in principle to the idea of freer international trade and capital transactions, including direct investments. Thus, with a strong initiative of private enterprises, cross-investments in manufacturing as well as in other industrial sectors between the two countries are likely to increase under the current condition.

7   SUMMARY
   AND CONCLUSIONS

This chapter summarizes and synthesizes major research findings reported in the preceding chapters. It is divided into three major sections: research objectives and methods, major findings of the research, and implications of the research findings.

RESEARCH OBJECTIVES AND METHODS

Before presenting a summary of major findings, it would be appropriate here to review briefly the objectives of the current research study and the research methods employed to accomplish these objectives. As reported in Chapter 1 and Chapter 3, the current study was undertaken with the following two major objectives relating to Japanese direct manufacturing investment in the United States: to investigate the investment decision-making process and the control system of Japanese parent companies that have established manufacturing plants in the United States and to examine the Japanese government-business interactions or inactions in relation to such direct manufacturing investment.

The first research objective is mainly concerned with behavioral and organizational aspects of Japanese corporations at the level of the firm. The second objective goes beyond the level of the firm and requires an analysis of complex relationships among macro- and micro-level actors. However, these two objectives complement each other in the attempt of the current research to increase the understanding of the phenomenon of a rapid increase in Japanese direct manufacturing investments in the United States.

As noted in Chapter 3, which provides a background review of existing research studies relating to the subject matter of the current research, the research undertaken previously on Japanese direct manufacturing investments in the United States has been sparse, especially that on the parent-subsidiary linkage in management areas. Furthermore, there has been some conflicting evidence and opinions in the United States with regard to the government-business relations in Japan. Due partly to a lack of understanding about Japan's government-business relations and industrial organization, there seems to exist in the United States a mixed feeling about the activities and behavior of Japanese corporations doing business internationally — admiration, fear, and suspicion. Examining only macro data and statistics cannot unveil the complex reality that actually exists. The current study, therefore, utilized personal interviews to get close to this reality. The interview survey was intended to find the inner workings of the investment decision-making process and the control system at the level of the firm as well as the interactions or lack of such between government and business. Interviewees were selected from three levels: 15 Japanese companies at the micro level that established manufacturing plants in the United States, the Keidanren at the meso level, and the MITI at the macro level.

Corporate behavior and macro-micro interactions may differ in different industries. In order to focus the attention of the current research, the 15 firms were selected from those Japanese companies that had invested in U.S. manufacturing plants in high-technology industries. This particular group of industries was selected because current industrial policy in Japan is centered around this group and because international competition in the industries — especially between the United States and Japan — will likely be intense in the future.

Prior to the field work in Japan in the summer of 1984, a preliminary survey was conducted with Japan specialists in New York and Washington, D.C., in March 1984. During the field work in Japan, personal interviews were also conducted with Japanese academicians and others in business fields. In addition to the interview survey, an extensive review of published materials in the United States and in Japan was conducted throughout the research in order to cross-check the interview data collected and to expand the understanding of the reality observed. The next section summarizes the major findings of the current research.

MAJOR RESEARCH FINDINGS

Although the 15 companies for the interview survey were selected from those Japanese parent firms that had invested in U.S. manufacturing plants in the high technology industries, they differed in corporate size and in the level of their international activities. There were some variations in the investment decision-making process and the control system among these firms. These variations were related mainly to the objective of the investment, the structure of domestic and international activities of the investing company, the personality of the top management, and other company-specific and product-specific factors.

It was observed that the investment decision was made and carried out unequivocally at the level of the firm without any interference or guidance from the macro-level actors. It was also noted that a new pattern of government-business relations and industrial organization has developed.

A summary of major findings is presented in the following pages in the same sequence as in the text: the investment decision-making process, structural linkage and the control system, and changes in government-business relations. For the purpose of presentation and discussions of the major research findings, the 15 Japanese companies are categorized into nine large and six small firms unless other classifications are deemed appropriate to reflect the underlying characteristics of the firms in question.

The Investment Decision-Making Process

Top management at some of the large companies and the majority of the small firms exhibited a strong initiating force for their initial manufacturing investments in the United States. These individuals at the top management level were in most cases the corporate founders. The top management at the companies with high export-dependency ratios also tended to recognize earlier the necessity of starting manufacturing operations in the United States to sell their products in the market. In the other cases, the initiating force came mainly from those individuals who were close to the marketing and/or information-gathering activities of the companies in the United States.

In all cases, each investment opportunity — whether it was startup of a new manufacturing plant or acquisition of an existing U.S. corporation — was considered and evaluated separately and in light of multiple reasons. The large U.S. market was an important motivational factor for the majority of the investments. However, it was a secondary factor for some investments, which were motivated primarily by the desire to secure access to technologies.

Aside from the large size of U.S. markets, which after all could be served by exports rather than local production, the following were three reasons most frequently cited by the 15 Japanese firms for their direct manufacturing investments in the United States: to establish close customer relations in the United States, to secure access to technologies, and to overcome trade barriers. The first reason was shared equally by the majority of the companies interviewed. The second reason was a "very important" factor for investments undertaken by some large firms and the majority of the small firms. The third reason was generally unimportant for the small companies.

At the majority of the companies, a project team was formed to investigate the feasibility of the manufacturing venture in the United States. Typically such a team was composed of five to ten individuals from the home office in charge of production, sales, accounting/finance, and corporate planning plus key employees from the U.S. sales subsidiary.

The type of information gathered during the feasibility study varied, depending on the mode of entry — acquisition or startup. In the case of acquisition, the major concerns were in assessing the technology level and the marketing ability of the target company. As Japanese banks doing business in the United States lacked know-how in corporate acquisitions in general, Japanese investors relied upon U.S. bankers.

In the case of startups, the major concern was labor-related issues such as the quality and availability of labor, the level of union activity, and the past history of management-employee relations in a particular locality within the United States. The Japanese investors were concerned primarily with differences in the employment system and cultural values as well as the production-related issue of how to maintain the reputation of good-quality products. Other factors considered during the investigation phase include the potential market for the product to be manufactured, the total capital requirement for the investment, tax and other incentives to be granted in a particular locality, and the existence of local subcontractors for intermediate products and supplies.

The feasibility study generally lasted for 6 to 12 months, and the planning horizon for the report of the study was set at a minimum of three years and maximum of ten years. The feasibility study was also instrumental for the practice of Nemawashi, the groundwork, among the interested parties in some cases.

Selection decisions on product lines and production processes were related importantly to investment rationales. Types of products to be manufactured were obvious in the case of defensive investments to overcome trade frictions. Here, the critical decision task lay in determining the scale of the manufacturing operation, that is, the production volume, the type of production process, and the level of processing. Product selection was a major concern for investments in market-sensitive products that would require close customer relations as well as for the companies whose major objective in investing in U.S. manufacturing operations was to diversify their product lines.

In comparison of product lines and production processes employed at the parent, the U.S. manufacturing subsidiary and the other overseas manufacturing plants, it was hypothesized that the more recent the investment, the more highly automated the production processes to be installed in order to assure product quality of the products and to save labor-related costs. Worldwide competitive pressures would also be likely to force the Japanese firms to produce newer and improved products at their manufacturing plants anywhere in the world. One implication here is that the Japanese companies will require more and more highly skilled, rather than unskilled, labor to operate such technically complex manufacturing plants, and thus they will prefer the United States, where highly trained technicians and professionals are relatively abundant, as a production site to the other overseas regions.

The majority of the firms preferred startup to acquisition as their mode of entry into U.S. manufacturing; in fact, seven of the nine large companies specifically stated that startup was their basic company policy for overseas direct investments. In the case of the small firms, acquisition of an existing U.S. firm was not considered at all, mainly because of their limited corporate resources.

Reasons for acquisitions were specific and related to tangible and intangible assets possessed by the acquired U.S. companies, for example, product technologies and marketing know-how of the acquired firms. One large company acquired a U.S. firm in the same industry prior to its initial startup manufacturing investment in order to learn the human resources management practiced at the acquired company. In general, acquisitions of existing companies were preferred by and satisfactory to those companies that had not possessed a strong marketing network within the U.S. market prior to the acquisitions.

Multiple reasons explain why the majority of the Japanese companies preferred startup manufacturing ventures. These reasons are utilization of their familiar production processes, adaptation and development of their own management practices, ease in linking the manufacturing plant to the U.S. sales subsidiary, flexibility in location selection and factory layout with a future plan for possible expansions, and the complete control over the amount and the timing of capital expenditures.

The majority of the firms, including those that acquired existing U.S. companies, preferred the strategy of 100 percent ownership. Here, the organizational control was a major reason for such preference.

In deciding where to locate, quality of labor, proximity to markets, and labor unionization were three major concerns for the large firms, while proximity to markets was the primary concern for the majority of the small firms, whose U.S. plants were characterized as assembly-type and/or service oriented.

The majority of the firms relied on subjective judgments, with varying degrees of quantitative and qualitative analyses, in making their final decisions to invest. The large companies with experience in overseas investments utilized more elaborate decision rules than the others.

The locus of decision making was concentrated at the top management level. Consensus building was carried out only among the top management at five large and four small companies and among top and middle managements in four large and two small firms. It was also found that the decision-making style (top-down versus bottom-up) varied depending on particular decision tasks and even among the companies. This may imply that the traditional decision-making process based on group participation has gradually been transformed into a mixed approach, where effectiveness and efficiency of decision making determine how the process should be structured.

In all cases, the decision to invest was made at the level of the firm without any consultation or deliberations with Japanese government officials or even with such related companies as group-member firms of those belonging to particular industrial groups, domestic subsidiaries, and affiliates. In the case of the large firms in particular industrial groups, the reason for not consulting with their group-member firms might be that the scale of investment was not large enough to require such consultation.

Structural Linkage and the Control System

Organization structure is important, as it defines a division of responsibility and regulates flows of information internally as well as between the parent and the subsidiary. Chapter 5 presented the organization structures of the companies interviewed. It also examined the structural linkage between the parent and the subsidiary as well as the control system from the parent perspective, that is, the locus of policy formulation, the communication methods, and the evaluation of subsidiary performance.

In general, as a corporation grows in size and in the breadth of product lines and markets to be served, it transforms its organization from a flat, functionally based structure to a more complex, multidivisional and/or matrix structure. This generally holds true to the companies interviewed. The majority of the firms adopted the multidivisional system, that is, the Jigyobusei, of management to organize their business activities, human resources, and communication channels.

The linkage between the parent and the subsidiary is difficult to design and to maintain. Communication gaps between Japanese and North Americans, due primarily to the difference in the two languages plus dissimilarity in perception and value judgment, have been a difficult barrier to overcome for the Japanese companies.

In the case of acquisitions of existing U.S. firms and ventures with U.S. entrepreneurs (the Japanese investors as venture capitalists), the Japanese parent companies have delegated substantial autonomy to their U.S. subsidiaries. The control system at the majority of the small firms was also found to be decentralized to a significant degree. As the U.S. subsidiaries of these small companies are primarily engaging in service-oriented and/or assembly operations as an extension of marketing activities, decentralization is a reasonable approach. Manufacturing operations, in contrast, require more coordinating efforts than marketing activities at the headquarters level.

The parent-subsidiary linkage at the small firms is maintained by one or two top executives at the home office. The large companies have organized the structural linkage generally through their product-based divisions. Some of these large companies maintain their corporate executives at their U.S. subsidiaries to strengthen the communication linkage at the top management level.

At those companies where the relevant product-based division maintains a structural linkage with the U.S. manufacturing plant, several other home-office divisions — such as the international division, the corporate planning division, the finance/accounting division, and the subsidiaries office — are also required to maintain some operational links in varying degrees. There appears to be a multiple communications link between the parent and the overseas subsidiaries in general; consequently, an extensive use of parent company nationals (PCNs) at these subsidiaries as observed by some researchers.

In the case of startup, wholly owned subsidiaries, frequent consultation and negotiations ensue between the parent and the subsidiary. However, this frequent communication does not necessarily mean an effective control and coordination. The areas of policy making, in which the parent's participation is strongest, are selection of products, product development (R & D), intercompany transfer prices, long-term financing, and selection of Japanese personnel to be transferred to the U.S. operations. Policies pertaining to local employees are highly decentralized. Marketing policies are in the domain of the U.S. sales subsidiary.

The majority of the companies sell their products manufactured or processed at their U.S. plants primarily within the United States. Although some U.S. manufacturing subsidiaries procure materials for processing from their related companies in Southeast Asia, this seemingly multiplant strategy is not coordinated at the headquarters level. Instead, such procurement policies are delegated to the U.S. subsidiaries.

All 15 companies require their U.S. manufacturing subsidiaries to submit written reports on a regular basis, that is, weekly, monthly, quarterly, semiannually, and annually. The large firms with more experience in international business tend to require more detailed and more frequent reports than the others. Monthly reports cover such topical matters as financial, production, personnel, and other business-related matters. (For details, see Chapter 5.) At some large companies, the subsidiary is required to submit a medium-range corporate plan or R & D-related activities and plans.

At the majority of the large firms and some small companies, regular conferences of management-level personnel of the parent and the subsidiary are considered as a "very important" method of communications. However, such joint management conferences are typically attended by mostly or only Japanese nationals. Cultural and language barriers are the major reason for this Japanese orientation, since most Japanese executives and managers find it difficult to interact freely with their U.S. counterparts at the formal business meetings.

As to evaluation of subsidiary performance, the majority of the firms prefer to use multiple measures with the highest importance attached to local profits. All of the large firms use contribution to consolidated profit and budget variance as performance evaluation measures, and the majority of these companies consider these measures as "very important." Market share is closely monitored at the sales subsidiary, in general, and considered a "very important" evaluation measure. Some large firms monitor such nonfinancial measures as productivity and employee turnover as performance evaluation measures.

Overall, the majority of the companies seem to rely on PCNs assigned for management control to their U.S. operations, and they seem to lack the organizational ability to control and coordinate various activities among the parent, the U.S. subsidiaries, and the other overseas subsidiaries. Efforts to better coordinate activities of the related firms have been made at some of the large companies. It also appears to be critically needed for the large companies to develop employees equipped with intercultural communications skills.

For those large firms that have several U.S. subsidiaries linked operationally to respective product-based divisions at the home office, it seems appropriate to establish a regional headquarters office in the United States because of the following reasons:

1. The size and the geographical spread of the U.S. market warrants coordination of marketing and manufacturing activities on a regional basis.

2. The extensive use of PCNs in each operating unit in the United States can be reduced by maintaining a limited number of able and key PCNs at the regional headquarters office. This will reduce the costs of maintaining expatriates, costs that tend to be higher than those of employing host-country nationals. It will also relieve the bottleneck (the limited number of Japanese employees assignable to overseas ventures) for overseas expansion. It is also important to avoid a possible criticism in host countries (perhaps more likely voiced in developing countries, such as in Southeast Asia, than in the United States) against the extensive use of PCNs.

3. Conflicts of interest among several manufacturing and sales subsidiaries can be arbitrated effectively and efficiently by the regional

headquarters with appropriate authorities and cooperation from the top management of the home office.

In addition, the regional headquarters approach will be instrumental in expediting preparation of such reports as consolidated financial statements, U.S. federal corporate income-tax returns, and other regulatory statements required to be filed. This approach will also help develop coherent policies and actions in the areas of government relations (in terms of responding positively and constructively to U.S. public policies and regulations), public relations, and community services, which all relate to the issue of social responsibility of a firm within the distinctive cultural setting and environment in the United States.

Changes in Government-Business Relations

In order to find the underlying force that might explain the rapid increase of Japanese direct manufacturing investment in the United States since the early 1970s, the current study examined the environmental condition and factors affecting Japanese companies' decisions to invest in the United States, namely the government-business relations. Since the problem at hand is concerned with Japanese companies' decisions and activities beyond the national boundary (that is, direct manufacturing investment in the United States), an environmental model was used to isolate major factors and actors. It is important to realize the complexity of interactions among macro- and micro-level actors, including not only domestic but also actors outside Japan.

Two major currents were identified as having worked to trigger Japanese direct manufacturing investment in the United States. One was a politically oriented current relating to Japan's drive for export-led growth during the period of more than two decades after the end of World War II and the resultant increase in political pressure from Japan's trading partners to liberalize restrictive trade and investment policies and practices. Another current was an enterprise-oriented one, characterized by private initiatives of Japanese companies and business leaders. Here, the period around the late 1960s was a turning point for Japan's economic management, which moved from the state-guided market system to the private-sector-led market system.

Chapter 6 recounted the important historical development of changes in the government controls on foreign exchange and international transactions of private business in Japan. It examined how and why MITI gained and subsequently lost by the early 1970s its powerful tools — the foreign exchange budget system and the centralized control system on foreign exchange — to manage and control the development of Japanese industries. Thus, it was observed that Japanese corporations had not been unduly constrained in their decisions to invest in overseas manufacturing ventures since the early 1970s.

The policy direction of the MITI has been shifting from micro-oriented (enterprise-oriented) to more macro-oriented, supportive, indirect policies in recent years. Chapter 6 studied MITI's structural reform in the early 1970s, its process of policy making, and its linkage with Japanese industries.

Keidanren is also concerned more with a long-range vision of the Japanese industries and economy rather than with trying to build consensus among Japanese business on immediate micro-level issues. However, it still seems to play a vital role as a gatekeeper between the business community and the government.

It was observed that there had been a significant development of a four-way communication channel among the two business communities and the governments in Japan and the United States. Although the pattern of communications is complex, it seems to have shifted from state-initiated to privately initiated interactions and discussions on bilateral economic issues. It was observed that such bilateral interactions began to spill over to the grassroots level, opening up communications and cross-membership in some trade associations of the two countries and increasing the emphasis on public relations activities of Japanese companies in the United States.

It was also observed that the traditional concept of Japan, Inc., had lost its ground and that a new pattern of industrial organization had been evolving in Japan. Chapter 6 identified and discussed various factors that would contribute further to the complex realignment of large and small companies in Japan.

Comparative data on Japan's foreign direct investment in general and her direct manufacturing investment in the United States in particular were presented and analyzed in relative terms in Chapter 6. A sharp increase in Japan's outward direct investment since the early 1970s was observed, corresponding to the relaxation of Japanese government policies on international capital transactions. It was also noted that Japanese direct investments in the United States were concentrated largely in wholesale trade industries and quite modestly in manufacturing industries in comparison to other industrialized countries. The macro data showed clearly the Japanese companies' historical orientation toward trade and sales activities in the United States.

Currently there is no consensus at MITI regarding the effect of Japanese outward direct investment on the Japanese economy. MITI has been receiving numerous requests from other industrialized countries, including the United States, to increase Japanese companies' direct manufacturing investments in their countries. As Japan's trade frictions with the United States have been persistent, MITI appears to welcome Japanese companies' outward direct investments and does not seem to interfere with their private initiatives.

IMPLICATIONS OF THE RESEARCH FINDINGS

The current research study focused on the investment decision and the control system of the 15 Japanese parent companies that had established U.S. manufacturing plants in high-technology industries. The analysis of the government-business relations was also focused mainly on the issues relating to Japan's outward direct investment. The interview survey on macro-micro interactions was pertinent primarily to the industrial sector characterized as high-technology (or growth) industries. Thus, the pictures emerging from the current study may be quite different for those companies and government-business interactions in such other industrial sectors as basic industries (steel, chemicals, metals, etc.) and natural resource-oriented sectors (mining, petroleum, fishery, etc.).

Before turning to policy implications of the current study, it is appropriate to list some suggestions for further research. As noted, corporate behavior and government-business relations are likely to be different in different industrial sectors. Therefore, the examination similar to the current study should be extended to other distinctive industries such as those indicated here. It would also be a worthwhile research endeavor to examine the decision-making process of companies that fall into the following categories: (1) those that considered seriously the possibility of direct manufacturing investment in the United States but decided not to undertake such investment; (2) those that undertook disinvestments from their U.S. manufacturing operations.

The methods used in the current research to measure the parent-subsidiary linkage can certainly be improved. The locus of policy formulation with respect to the subsidiary's strategic and operational decisions can, for example, be measured in terms of more-refined scaling than the trichotomy (the headquarters, the subsidiary, and the joint) used in the current research.

The parent-subsidiary linkage should also be studied from the subsidiary perspective, and the experience at the subsidiary level should be compared with the parent's perspective to understand how the control mechanism actually works at the operational level. It would also be quite a valuable research endeavor to investigate how Japanese-owned manufacturing subsidiaries motivate, successfully or unsuccessfully, U.S. workers (skilled and unskilled) in order to raise productivity at their U.S. manufacturing plants.

The current study has touched upon various areas of importance relating to Japanese direct manufacturing investment in the United States to serve as an exploratory and descriptive research study, not as a hypothesis-testing one. However, it is hoped that the study will generate greater understandings of the issue at hand and encourage further research.

Policy implications of the current study are suggestive and future oriented. Although several implications for corporate policies have already been mentioned in the earlier section reporting major findings of the current research, the following summarizes major policy implications.

Overall, the Japanese companies interviewed have not yet been able to come up with coherent policies to coordinate their home and overseas manufacturing activities. The majority of the firms strive for plant-level optimization. Although some large companies have been moving toward regional optimization by creating their regional headquarters in the United States, none of the firms seems yet to have developed a strategy of global optimization. Multinationalization of production and marketing strategies will be the greatest organizational challenge for the Japanese companies.

There is an infinite number of alternative organizational structures, ranging from centralization to decentralization, in managing foreign subsidiaries. Organizational fragmentation should be transformed into an effectively decentralized structure with an adequate coordinating mechanism. In order to strike a well-balanced mix of policies and practices, the corporate top management must pay constant attention to strategic planning and structural adaptations. A team of experts, who are independent and impartial of the interest of each individual operating unit, can assist the top management in the assessment of the strengths and weaknesses of the existing system in order to remedy and improve the effectiveness and efficiency of the organization as an integrated whole.

Computerization, and the systems approach accompanied with it, will certainly continue to affect the control system in the future. The Japanese management will be likely to perceive the process of corporate management in terms of sequential and logical steps as practiced in the West. This implies that planning and organizational controls will become more structured and standardized. Yet the decision-making process and the implementation of decisions involve more than computer-processed information. Final decisions are influenced by judgments or hunches based on the experiences (special knowledge acquired through cognitive processes) and the attitudes (including philosophical values) of the decision makers. Furthermore, the actual implementation of these decisions is affected by the caliber (intellectual capacity, the extent of which depends on the type of a particular job) and the motivational factors associated with the people who are to operationalize the decisions.

In a multinational setting, a corporate decision must be articulated so that the implementation can be operationalized satisfactorily by local employees who have backgrounds and values different from the parent company nationals (PCNs). As detailed in Chapter 5 as well as in the earlier section on major findings, a regional headquarters approach is recommended. Thus, a large Japanese company with several subsidiaries and units of operations established in the United States will be linked operationally to the respective product-based divisions at the parent.

To fill the communications gap between the Japanese parent and the U.S. subsidiary, each of which is located in a distinctively different cultural environment, it becomes critically important to develop and assign able PCNs with intercultural communications skills to the subsidiary. This is also true for U.S. companies doing business in Japan. In this respect, it is noteworthy that International Business Machines Corporation (IBM) underwent a massive reorganization of its Far East operations and established its Tokyo-based regional headquarters in the summer of 1984.[1] As a part of this reorganization, IBM transferred approximately 200 PCNs to its Japanese headquarters (IBM Japan) in July 1984 to strengthen the decentralized operations in the Asia-Pacific region with its eye particularly on the large and growing markets in Japan and China.

The high-technology industries are characterized by large costs of R & D and products with short life cycles. This requires a careful planning and coordination of activities of various units of operations on the part of the corporate headquarters. Undivided attention of the top management in this area of strategic planning should be recognized as vitally important. Organizational structure and the control system should achieve a goal congruence in this respect.

The private initiative currently underway in Japan should be strengthened to encourage innovative adaptations of private enterprises to the rapidly changing market environments. Private firms, with a minimum intervention from nation states, should search for a proper mix of their own international division of labor based on their knowledge of their specialized business fields. Here, however, the macro- and meso-level actors can and should provide quality information that cannot be collected or would be too costly to collect at the level of the individual firm, for example, macro-level statistical data on domestic and international economies. Thus, MITI's long-range vision of the Japanese economy and Keidanren's study on a medium- to long-term vision of the Japanese industries and economy are constructive in this respect.

Economic policy making in Japan has almost been equivalent to military-defense policy making in the United States in terms of the importance, or priority attached to the respective policy area by each nation under the name of national security. Both nations subscribe to the market economy with private initiatives in principle. A competitive environment based on a market-oriented system is dynamic and beneficial for the economy in the long run.[2]

As the current U.S. trade deficits with Japan have grown to an almost politically intolerable level for the United States, measures to limit imports from Japan have been receiving strong support from both the Senate and the House on Capitol Hill.[3] The U.S. side contends that the Japanese markets are not so open to U.S. exports as the U.S. markets are to Japanese products.[4] The Japanese side argues that the huge federal budget deficits keep interest rates high in the United States and the U.S. dollars strong vis-à-vis the Japanese yen, making U.S. goods uncompetitive in the international markets.

It was observed in Chapter 4 that the majority of the Japanese firms considered the large market size of the United States a precondition for their decisions to establish their U.S. manufacturing plants. Prior to their startup ventures, these companies had been exporting their products to the United States through their U.S. sales subsidiaries. Their direct manufacturing investments were, therefore, undertaken to expand further their market presence in the United States. Furthermore, it was noted in Chapter 5 that the Japanese manufacturing subsidiaries in the United States depend in varying degrees on supply of equipment, parts, and other intermediate products from their parent and related firms in

Southeast Asia. Such imports of intermediate products are necessary for these subsidiaries to compete in U.S. markets in terms of product quality and price (as affected by economies of scale). Thus, such protectionist measures as local content legislation proposed in the U.S. Congress might likely complicate the further development — and perhaps even future establishment — of Japanese manufacturing operations in the United States.

Direct investments and international trade are interrelated, and the former does not necessarily replace the latter. Public policies in the United States and Japan with respect to international trade and investment will affect the economic well-being of both countries and so will have to be evaluated on such criteria as allocative efficiency, equity in the distribution of income, stability of employment and prices, and economic growth.

Cross-investments between the United States and Japan should be encouraged. These will likely strengthen the bilateral relations and lessen economic conflicts associated with national (parochial) interests. Bilateral trade is exchange of goods and materials, while cross-investments involve direct exchange of technologies as well as managerial talents and values. Thus, if they are conducted with good faith on both sides, they will likely enhance mutual understanding of the two countries.

The future requires systemic and innovative adaptations to the changing environment. The increase in Japanese direct manufacturing investments in the United States can be viewed as portending a turning point in U.S.-Japanese relations. This transitional period will require plenty of communications and coordination among rule-making bodies of the two countries on both public and private levels in such areas of policies and practices as trade, investment, taxation, employment, and disclosure requirements (accounting rules), to name a few. Continuing dialogues and protracted, intensive negotiations among the public and private sectors of the two nations are essential in order to come to terms with mutually agreeable and beneficial conditions and results in these policy and practice areas.

APPENDIXES

A   List of Participating Firms and Organizations: Personnel Interviewed

FIRMS

Canon Inc.	General Manager Business Machines Operations Chief Executive Office	July 19, 1984
	General Manager Productive Management Administration Division	July 19, 1984
	Doctor of Engineering Sayanagi Laboratory Canon Research Center	July 27, 1984

Dainippon Ink &
    Chemicals, Inc.
	General Manager
	Corporate Administration
		June 29, 1984, &
		    July 26, 1984

	Manager	June 29, 1984, & July 26, 1984
	Staff Corporate Administration	June 29, 1984
Hitachi, Ltd.	Manager North American Department Overseas License and Business Support Division	July 25, 1984
	Section Manager North American Department Overseas License and Business Support Division	July 25, 1984

	Staff North American Department Overseas License and Business Support Division	July 25, 1984
Kel Corporation	President	July 3, 1984
Kikusui Electronics Corporation	Executive Vice-President	August 1, 1984
Mitsubishi Chemical Industries, Ltd.	Director Overseas Department	July 5, 1984
Mitutoyo Mfg. Co., Ltd.	Director Export Division	July 23, 1984
NEC Corporation	General Manager Long-Range Planning Division	July 4, 1984
	Manager Corporate Planning Division	July 4, 1984, & July 26, 1984
	Program Manager Overseas Affiliates Auditing Division	July 4, 1984
	Supervisor Corporate Planning Division	July 26, 1984
Ricoh Company, Ltd.	General Manager Staff Office of Planning	July 11, 1984
	Assistant General Manager Accounting Department	July 11, 1984
Seiko Instruments & Electronics, Ltd.	President	August 15, 1984
	Director General Administrative Department	July 10, 1984, & August 15, 1984
	General Manager Overseas Corporate Planning	July 10, 1984
Sony Corporation	Manager Press and Public Relations	July 2, 1984

TDK Corporation	Manager Corporate Planning Office	July 9, 1984
Tokyo Aircraft Instruments Co., Ltd.	Director General Planning Department	July 18, 1984
	President of the U.S. Subsidiary	July 18, 1984
Toshiba Corporation	Assistant General Manager Corporate Planning Office	July 19, 1984, & July 31, 1984
ULVAC Corporation	Executive Vice-President President of the U.S. Subsidiary	July 13, 1984

OTHER ORGANIZATIONS

Keidanren	Senior Assistant Director Energy & Industrial Affairs Department	July 17, 1984, & July 25, 1984

Ministry of
  International Trade
  and Industry
	Deputy Director
	International Business Affairs
	  Division
	Industrial Policy Bureau
		July 16, 1984

	Deputy Director Industrial Structure Division Industrial Policy Bureau	August 2, 1984

B   Questionnaire

INSTRUCTION

1. Please complete this questionnaire *prior* to our meeting.

2. The purpose of this questionnaire survey is to explore the decision-making process and the control system of Japanese firms investing in manufacturing operations in the United States. For the purpose of this research, a direct investment means that (a) your company owns more than 25 percent of the equity of the new or existing foreign operation; (b) this ownership share was acquired at the time of the initial investment in the foreign affiliate; (c) this ownership share includes equity participation directly from the parent company and also indirectly via other foreign affiliates.

3. The survey includes 40 questions and is divided into seven sections:
    1) The Initiating Forces
    2) Investigation
    3) Decision Making
    4) Implementation & Control
    5) Evaluation Practices
    6) Company Information
    7) Interviewee Information

4. For some questions the survey asks for information on your company's direct investment decision-making practices for your most recent manufacturing plant in the United States as well as your original (first-time) manufacturing plant in the United States. So, if you have more than one manufacturing plant in the United States, please record for your most recent and original manufacturing plants as indicated in this questionnaire.

5. Even if for any reason you do not complete the entire questionnaire, please return it anyway at the time of our meeting. Even partial information provides important input for my conducting our actual interview.

6. All individual responses will be kept strictly confidential. Thus, I hope you will be completely candid.

THANK YOU VERY MUCH FOR YOUR COOPERATION IN THIS RESEARCH ENDEAVOR.

Section 1: The Initiating Forces

1. Who proposed the possibility of establishing a manufacturing plant in the United States? Plese note first the year of plant opening, the location within the United States, and the type of entry (new or acquisition) of each of your most recent and original manufacturing plants. Then, please check (X) who proposed the direct manufacturing investment(s) in the United States.

	Year	Location	Mode of Entry
(1) Most Recent	____	_____	_____
(2) Original	____	_____	_____

	(1) Most Recent	(2) Initial
(a) Chairman		
(b) President		
(c) Board of Directors		
(d) Council of Managing Directors		
(d) Sales Division		
(f) Production Division		
(g) Sales Office (Subsidiary) in the United States		
(h) Customer in the United States		
(i) Trading Company		
(j) Other, please specify		

2. What were the reasons contemplated for such direct investment rather than exporting to serve the U.S. market? Please indicate the relative importance of the following items according to the scale 1 = Very Important, 2 = Important, 3 = Less Important, and 4 = Not Important.

	(1) Most Recent	(2) Initial
(a) Diversify risk		
(b) Overcome trade restrictions		
(c) Save labor cost		
(d) Save shipping cost		
(e) Save land cost		
(f) Secure access to raw materials		
(g) Secure access to capital		
(h) Secure access to technology		
(i) Look for the large market		
(j) Look for the political stability		
(k) Look for the well-established infrastructure		
(l) Follow the competitors		
(m) Establish closer relations with customers in the United States		
(n) Take advantage of currency fluctuation		
(o) Other, please specify		

Section 2: Investigation
  1. Please check who carried out the investigation (the feasibility study).

  (1) Most Recent   (2) Initial
  (a) Ad-hoc project team
  (b) International Division
  (c) Corporate Planning Division
  (d) Sales office (subsidiary) in the
      United States
  (e) Outside consultants
  (f) Other, please specify

  2. If you checked (a) to the question above, please specify the composition (members) of the project team, according to functional specializations, that is, production, engineering, finance, accounting, personnel, and so on.

  3. Please list five most important types of information gathered (1) for your most recent manufacturing plant in the United States and (2) for your initial manufacturing plant in the United States.
  (1) Most Recent
      (a)
      (b)
      (c)
      (d)
      (e)
  (2) Initial
      (a)
      (b)
      (c)
      (d)
      (e)

  4. In preparing the report of the investigation, what was your planning horizon in number of years?
  (1) Most Recent   _____ years
  (2) Initial   _____ years

  5. How long in number of months did it take to complete the investigation?
  (1) Most Recent   _____ months
  (2) Initial   _____ months

Section 3: Decision Making
  1. Please check who made the final go/no go decision.

  (1) Most Recent   (2) Initial
  (a) Chairman
  (b) President
  (c) Board of Directors

(d) Area manager

(e) Other, please specify

2. Please check all the parties consulted, showing the extent of consensus reached regarding the investments.

	(1) Most Recent	(2) Initial
(a) Top management (chief executives and directors)		
(b) Upper-middle management (department heads and plant managers)		
(c) Lower-middle management (section chiefs)		
(d) Lower management (supervisors and foremen)		
(e) All employees		

3. How did the decision makers measure business risk associated with the investment?

	(1) Most Recent	(2) Initial
(a) Make a subjective evaluation of risk		
(b) Project a probability distribution of cash flows		
(c) Perform a sensitivity analysis		
(d) Make no risk assessment		
(e) Other, please specify		

4. Please check as appropriate regarding your most recent plant whether you _____ opened a new plant, or _____ bought an existing plant. Then, please note below three most important factors for the action you took.

(a)

(b)

(c)

Please note below three most important reasons for the alternative action you rejected.

(a)

(b)

(c)

5. Please check as appropriate regarding your initial plant whether you _____ opened a new plant, or _____ bought an existing plant. Then, please note below three most important factors for the action you took.

(a)

(b)

(c)

Please note below three most important reasons for the alternative action you rejected.

(a)

(b)

(c)

6. Please indicate the relative importance of the following factors in selecting a location for your manufacturing plants within the United States, using the scale 1 = Very Important, 2 = Important, 3 = Less Important, and 4 = Not Important.

(1) Most Recent   (2) Initial

(a) Cost of land
(b) Cost of labor
(c) Quality of labor
(d) Nonlabor unionization
(e) Proximity to markets
(f) Proximity to suppliers
(g) Proximity to a Japanese community
(h) Proximity to competitors
(i) Proximity to educational and research institutions
(j) Quality of life (air, nature, weather, etc.)
(k) Special tax incentives
(l) Other state and local government incentives
(m) Other, please specify

7. Please check from which of the following parties you sought opinions or advice in making the final decision to invest.

(1) Most Recent   (2) Initial

(a) Subsidiary firms (*Kogaisha*)
(b) Affiliated firms (*Keiretsugaisha*)
(c) Associated firms (*Kankeigaisha*)
(d) Main bank
(e) Trade associations (*Keidanren*, etc.)
(f) Japanese government or its agencies (MITI, MOF, etc.)
(g) Other, please specify

8. Please indicate how long in number of months it took to reach the final decision to invest in U.S. manufacturing after the feasibility study had been completed.
(1) Most Recent   _____ months
(2) Initial   _____ months

9. Please indicate how long in number of months it took to open the plant after the final decision had been made.
(1) Most Recent   _____ months
(2) Initial   _____ months

Section 4: Implementation and Control

1. Please check which of the following statements best describes your current operating policy with regard to your manufacturing operations in the United States.

    (a) ( ) U.S. operations are tightly controlled from the corporate headquarters

    (b) ( ) U.S. operations are permitted a substantial degree of local autonomy

    (c) ( ) U.S. operations are managed jointly by the corporate headquarters and the local staff.

2. Are your manufacturing operations in the United States a strategic component of an integrated system?

    (a) ( ) Yes

    (b) ( ) No

3. Please check which of the following divisions of your company regularly monitor the activities of your manufacturing plants in the United States.

    (a) ( ) President's Office

    (b) ( ) International Division

    (c) ( ) Export Division

    (d) ( ) Production Division

    (e) ( ) Finance and Accounting Division

    (f) ( ) Other, please specify

4. Please check which of the following functions at the plant level are monitored by the headquarters.

    (a) ( ) Production volume

    (b) ( ) Sales

    (c) ( ) Advertisement

    (d) ( ) Finance

    (e) ( ) Accounting

    (f) ( ) Personnel — Japanese

    (g) ( ) Personnel — local management and technical specialists

    (h) ( ) Other, please specify

5. Please check the appropriate level in which the following policies are determined: (1) the headquarters level, (2) the local level, and (3) jointly.

                             (1) Headquarters   (2) Local   (3) Joint

    (a) Selection of products to be manufactured or processed

    (b) Product development (R & D)

    (c) Product modification

    (d) Selection of process technology

    (e) Production volume

    (f) Procurement of materials for production

    (g) Marketing strategy

(h) Transfer pricing of materials/
    components
(i) Pricing of the products
    manufactured or assembled
(j) Long-term financing
(k) Short-term financing
(l) Major capital expenditures
(m) Dividend payout
(n) Personnel — Japanese
(o) Personnel — local management
    and technical specialists
(p) Personnel — local factory workers

6. Please check (1) in the first column which of the following communication methods you normally use to facilitate the implementation of your overall corporate objectives at the subsidiary level and also indicate (2) in the second column the relative importance of each communication method according to the scale 1 = Very Important, 2 = Important, 3 = Less Important, and 4 = Not Important.

(a) ( ) ( ) Training and indoctrination of the key individuals of the subsidiary
            prior to task assignments
(b) ( ) ( ) Regular conferences of all management from both the headquarters
            and the subsidiary either in Japan or in the United States
(c) ( ) ( ) Personal visits by decision-making personnel to the subsidiary
            whenever problems arise
(d) ( ) ( ) Written statements of performance on a regular basis, for example,
            monthly reports including financial statements
(e) ( ) ( ) Frequent communication via telephone and/or telex.
(f) ( ) ( ) Other, please specify

7. Please check which of the following distribution channels your company uses to sell products in the United States (1) before and (2) after the establishment of your initial manufacturing plant in the United States.

	(1) Before	(2) After
(a) Through trading companies		
(b) Through own sales branches		
(c) Through U.S. distributors		

8. Who are the main suppliers of (1) raw material, (2) parts, and (3) subassemblies (intermediate materials) for production at your manufacturing plants in the United States? Please specify approximate percentage of procurement from each of the following possible sources to the total procurement for your U.S. production.

	(1) Raw materials	(2) Parts	(3) Subassemblies
(a) Parent company in Japan	%	%	%
(b) Subsidiary firms in Japan and abroad	%	%	%
(c) U.S. firms	%	%	%

(d) Firms other than Japanese
    or U.S.   %   %   %
(e) Other, please specify   %   %   %
                                    100%   100%   100%

9. Where are the main customers for your products manufactured in the United States? Please specify approximate percentage of sales to the following possible destinations.

  (a) The United States   %
  (b) Japan   %
  (c) Europe   %
  (d) Other, please specify   %
                                      100%

10. Please check whether in terms of the following measures you have (1) expanded or (2) contracted your manufacturing operations *in the United States* since the opening of your initial manufacturing plant in the United States.

                                     (1) Expanded   (2) Contracted
  (a) Production volume
  (b) Employment level

11. Please check whether in terms of the following measures you have (1) expanded or (2) contracted your manufacturing operations *in Japan* since the opening of your initial manufacturing plant in the United States.

                                     (1) Expanded   (2) Contracted
  (a) Production volume
  (b) Employment level

12. Please note what relationships, if any, there are between your answers to the questions 10 and 11 above.

Section 5: Evaluation Practices

1. Please indicate the relative importance of the following measures which you normally use to evaluate the performance of your U.S. manufacturing unit according to the scale 1 = Very Important, 2 = Important, 3 = Less Important, and 4 = Not Important. If you do not use any one of the following measures, please indicate by placing "X."

  (a) ( ) Local profit
  (b) ( ) Contribution to consolidated profit
  (c) ( ) Return on investment
  (d) ( ) All cash flows to the parent
  (e) ( ) Market share
  (f) ( ) Productivity
  (g) ( ) Budget variance

(h) ( ) Employee turnover
(i) ( ) Other, please specify

2. Please check which of the following statements best describes the reasons for differences between performance evaluation practices you normally use for your U.S. manufacturing operations and those you use for your other manufacturing operations.

(a) ( ) There are no differences.
(b) ( ) Practices differ because the business environment in the United States is unique.
(c) ( ) Practices differ because the activity of the U.S. manufacturing plant is different from that of the other manufacturing plants.
(d) ( ) Other, please specify

3. Please list what types of information and reports are required to be transmitted to the corporate headquarters in Japan from your manufacturing subsidiary in the United States. Please note also how often each of the reports is required.

Section 6: Company Information

1. Please indicate (1) in the first column the number of manufacturing plants in which your company and other affiliates own more than 25 percent of equity share and (2) in the second column the average number of factory workers for the most recent fiscal period in each of the following areas.

(1) Number of Plants   (2) Factory Workers

(a) Japan
(b) The United States
(c) Europe
(d) Southeast Asia
(e) Other

2. Please indicate (1) in the first column the proportion of your total overseas manufacturing operations and (2) in the second column the proportion of your U.S. manufacturing operations, each relative to the consolidated total of your manufacturing operations in terms of each of the following measures.

	(1) Total Overseas	(2) U.S.A.
(a) Assets	%	%
(b) Gross Sales	%	%
(c) Net Profit	%	%
(d) Number of full-time employees	%	%

3. Please compare the nature of your manufacturing operations in the United States with your (1) domestic and (2) other overseas manufacturing plants.

(1) Domestic   (2) Other Overseas

Products
(a) More mature
(b) Newer

    (c) Same

Production Process
    (a) More capital intensive
    (b) More labor intensive
    (c) Same

Labor
    (a) More skilled
    (b) Less Skilled
    (c) Same

Productivity
    (a) Better
    (b) Worse
    (c) Same

4. Please state the title, according to the organizational hierarchy at the corporate headquarters, of the person who was transferred to the United States as the head of the manufacturing unit at the time of his transfer.

5. Please check which of the following organizational structures your company is currently based upon.
    (a) ( ) Organized globally by product lines
    (b) ( ) Organized globally by geographic divisions
    (c) ( ) Organized globally by functional areas
    (d) ( ) Using an international division
    (e) ( ) Other, please specify

6. In each of the following categories of functional specialization, please indicate the number of decision makers at the highest decision-making level of your company.

                                       Number
    (a) Finance
    (b) Marketing
    (c) Personnel
    (d) Engineer
    (e) Scientist
    (f) Legal
    (g) General management
    (h) Outside members
    (i) Other, please specify

Section 7: Interviewee Information
The questionnaire in this section was adapted from Frank A. Heller and Bernhard Wilpert, *Competence and Power in Managerial Decision-Making: A Study of Senior Levels of Organization in Eight Countries,* pp. 202–3 and p. 207. Copyright 1981. Reprinted by permission of John Wiley & Sons, Ltd.

1. In the first two questions, the word *change* will include (1) technological, (2) organizational, and (3) human relations changes that could conceivably apply to your own industry. Please answer with your estimate.

(1) *Looking at the facts,* what rate of change do you expect in your own industry during the next five years?

(1) Technology   (2) Organization   (3) Human Relations

- (a) Very slow
- (b) Slow
- (c) Moderate
- (d) Rapid
- (e) Very rapid

(2) *Do you feel* that this rate of change will be too rapid or too slow?

(1) Technology   (2) Organization   (3) Human Relations

- (a) Too slow
- (b) Slow
- (c) Adequate
- (d) Rapid
- (e) Too rapid

(3) Do you believe that in the future, let us say the next ten years, corporate managers will be different in terms of managerial ability?

- (a) ( ) Much better
- (b) ( ) Better
- (c) ( ) Same
- (d) ( ) Bad
- (e) ( ) Worse

2. The following questionnaire is not related to your direct investment decision but is concerned with 12 possible decisions to be made by your immediate superior in relation to you. Please read first the following five methods of making decisions. The word *him* or *his* always refers to your superior.

Five Methods of Making Decisions
(a)   HIS DECISION without detailed explanation
These are decisions made by him without previous discussion or consultation with his subordinates and no special meeting or memorandum is used to explain the decision. This method includes decisions made after consulting with managers at the same level or superiors.
(b)   HIS DECISION with detailed explanation
The same as above, but afterwards he explains the problem and the reasons for his choice in a memorandum or in a special meeting.
(c)   PRIOR CONSULTATION with you
Before the decision is taken, he explains the problem to you and asks for your advice and help. He then makes the decision by himself. His final choice may or may not reflect your influence.

(d) JOINT DECISION MAKING with you

He and you together analyze the problem and come to a decision. You usually have as much influence over the final choice as he. When there are more than two in the discussion, the decision of the majority is accepted more often than not.

(e) DELEGATION of decision to you

He asks you to make the decisions regarding a particular subject. He may or may not request you to report your decisions to him. He seldom vetos your decision.

Below is a set of decision tasks. If your immediate superior does not have the authority to make the final decision, or if the subject is not relevant, please check the box marked "Not Applicable." However, if the decision is applicable, please indicate which of the various methods of making decisions described above he uses to arrive at the decision. If he uses more than one procedure, please split the percentages accordingly. Most usually, however, you will put 100 percent next to one of the five alternatives.

(1) The decision to increase your salary

( ) Not Applicable*

(a) _____ % HIS DECISION without detailed explanation

(b) _____ % HIS DECISION with detailed explanation

(c) _____ % PRIOR CONSULTATION with you

(d) _____ % JOINT DECISION-MAKING with you

(e) _____ % DELEGATION of decision to you

*Same response categories for the remaining decision tasks

(2) The decision to increase the number of employees working for you

(3) The decision to hire one of several applicants to work for you

(4) The decision on the style and layout of written letters in your office

(5) The decision relating to the purchase of a piece of equipment for your department at a cost within his budgetary discretion

(6) The decision to promote one of the employees working for you

(7) The decision to give a merit pay increase to one of your subordinates

(8) The decision to change the money allocation for your department during the preparation of the company budget

(9) The decision to discharge one of your staff

(10) The decision to change an operating procedure followed by you

(11) The decision to assign you to a different job (on same salary) under his jurisdiction

(12) The decision regarding what goals or standards of performance should be set for you

3. Please indicate your name, the nature of your work, job title, and number of years with the company.

(a) Name

(b) Nature of work

(c) Title

(d) Number of years

C   Interview Questions

FIRMS

1. Please describe your company's organizational structure and your role in the organization.

2. Please describe briefly the historical evolution of your firm, especially since 1970.

3. Please describe the competitive environment of your business, that is, your firm's competitors, the competitive edge of your firm, and the future of the industry.

4. Please state the top five of your firm's goals.

5. Please describe how your company's decision to invest in U.S. manufacturing was made, that is, the initiating forces, the decision-making process, and the decision rules.

6. Please describe how you considered the effects of your company's outward investment on domestic economy, domestic employment, and other firms in the corporate group during the process of making the decision to invest in U.S. manufacturing.

7. Please describe how your U.S. manufacturing operation fits in to your company's overall corporate objectives organizationally and operationally.

8. Please describe your management control system to monitor the manufacturing operation in the United States from your headquarters in Japan. Is the control system different from the one you normally use to monitor your domestic or other foreign subsidiaries?

9. How does the U.S. subsidiary's performance live up to the parent company's expectations?

10. Please describe your U.S. subsidiary's competitive edge and how it is sustained.

11. In which areas of your management control system at the corporate headquarters level would you like to see improvements to better control your overseas operations?

12. Please describe your company's working relationship with the Japanese government agencies and economic organizations and explain to what extent your decision to invest in U.S. manufacturing was influenced by these institutions.

13. In your opinion, what should be the roles of the government and economic organizations with respect to corporate business activities?

14. What are some of the major opportunities and problems you foresee in your company's manufacturing operations in the United States?

KEIDANREN

1. Please describe the current organizational structure of Keidanren and your role in the organization.

2. Please describe major changes in Keidanren's structure since 1970.

3. Please describe some of the major international economic problems your organization is currently concerned about.

4. Please describe, using one such problem as an example, how your organization generated alternative solutions, came up with a policy statement, and implemented measures to carry out the policy.

5. Please state your opinion regarding MITI's policies to adjust the Japanese industrial structure toward the one based on the more knowledge-intensive industries.

6. Since the early 1970s there has been a tremendous increase in the number of Japanese firms investing in U.S. manufacturing. In your opinion, what are the major reasons for such increase? What do you think about this phenomenon?

7. Please describe some of your important guiding principles in monitoring the overseas activities of Japanese manufacturing firms.

8. What are some of the major opportunities and problems you foresee in Japanese manufacturing firms in the United States?

MITI

1. Please describe the current organizational structure of MITI and your role in the organization.

2. Please describe major changes in MITI's organizational structure since 1970.

3. Please describe how you coordinate the administrative objectives of MITI and the business objectives of private enterprises.

4. Please describe the important factors conducive to or hindering structural adjustment of the Japanese economy toward an economic structure based on knowledge-intensive industries.

5. Since the early 1970s there has been a tremendous increase in the number of Japanese firms investing in U.S. manufacturing. In your opinion, what are the major reasons for such increase? What do you think about this phenomenon?

6. Please describe your methods, if any, to encourage or discourage any specific industries or firms in opening manufacturing plants in the United States.

7. Please describe in conjunction with your industrial policies some of your important guiding principles in monitoring or administering the overseas activities of Japanese manufacturing firms.

8. What are some of the major opportunities and problems you foresee in the overseas activities of Japanese manufacturing firms?

D Japanese-owned U.S. Manufacturing Plants: Mode of Entry and Ownership Structure by Industry

			Mode of Entry		Ownership Structure		
Code	Industry	Total	Acqui-sition	Startup	Wholly Owned	Japanese Partner(s) Only	U.S.* Partners Involved
20	Food and Kindred Products	83	49	34	51	7	25
22	Textile Mill Products	13	3	10	5	4	4
23	Apparel and Other Textile Products	12	11	1	2	0	10
24	Lumber and Wood Products	7	3	4	3	4	0
25	Furniture and Fixture	2	1	1	2	0	0
26	Paper and Allied Products	2	0	2	1	0	1
27	Printing and Publishing	5	1	4	4	0	1
28	Chemicals and Allied Products	46	33	13	27	1	18
29	Petroleum and Coal Products	1	1	0	0	0	1
30	Rubber and Plastics Products	21	8	13	14	3	4
32	Stone, Clay, and Glass Products	7	4	3	5	0	2
33	Primary Metal Products	48	34	14	3	6	39
34	Fabricated Metal Products	81	57	24	18	2	61
35	Nonelectrical Machinery	48	21	27	32	4	12
36	Electrical Equipment and Supplies	79	26	53	68	2	9
37	Transportation Equipment	21	3	18	15	2	4
38	Instruments and Related Products	27	5	22	22	0	5

			Mode of Entry		Ownership Structure		
Code	Industry	Total	Acqui-sition	Startup	Wholly Owned	Japanese Partner(s) Only	U.S.* Partners Involved
39	Miscellaneous Manufacturing	18	3	15	17	1	0
	Total	521	263	258	289	36	196

*Includes two manufacturing plants with involvement of non-Japanese non-U.S. partners.

Source: Compiled from census data published by Japan Economic Institute of America, Washington, D.C., "Japan's Expanding Manufacturing Presence in the United States: A Profile," April 17, 1981, and "Japan's Expanding Manufacturing Presence: 1983 Update," April 13, 1984.

E   Chronology of Japan-U.S. Trade Frictions

Year

1955   The Japanese-made "one-dollar blouse" became an issue in the United States.

1956   Japan implemented voluntary restraints of exports of cotton goods to the United States.

1957   A Japan-U.S. cotton goods agreement was signed.

1969   Japan agreed to implement the first voluntary restriction on shipments of steel products to the United States.
Japan-U.S. negotiations on limiting Japanese exports of textiles started.

1970   A U.S. company brought suit against Japanese color-TV manufacturers on antitrust grounds and sought compensation duties on imports of Japanese-made color TVs.

1971   The Japanese textile industry declared unilateral restriction of exports to the United States of cotton, woolen, and synthetic textile products.

1972   A Japan-U.S. textile trade agreement was signed.
Japan started the second voluntary restriction of steel exports to the United States for the period from January 1972 to December 1974.

1975   The United States brought suit against Toyota on antitrust grounds and began examination of possible dumping of Japanese automobiles in the U.S. market.

1976   The Japan-U.S. orderly marketing agreement on specialty steels was signed, effective for the period from June 1976 to February 1980.

1977　The Japan-U.S. orderly marketing agreement on color TVs was signed, effective for the period from July 1977 to June 1980.

The Japan-U.S. Trade Facilitation Committee was created.

1978　Japan sent a delegation to the United States to find ways to promote imports of U.S. products.

The United States introduced the Trigger Price Mechanism for steel imports.

The United States requested to open to foreign firms of Nippon Telegraph & Telephone Public Corporation's (NTT) bidding for procurement of materials and equipment.

Japan-U.S. negotiations of trade on farm produce were concluded.

1979　The agreement of the Tokyo Round of Multilateral Trade Negotiations was signed.

An agreement between Japan and the United States was reached on government procurement policies and trade on tobacco and coal.

1980　Requests for restrictions of imports of Japanese-made automobiles gathered momentum in the United States.

The Japanese and U.S. governments developed a formula for the process of NTT procurement.

The United States began levying high import duties on Japanese-made pickup trucks.

1981　Japan started voluntary restrictions of exports of automobiles to the United States, effective for the period from April 1981 to March 1984.

1982　Calls on Japan to open further her domestic market began to mount in the U.S. government. Some senators proposed a local content legislation and the concept of reciprocity in trade.

Houdaille Industries, Inc., filed with U.S. trade representatives a petition to deny eligibility for the income-tax credit on Japanese-made machine tools — a beginning of heated debates on Japan's industrial policies.

Japan announced two consecutive packages of market-opening measures.

Following the recommendation in 1981 by the Japan-U.S. Economic Relations Group, the Japanese cabinet agreed to establish an Office of Trade ombudsman to provide an institutionalized window to handle trade-related complaints.

1983   Negotiations on trade in farm produce were resumed.
       The United States imposed import surcharges on Japanese-made
       motorcycles (the highest rate of 45 percent).
1984   The voluntary restraints program of exports of automobiles to the
       United States was extended, effective for the period from April
       1984 to March 1985.

Source: Based primarily on the *Japan Economic Journal,* November 8, 1983, p. 25;
and Yoshi Tsurumi, *Ikareru Amerika: Nihon no Kigyosenryaku Saitenken* (Angry
America: Reevaluation of Japanese Corporate Strategies) (Tokyo: Toyo Keizai
Shinposha, 1983), pp. 235–42.

F Structural Reform of MITI: Comparison of Old and New Structures

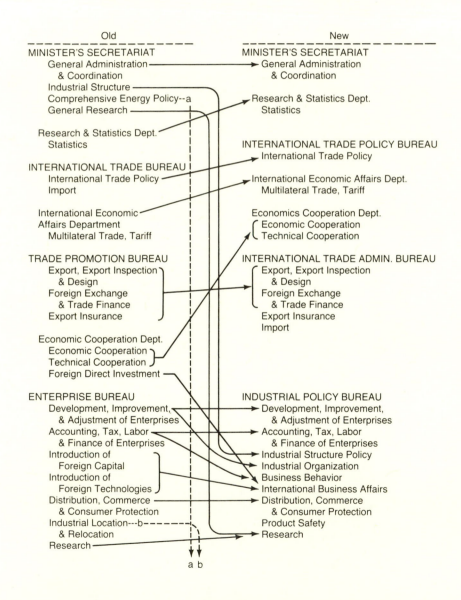

Old

MINISTER'S SECRETARIAT
- General Administration
  - & Coordination
- Industrial Structure
- Comprehensive Energy Policy--a
- General Research

Research & Statistics Dept.
- Statistics

INTERNATIONAL TRADE BUREAU
- International Trade Policy
- Import

International Economic
Affairs Department
- Multilateral Trade, Tariff

TRADE PROMOTION BUREAU
- Export, Export Inspection
  - & Design
- Foreign Exchange
  - & Trade Finance
- Export Insurance

Economic Cooperation Dept.
- Economic Cooperation
- Technical Cooperation
- Foreign Direct Investment

ENTERPRISE BUREAU
- Development, Improvement,
  - & Adjustment of Enterprises
- Accounting, Tax, Labor
  - & Finance of Enterprises
- Introduction of
  - Foreign Capital
- Introduction of
  - Foreign Technologies
- Distribution, Commerce
  - & Consumer Protection
- Industrial Location---b
  - & Relocation
- Research

a b

New

MINISTER'S SECRETARIAT
- General Administration
  - & Coordination

Research & Statistics Dept.
- Statistics

INTERNATIONAL TRADE POLICY BUREAU
- International Trade Policy

International Economic Affairs Dept.
- Multilateral Trade, Tariff

Economics Cooperation Dept.
- Economic Cooperation
- Technical Cooperation

INTERNATIONAL TRADE ADMIN. BUREAU
- Export, Export Inspection
  - & Design
- Foreign Exchange
  - & Trade Finance
- Export Insurance
- Import

INDUSTRIAL POLICY BUREAU
- Development, Improvement,
  - & Adjustment of Enterprises
- Accounting, Tax, Labor
  - & Finance of Enterprises
- Industrial Structure Policy
- Industrial Organization
- Business Behavior
- International Business Affairs
- Distribution, Commerce
  - & Consumer Protection
- Product Safety
- Research

194

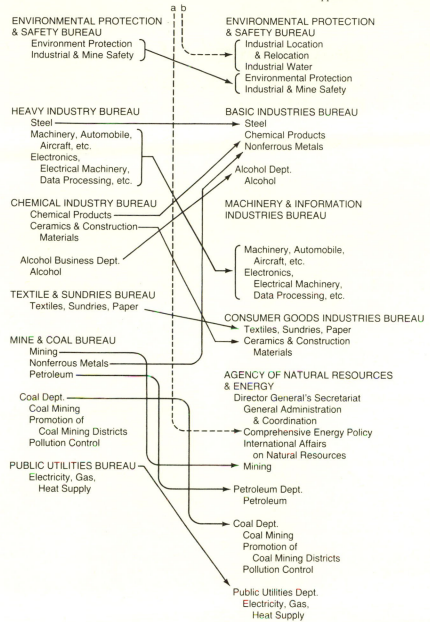

a b

ENVIRONMENTAL PROTECTION
& SAFETY BUREAU
    Environment Protection
    Industrial & Mine Safety

ENVIRONMENTAL PROTECTION
& SAFETY BUREAU
    Industrial Location
        & Relocation
    Industrial Water
    Environmental Protection
    Industrial & Mine Safety

HEAVY INDUSTRY BUREAU
    Steel
    Machinery, Automobile,
        Aircraft, etc.
    Electronics,
        Electrical Machinery,
        Data Processing, etc.

BASIC INDUSTRIES BUREAU
    Steel
    Chemical Products
    Nonferrous Metals

    Alcohol Dept.
    Alcohol

CHEMICAL INDUSTRY BUREAU
    Chemical Products
    Ceramics & Construction
        Materials

    Alcohol Business Dept.
    Alcohol

MACHINERY & INFORMATION
INDUSTRIES BUREAU

    Machinery, Automobile,
        Aircraft, etc.
    Electronics,
        Electrical Machinery,
        Data Processing, etc.

TEXTILE & SUNDRIES BUREAU
    Textiles, Sundries, Paper

CONSUMER GOODS INDUSTRIES BUREAU
    Textiles, Sundries, Paper
    Ceramics & Construction
        Materials

MINE & COAL BUREAU
    Mining
    Nonferrous Metals
    Petroleum

    Coal Dept.
    Coal Mining
    Promotion of
        Coal Mining Districts
    Pollution Control

AGENCY OF NATURAL RESOURCES
& ENERGY
    Director General's Secretariat
    General Administration
        & Coordination
    Comprehensive Energy Policy
    International Affairs
        on Natural Resources
    Mining

PUBLIC UTILITIES BUREAU
    Electricity, Gas,
        Heat Supply

    Petroleum Dept.
    Petroleum

    Coal Dept.
    Coal Mining
    Promotion of
        Coal Mining Districts
    Pollution Control

    Public Utilities Dept.
    Electricity, Gas,
        Heat Supply

Source: Internal memorandum of the Ministry of International Trade and
Industry.

G List of Members of U.S.-Japan Advisory Commission

American Members

David Packard (Co-Chairman)
Chairman of the Board
Hewlett-Packard, Inc.

Donald Rumsfeld
President
G. D. Searle and Company

James Hodgson
Former Ambassador to Japan

Douglas Fraser
President Emeritus
United Automobile, Aerospace and
    Agricultural Workers of America

Daryl Arnold
Chairman
Western Growers Association

James Bere
Chairman
Borg-Warner Corporation

William Timmons
President
Timmons and Company

Japanese Members

Nobuhiko Ushiba (Co-Chairman)
Advisor to the Minister for Foreign
    Affairs

Akio Morita
Chairman and Chief Executive Officer
Sony Corporation

Yotaro Kobayashi
President
Fuji Xerox Co., Ltd.

Saburo Okita
Chairman
Institute for Domestic and International
    Policy Studies

Seizaburo Sato
Professor of Political Science
University of Tokyo

Ichiro Shioji
Chairman
Confederation of Japan Automobile
    Workers' Union

Isamu Yamashita
Director and Chairman
Mitsui Engineering & Shipbuilding
    Co., Ltd.

Source: Interview with Mr. Albert L. Seligmann, executive director, United States-Japan Advisory Commission, Washington, D.C., March 6, 1984.

Notes

1 — INTRODUCTION

1. Data based on the reports compiled by Susan MacKnight and published by the Japan Economic Institute of America, Washington, D.C., "Japan's Expanding Manufacturing Presence in the United States: A Profile," April 17, 1981, and "Japan's Expanding Manufacturing Presence: 1983 Update," April 13, 1984. For the purpose of the current study, only those manufacturing plants located in the 50 states are included; the 5 manufacturing plants located in Puerto Rico are not included in the total of 521 plants.

2. "Japanese Multinationals: Covering the World with Investment," *Business Week,* June 16, 1980, pp. 92–102; "Japan's Strategy for the '80s," *Business Week,* December 14, 1981, pp. 39–120. For a recent debate on Japanese factory ventures in the United States, see Winston Williams, "Japanese Investment, a New Worry," *New York Times,* May 6, 1984, F1 and F23.

3. I. M. Destler, Hideo Sato, Priscilla Clapp, and Haruhiro Fukui, *Managing an Alliance: The Politics of U.S.-Japanese Relations* (Washington, D.C.: The Brookings Institution, 1976) pp. 42–43.

4. There are several articles on increased competition and bilateral negotiations on trade in high-technology products between Japan and the United States. See, for example, Lionel H. Olmer, "Japan's Drive for Technological Preeminence Challenges U.S.," *Business America,* January 24, 1983, pp. 610–15; Timothy J. Curran, "Politics and High Technology: The NTT Case," in *Coping with U.S.-Japanese Economic Conflicts,* ed. I. M. Destler and Hideo Sato (Lexington, Mass.: Lexington Books, 1982), pp. 185–241; and Hideo Tamura, "High Technology Patent Disputes Proliferate between Japan and U.S.," *The Japan Economic Journal,* May 8, 1984, p. 4.

5. Julian Gresser, *High Technology and Japanese Industrial Policy: A Strategy for U.S. Policymakers,* Subcommittee on Trade of the Committee on Ways and Means, U.S. House of Representatives (Washington, D.C.: U.S. Government Printing Office, 1980).

2 — BACKGROUND

1. Peter F. Drucker, "Economic Realities and Enterprise Strategy," in *Modern Japanese Organization and Decision-Making,* ed. Ezra F. Vogel (Berkeley: University of California Press, 1975), p. 243.

2. Eugene J. Kaplan, *Japan: The Government-Business Relationship, A Guide for the American Businessman,* U.S. Department of Commerce, Bureau of International Commerce (Washington, D.C.: U.S. Government Printing Office, 1972), p. 10.

3. Chitoshi Yanaga, *Big Business in Japanese Politics* (New Haven, Conn.: Yale University Press, 1968), p. 28.

4. Chalmers Johnson, *MITI and the Japanese Miracle: The Growth of Industrial Policy, 1925–1975* (Stanford, Calif.: Stanford University Press, 1982), p. 307.

5. For a comparison of the prewar and the postwar Japanese industrial structures as well as the dissolution of Zaibatsu by the Occupation after World War II, see Michael Y. Yoshino, *Japan's Managerial System: Tradition and Innovation* (Cambridge, Mass.: The MIT Press, 1968), chap. 5.

6. Dodwell Marketing Consultants, *Industrial Groupings in Japan, 1982/83,* rev. ed. (Tokyo: Dodwell Marketing Consultants, 1982), p. 7.

7. Ibid.

8. Naoto Sasaki, *Management and Industrial Structure in Japan* (Oxford: Pergamon Press, 1981), chap. 5.

9. Ibid., p. 85.

10. For a review of the major theories advanced by Western economists to explain the behavior of Western multinationals, see Terutomo Ozawa, *Multinationalism, Japanese Style: The Political Economy of Outward Dependency* (Princeton, N.J.: Princeton University Press, 1979), chap. 2. For a concise summary of various theories of foreign investments, see Kiyoshi Kojima, *Direct Foreign Investment: A Japanese Model of Multinational Business Operations* (New York: Praeger, 1978), chap. 3.

11. Stephen Hymer, *The International Operations of National Firms: A Study of Direct Foreign Investment* (Cambridge, Mass.: The MIT Press, 1976). A doctoral dissertation originally completed in 1961.

12. Charles P. Kindleberger, *American Business Abroad* (New Haven, Conn.: Yale University Press, 1969), pp. 13–14.

13. Ibid.

14. Raymond Vernon, "International Investment and the Product Life Cycle," *Quarterly Journal of Economics,* vol. 80 (May 1966), pp. 190–207.

15. Frederick Knickerbocker, *Oligopolistic Reaction and Multinational Enterprise* (Cambridge, Mass.: Harvard University Press, 1974).

16. Edward Brown Flowers, "Oligopolistic Reactions in European and Canadian Direct Investment in the United States," *Journal of International Studies,* Fall/Winter 1976, p. 43–55.

17. John D. Daniels, *Recent Foreign Direct Manufacturing Investment in the United States: An Interview Study of the Decision Process* (New York: Praeger, 1971), p. 13 and p. 86.

18. Kojima, *Direct Foreign Investment.*

19. Harry G. Johnson, "The Efficiency and Welfare Implications of the International Corporations," in *The International Corporation,* ed. C. P. Kindleberger (Cambridge, Mass.: The MIT Press, 1970).

20. Kojima, *Direct Foreign Investment,* pp. 103–4.

21. Ibid., p. 172.

22. John E. Roemer, *U.S.-Japanese Competition in International Markets: A Study of the Trade-Investment Cycle in Modern Capitalism,* Institute of International Studies, Research Series, no. 22 (Berkeley: The University of California, 1975).

23. Ibid., p. 131.

24. Ibid., pp. 177–78.

25. Yoshi Tsurumi, *The Japanese Are Coming: A Multinational Interaction of Firms and Politics* (Cambridge, Mass.: Ballinger, 1976), p. 104.

26. Ibid., pp. 115–16.

27. Michael Y. Yoshino, *Japan's Multinational Enterprises* (Cambridge, Mass.: Harvard University Press, 1976), p. 90.

28. Ozawa, *Multinationalism,* p. 25.

29. Ibid., p. 69.

30. Ibid., p. 229.

31. Richard D. Robinson, *International Business Management: A Guide to Decision Making,* 2d ed. (Hinsdale, Ill.: The Dryden Press, 1978), pp. 22–26.

32. Ibid., p. 22.

33. Ibid., p. 27.

34. Yair Aharoni, *The Foreign Investment Decision Process* (Boston: Harvard University Press, 1966), p. 15.

35. Ibid., p. 3.

36. Yoshino, *Japan's Managerial System,* p. 258.

37. Rodney Clark, *The Japanese Company* (New Haven, Conn.: Yale University Press, 1979), p. 129.

38. Robinson, *International Business Management,* p. 635.

39. Robert N. Anthony, *Planning and Control Systems: A Framework for Analysis* (Boston: Division of Research, Graduate School of Business Administration, Harvard University, 1965).

40. Ibid., p. 16.

41. Ibid., p. 17.

42. Ibid., p. 18.

43. John Snow Schwendiman, *Strategic and Long-Range Planning for the Multinational Corporation* (New York: Praeger, 1973), p. 15.

44. Alfred D. Chandler, Jr., *Strategy and Structure: Chapters in the History of the Industrial Enterprise* (Cambridge, Mass.: The MIT Press, 1962), p. 14.

45. John M. Stopford and Louis T. Wells, Jr., *Managing the Multinational Enterprise: Organization of the Firm and Ownership* (New York: Basic Books, 1972), p. 19.

46. Ibid., pp. 21–29.

47. Yoshino, *Japan's Multinational Enterprises,* p. 132.

48. Ibid., p. 142.

3 — RESEARCH DESIGN

1. Richard N. Farmer and Barry M. Richman, *International Business: An Operational Theory* (Bloomington, Ind.: Cedarwood Press, 1974).

2. For the concept of gatekeepers, see David Easton, *A Systems Analysis of Political Life* (New York: John Wiley & Sons, 1965), pp. 86–96.

3. Frank A. Heller and Bernhard Wilpert, *Competence and Power in Managerial Decision-Making: A Study of Senior Levels of Organization in Eight Countries* (New

York: John Wiley & Sons, 1981), p. 57. They paraphrased the point made by D. J. Moberg and J. L. Koch, "A Critical Appraisal of Integrated Treatments of Contingency Findings," *Academy of Management Journal* 18 (1975), pp. 109–24.

4.   Robert Doktor, "Some Tentative Comments on Japanese and American Decision Making," *Decision Sciences,* vol. 14 (1983), pp. 607–12.

5.   Nan Lin, *Foundation of Social Research* (New York: McGraw-Hill, 1976), p. 203.

6.   "Japan's Expanding Manufacturing Presence in the United States: A Profile," April 17, 1981, and its annual updates compiled and published by the Japan Economic Institute of America, Washington, D.C.

7.   These primary Japanese investing companies are listed in *Industrial Groupings in Japan,* 1982/83 rev. ed. (Tokyo: Dodwell Marketing Consultants, 1982), part 3.

8.   *Kaisha Shikiho* (Japanese Company Handbook) (Tokyo: Toyo Keizai Shinposha, September 1983).

9.   The Statistical Package for Social Science (SPSS) was used.

10.   Eugene J. Kaplan, *Japan: The Government-Business Relationship, A Guide for the American Businessman* (Washington, D.C.: U.S. Government Printing Office, 1972), p. 34.

11.   Richard W. Riche, Daniel E. Hecker, and John U. Burgan, "High Technology Today and Tomorrow: A Small Slice of the Employment Pie," *Monthly Labor Review,* November 1983, pp. 50–58.

12.   U.S. Department of Commerce, International Trade Administration, *An Assessment of U.S. Competitiveness in High Technology Industries* (Washington, D.C.: U.S. Government Printing Office, 1983).

13.   Roger W. Schmenner, *Making Business Location Decisions* (Englewood Cliffs, N.J.: Prentice-Hall, 1982).

14.   Heller and Wilpert, *Competence and Power,* pp. 202–3 and p. 207.

15.   U.S. Department of Commerce, International Trade Administration, *Attracting Foreign Investment to the United States: A Guide for Government* (Washington, D.C.: U.S. Government Printing Office, 1981), pp. II, 1, 2.

4 — THE INVESTMENT DECISION-MAKING PROCESS

1.   Yair Aharoni, *The Foreign Investment Decision Process* (Boston: Harvard University Press, 1966), p. 55.

2.   The normalization process was not used, since it obscures the intuitive meaning of the original measurement scale. It also tends to make comparison of more than one group of samples difficult, for example, large firms versus small firms in the current study.

    For example, two respondents, X and Y, are requested to rate the importance of five items each for their decision making, using a four-point scale ranging from "very important" to "not important." X rates the first item as "very important" (point 4 in the scale) and the remaining items as "important" (point 3 in the scale). The average of X's scores on the five items is 3.2, and thus the normalized score for the first item is 0.8 and that for each of the remaining items is –0.2. In contrast, respondent Y rates the first item as "very important" and the remaining items as "not important" or "not considered" (point 1 in the scale). The average of Y's scores on the five items is 1.6, and thus the normalized score for the first item is 2.4 and that for each of the remaining items is –0.6. X and Y may attach the same level of importance to the first item, but the normalized scores for the item are 0.8 and 2.4, respectively. Here, it is impossible to know if these normalized scores mean "important" or "not important." Furthermore, it might be that X truly considers *more items* as important for his decision making than Y, but his normalized scores for items 2 to 5 show –0.2, which gives an impression that these remaining items are not important for X's decision making. The implicit fact can be well preserved if the overall average ratings of the five items, 3.2 for X which is *more* than 1.6 for Y, are presented with the indicated scores (original rather than normalized scores). This method of reporting average scores for individual items as well as for all items, instead of the normalization process, seems also desirable when X and Y represent two different groups, each consisting of more than one sample, as in the current study.

However, some researchers recommend the normalization process with good reasons. See, for example, John M. Stopford and Louis T. Wells, Jr., *Managing the Multinational Enterprise: Organization of the Firm and Ownership* (New York: Basic Books, 1972), pp. 104–5; and Michael Y. Yoshino, *Japan's Multinational Enterprises* (Cambridge, Mass.: Harvard University Press, 1976), pp. 148–49.

3.   Yoshino, *Japan's Multinational Enterprises*, p. 81.

4.   Lawrence G. Franko, *The European Multinationals* (Stamford, Conn.: Greylock Press, 1976), chap. 7.

5.   Tsurumi also noted that leading firms in the United States and in Europe began to refuse to license new products and process technologies to Japanese companies, which had become successful in competing in the world markets. He also observed that some Japanese firms began to open R & D-related manufacturing operations in the United States and in Europe in the early 1970s. Yoshi Tsurumi, *The Japanese Are Coming: A Multinational Interaction of Firms and Politics* (Cambridge, Mass.: Ballinger, 1976), pp. 117–18. See also Yoshino, *Japan's Multinational Enterprises*, p. 83.

6.   "Major Japanese Firms Setting up Research Offshoots in U.S.," *The Japan Economic Journal*, September 18, 1984, p. 11.

7.   For the textile dispute tangled with the issue of the reversion of Okinawa, see I. M. Destler, Hideo Sato, Priscilla Clapp, and Haruhiro Fukui, *Managing an Alliance: The Politics of U.S.-Japanese Relations* (Washington, D.C.: The Brookings Institution, 1976). For such politically volatile issues developed in the 1970s as steel, automobiles, and telecommunications equipment, see I. M. Destler and Hideo Sato, eds., *Coping with U.S.-Japanese Economic Conflicts* (Lexington, Mass.: Lexington Books, 1982).

8.   "The Industrial Policies and Practices of Japan and the U.S. — A Businessmen's View" (Advisory Council on Japan-U.S. Economic Relations and Japan-U.S. Economic Council, July 1984), p. 16. (Mimeographed.) The Japan Economic Institute of America surveyed and reported that the number of states with Buy American practices limiting the purchase of foreign-made products increased from

23 in 1973 to 36 in 1982. The results of its survey are summarized in *Yearbook of U.S.-Japan Economic Relations in 1982* (Washington, D.C.: Japan Economic Institute of America, June 1983), pp. 81–84.

9.   Masahiko Ishizuka, "Are Japanese Investments Welcome?" *The Japan Economic Journal*, May 8, 1984, p. 6.

10.   The Nikko Research Center, *Japan's Direct Investment in the United States: Summary of the Study* (Tokyo: The Nikko Research Center, 1979), p. 10.

11.   Duane Kujawa, "Production Practices and Strategies of Foreign Multinationals in the United States — Case Studies with a Special Focus on the Japanese, Volume I: Analysis" (a final report submitted to the Office of Foreign Economic Research, International Labor Affairs Bureau, U.S. Department of Labor, December 1984), p. 84. (Mimeographed.)

12.   Japan External Trade Organization, "Japanese Manufacturing Operations in the United States: Results of the First Comprehensive Field Study" (New York: Japan Trade Center, 1981), pp. 57–58. (Mimeographed.)

13.   Kujawa, "Production Practices," pp. 22–23.

14.   Ibid., p. 23.

15.   Tsurumi, *The Japanese*, p. 210.

16.   Kujawa, "Production Practices," p. 22.

17.   Tsurumi, *The Japanese*, p. 123.

18.   "How U.S. States Can Lose Business Investment: Keidanren Statement on Worldwide Unitary Taxation," *KKC Brief*, no. 17 (March 1984). *KKC Brief* is an occasional publication of the Japan Institute for Social and Economic Affairs (Keizai Koho Center), which is a private nonprofit organization attached to Keidanren.

19.   Two articles relating to Japanese investments in Oregon and Indiana appeared in *The Japan Economic Journal*, September 19, 1984, "Due to Absence of Unitary Tax, Fujitsu Chooses Oregon to Build Two Plants" and "Japan Businesses Are Increasingly Explicit in International Talks."

20.   Marie E. Wicks Kelly and George C. Philippatos, "Comparative Analysis of the Foreign Investment Evaluation Practices by U.S.-Based Manufacturing Multinational Companies," *Journal of International Business Studies*, Winter 1982, pp. 19–42.

21.   Tsurumi, *The Japanese*, p. 237.

5 — STRUCTURAL LINKAGE AND THE CONTROL SYSTEM

1.   Yoshi Tsurumi, *The Japanese Are Coming: A Multinational Interaction of Firms and Politics* (Cambridge, Mass.: Ballinger, 1976), pp. 236–37.

2.   The workshop was created originally in response to an informal request from MITI in 1971. It completed a comparative study of the level of internationalization of Japanese and Western multinational enterprises in 1978. For the results of the study, see Noritake Kobayashi, *Nihon no Takokuseki Kigyo* (Japanese Multinational Enterprises), 2nd. ed. (Tokyo: Chuo Keizaisha, 1983). The workshop is still active at the academic level and its members consist mainly of distinguished Japanese scholars

in international economics and business from several leading Japanese universities. The present author had an opportunity to attend its meeting in Tokyo during his field work conducted in Japan in the summer of 1984.

3. Kobayashi, *Nihon no Takokuseki Kigyo*, pp. 396–99.

4. Tsurumi, *The Japanese*, p. 236.

5. Michael Y. Yoshino, *Japan's Multinational Enterprises* (Cambridge, Mass.: Harvard University Press, 1976). p. 142.

6. Tsurumi, *The Japanese*, p. 240.

7. Duane Kujawa, "Production Practices and Strategies of Foreign Multinationals in the United States — Case Studies with a Special Focus on the Japanese, Volume I: Analysis" (a final report submitted to the Office of Foreign Economic Research, International Labor Affairs Bureau, U.S. Department of Labor, December 1984), p. 42. (Mimeographed.)

8. Tsurumi, *The Japanese*, p. 261.

9. Yoshino, *Japan's Multinational Enterprises*, p. 169.

10. Michael Y. Yoshino, *Japan's Managerial System: Tradition and Innovation* (Cambridge, Mass.: The MIT Press, 1968), p. 223.

11. Ibid., p. 207.

12. Ibid., pp. 150–52.

13. Noboru Makino and Yukio Shimura, *Nichi-Bei Gijutsu Senso* (The Japan-U.S. Conflicts on High Technology) (Tokyo: Nihon Keizai Shinbunsha, 1984), p. 218.

14. Kujawa, "Production Practices," pp. 59–64.

15. Roger Y. W. Tang, C. K. Walter, and Robert H. Raymond, "Transfer Pricing: Japanese vs. American Style," *Management Accounting*, vol. 60 (January 1979), pp. 12–16.

16. See, for example, "Aimed at Multinationals: Transfer Taxation May Be Implemented," *The Japan Economic Journal*, March 13, 1984, p. 3; and "Naikokusainyuho 482 Jo: Nichi-Bei Zeikinmasatsu no Osoremo" (Section 482 of the Internal Revenue Code: A Possibility of Japan-U.S. Taxation Conflicts), *Nihon Keizai Shinbun*, August 2, 1984, p. 13.

17. Sidney M. Robbins and Robert B. Stobaugh, *Money in the Multinational Enterprise: A Study of Financial Policy* (New York: Basic Books, 1973), pp. 37–44.

18. Ibid., p. 37.

19. Ibid., p. 40.

20. Ibid., p. 43.

21. For example, Yoshino observed that "companies usually continue to assume responsibility for the personal welfare of their employees even after they retire. They are usually named to positions appropriate to their status in one of the company's subsidiaries. The permanent employment practice also makes it necessary to find appropriate assignments for those who do not fit into the parent company. They are often shifted to foreign subsidiaries, sometimes in mid-career, just as domestic subsidiaries have been known to be used for such a purpose." Yoshino, *Japan's Multinational Enterprises*, p. 169.

22. Kujawa, "Production Practices," p. 35.

23. Yoshino, *Japan's Multinational Enterprises*, pp. 70–71.

24. "Computer-aided Decision-making More Popular among Top Managers," *The Japan Economic Journal,* June 19, 1984, p. 7.

25. Robbins and Stobaugh, *Money,* p. 153.

26. Helen G. Morsicato and Lee H. Radebaugh, "Internal Performance Evaluation of Multinational Enterprise Operations," *The International Journal of Accounting Education and Research,* vol. 15 (Fall 1977), pp. 92–93.

6 — CHANGES IN GOVERNMENT-BUSINESS RELATIONS

1. For further information on the revised law on foreign exchange and foreign trade as well as on the comparison between the original and the new laws, see Kaname Seki and Noriyuki Watanabe, *Atarashii Gaikokukawase Kanriho* (The New Law on Foreign Exchange Control), rev. ed. (Tokyo: Zaikei Shohosha, 1982).

2. These selection criteria have been well known inside and outside Japan. See, for example, Y. Ojimi (then-vice-minister of international trade and industry), "Basic Philosophy and Objectives of Japanese Industrial Policy," in *The Industrial Policy of Japan,* Organization for Economic Cooperation and Development (OECD) (Paris, 1972), pp. 11–31; and G. C. Allen, *The Japanese Economy* (New York: St. Martin's Press, 1981), chap. 7.

3. In addition to the materials cited in note 2 above, see the following publications for further information on how Japan's industrial policies have been implemented: G. C. Allen, "Industrial Policy and Innovation in Japan," in *Industrial Policy and Innovation,* ed. Charles Carter (London: Heinemann Educational Books, 1981); F. Gerard Adams and Shinichi Ichimura, "Industrial Policy in Japan," in *Industrial Policies for Growth and Competitiveness: An Economic Perspective,* ed. F. Gerard Adams and Lawrence R. Klein, the Wharton Econometric Studies Series (Lexington, Mass.: Lexington Books, 1983); and the Japan Economic Institute of America, *Japan's Industrial Policies* (Washington, D.C.: The Japan Economic Institute of America, 1984).

4. Seki and Watanabe, *Atarashii,* p. 26.

5. Chalmers Johnson, *MITI and the Japanese Miracle: The Growth of Industrial Policy, 1925–1975* (Stanford, Calif.: Stanford University Press, 1982), pp. 194–95.

6. Allen, *The Japanese Economy,* p. 159.

7. Johnson, *MITI,* p. 292.

8. I. M. Destler, Hideo Sato, Priscilla Clapp, and Haruhiro Fukui, *Managing an Alliance: The Politics of U.S.-Japanese Relations* (Washington, D.C.: The Brookings Institution, 1976) p. 195.

9. Ibid., p. 37.

10. Allen, *The Japanese Economy,* p. 168.

11. Johnson, *MITI,* p. 263.

12. OECD, *The Industrial Policy of Japan,* pp. 113–14.

13. Isaiah Frank and Ryokichi Hirono, ed., *How the United States and Japan See Each Other's Economy: An Exchange of Views between the American and Japanese*

Committees for Economic Development (New York: Committee for Economic Development, 1974), p. 58.

14. Seki and Watanabe, *Atarashii*, p. 26.

15. Ibid., p. 115.

16. Ibid. For regulations on outward direct investments, see pp. 153–55 and pp. 260–61.

17. Interview, for preliminary research for the current study, with Mr. Hajimu Hori, director of research at the Japan Trade Center in New York City, March 9, 1984. He was on assignment from the Economic Planning Agency of the Japanese government. He commented further, "Currently, the Japanese government does not have any restrictive measures on Japanese companies' overseas investments. It provides information only, such as investment climate overseas, to the companies which seek such information and advice."

18. Johnson, *MITI*, pp. 283–84.

19. Ibid., pp. 289–91.

20. Based on MITI's internal memorandum.

21. Interview with Mr. Hori; see note 17 above.

22. Yoshihisa Ojimi, "A Government Ministry: The Case of the Ministry of International Trade and Industry," in *Modern Japanese Organization and Decision-Making*, ed. Ezra F. Vogel (Berkeley: University of California Press, 1975), p. 102.

23. Interview with Mr. Yoshiharu Kunogi at MITI, Tokyo, Japan, July 16, 1984.

24. Interview with Mr. Hori. See note 17 above.

25. Frank and Hirono, *How the United States and Japan See Each Other's Economy*, p. 47.

26. For details, see MITI, *Tsusho Sangyo Roppo* (Japanese Laws on International Trade and Industry) (Tokyo: Tsusho Sangyo Chosakai, 1984).

27. Interview with Mr. Kunogi. See note 23 above.

28. For further discussions on the role of deliberation councils, see Muneyuki Shindo, "Seisakukettei no Shisutem: Shingikai, Shimonkikan, Shinkutanku no Yakuwari" (Policy-Making System: The Roles of Deliberation Councils, Advisory Organs, and Think-Tanks), *Jurist*, no. 29 (Winter 1983), pp. 246–51.

29. "MITI Starts Lending an Ear to U.S. Businessmen," *The Japan Economic Journal*, September 18, 1984, p. 4.

30. "MITI Invites U.S. and European Businessmen to Industrial Structure Council Meeting," *The Japan Economic Journal*, November 6, 1984, p. 4.

31. This point is also explained in Johnson, *MITI*, p. 222.

32. According to economic theories, "excess competition" does not possibly occur. However, the business environment among Japanese companies is often characterized as "excessively competitive." See, for example, Yasusuke Murakami, "Sengo Nihon no Keizai Shisutemu: Kyoso to Kainyu no Fukusokozo o Bunsekisuru" (The Economic System of Postwar Japan: An Analysis of the Multilayer Structure of Competition and Intervention), *Economisuto*, June 14, 1982, pp. 38–54.

33. T. F. M. Adams and Noritake Kobayashi, *The World of Japanese Business* (Tokyo: Kodansha International, 1969), p. 235.

34. *Keidanren 1983* (Tokyo: Keidanren, October 1983).

35.   Johnson, *MITI*, pp. 295–96.

36.   *Keidanren 1983*, p. 14.

37.   The Business Roundtable was founded in 1972 and is considered to be the most influential organization representing the interests of leading corporations in the United States. For further information, see A. Lee Fritschler and Bernard H. Ross, *Business Regulation and Government Decision-Making* (Boston: Little, Brown, 1980), pp. 48–51.

38.   For more information on these four economic organizations, see William Ouchi, *The M-Form Society: How American Teamwork Can Recapture the Competitive Edge* (Reading, Mass.: Addison-Wesley, 1984), pp. 43–48.

39.   This point was also observed by Gerald L. Curtis, "Big Business and Political Influence," in *Modern Japanese Organization and Decision-Making,* ed. Ezra F. Vogel (Berkeley: University of California Press, 1975), p. 61 and pp. 64–65.

40.   Takehiko Kamo, "The Behavior of Transnational Organizations between the United States and Japan" (Ph.D. dissertation, Yale University, 1977), pp. 166–67 and p. 255.

41.   Ibid. For a detailed story of how the Japan-U.S. Economic Council was created, see pp. 194–237.

42.   Ibid., pp. 202–3.

43.   Japan-U.S. Businessmen's Conference, *Agenda for Action,* Joint Task Force Report (Washington, D.C.: Advisory Council on Japan-U.S. Economic Relations, 1983).

44.   For the results of the commissioned study, see *Coping with U.S.-Japanese Economic Conflicts,* ed. I. M. Destler and Hideo Sato (Lexington, Mass.: Lexington Books, 1982).

45.   Japan-U.S. Businessmen's Conference, *Agenda.*

46.   Interview with Mr. Albert L. Seligmann, executive director, U.S.-Japan Advisory Commission in Washington, D.C., March 6, 1984.

47.   United States-Japan Advisory Commission, "Press Release on Report to President Reagan and Prime Minister Nakasone," October 18, 1983, p. 4. (Mimeographed.)

48.   "Japan Business Circles Promote More PR Activities in U.S.," *The Japan Economic Journal,* August 21, 1984, p. 11 and p. 13. In contrast to U.S. firms, Japanese companies in general have not been active in public relations in the past. In 1983, Tsurumi expressed his view in his publication written in Japanese: Japanese companies have not realized that public relations at the government level is counterproductive. Top management should become more concerned with the importance of public relations at the private level. See Yoshi Tsurumi, *Ikareru Amerika: Nihon no Kigyosenryaku Saitenken* (Angry America: Reevaluation of Japanese Corporate Strategies) (Tokyo: Toyokeizai Shinposha, 1983), pp. 189–204.

49.   Masahiko Aoki, "Giji-Tsuriikozo o Tsujiru Kakushinteki Taio: Nihon no Sangyososhiki no Shinkyokumen" (Innovative Adaptation through the Quasi-Tree Structure: An Emerging Aspect of Japan's Industrial Structure), *Kikan Gendaikeizai (Contemporary Economics),* no. 58 (Summer 1984), pp. 59–72.

50.   David R. Belli, "Foreign Direct Investment in the United States: Highlights from the 1980 Benchmark Survey," *Survey of Current Business* 63, no. 10 (October 1983), p. 25.

51. Ibid.
52. Ibid., p. 26.
53. The issue of the employment effect of foreign direct investment is controversial. In his study of the U.S. employment effects of U.S. multinational enterprises (MNEs) and those of foreign MNEs, Kujawa argues that there are two significant trends affecting MNEs' choice of the situs of production and, thus, employment. These trends are resource scarcity and declining innovation, the latter characterized by the maturing of products and industries. He contends further that "this in turn implies that production employment will be less stable for any single location, and that growth in jobs may well be won at the expense of growth in income — and increasing pressures for political subsidies to sustain both employment and incomes. In this regard, the future may well be a test of the political maturity of the industrialized nations (which are both the major donors and recipients of direct foreign investment), and of their ability to constrain within reasonable bounds the noncompetitive subsidies and other potential pressures they could develop to yield shortrun, politically rewarding solutions to longterm, difficult and extremely significant economic and social problems." Duane Kujawa, "Employment Effects of Multinational Enterprises: A United States Case Study" (a report submitted to the International Labor Office, Geneva, for publication as Working Paper 12 in its research project Employment Effects of Multinational Enterprises), pp. 35–36.

7 — SUMMARY AND CONCLUSIONS

1. For IBM's recent reorganization and strategies, see "Nihon I.B.M. no Jinji Jinmyaku Kenkyu" (A Study of Personnel and Human Linkages at IBM Japan), a special feature article in *Zaikai Tembo*, September 1984, pp. 105–43; and "Cover Story — IBM: More Worlds to Conquer," *Business Week*, February 18, 1985, pp. 84–98.

2. For private initiatives in the United States in reducing waste and fraud in U.S. government agencies, see, for example, "War on Waste: Nobody Has Any Guts in Washington," interview with J. Peter Grace, chairman, President's Private Sector Survey on Cost Control, *U.S. News & World Report*, July 25, 1983, p. 53; and Jeffery L. Sheler, "Federal Waste: The Finger Points at Congress," *U.S. News & World Report*, January 23, 1984, p. 55.

3. See, for example, "Cover Story — Collision Course: Can the U.S. Avert a Trade War with Japan?" *Business Week*, April 8, 1985, pp. 50–55; and "Trade War with Japan?" *U.S. News & World Report*, April 15, 1985, pp. 22–23.

4. On this point, however, Tsurumi argues that the Japanese market now is very much open to foreign businesses and that the success of U.S. firms in penetrating the Japanese markets (that is, the increase in U.S. exports to Japan) depends on understanding the consumer and industrial marketing systems, including supplier-customer relations, in Japan. See Yoshi Tsurumi, "Managing Consumer and Industrial Marketing Systems in Japan," *Sloan Management Review*, Fall 1982, pp. 41–50.

Selected Bibliography

Adams, F. Gerard, and Lawrence R. Klein, eds. *Industrial Policies for Growth and Competitiveness: An Economic Perspective.* The Wharton Econometric Studies Series. Lexington, Mass.: Lexington Books, 1983.

Adams, T. F. M., and Noritake Kobayashi. *The World of Japanese Business.* Tokyo: Kodansha International, 1969.

Aharoni, Yair. *The Foreign Investment Decision Process.* Boston: Harvard University Press, 1966.

Allen, G. C. *The Japanese Economy.* New York: St. Martin's Press, 1981.

_____. "Industrial Policy and Innovation in Japan." In *Industrial Policy and Innovation,* ed. Charles Carter. London: Heinemann Educational Books, 1981.

Anthony, Robert N. *Planning and Control Systems: A Framework for Analysis.* Boston: Division of Research, Graduate School of Business Administration, Harvard University, 1965.

Aoki, Masahiko. "Giji-Tsuriikozo o Tsujiru Kakushinteki Taio: Nihon no Sangyososhiki no Shinkyokumen," (Innovative Adaptation through the Quasi-Tree Structure: An Emerging Aspect of Japan's Industrial Structure) *Kikan Gendaikeizai (Contemporary Economics),* no. 58 (Summer 1984): 59–72.

Balance of Payments Yearbook. International Monetary Fund, various issues.

Barnds, William J., ed. *Japan and the United States: Challenges and Opportunities.* A Council on Foreign Relations Book. New York: New York University Press, 1979.

Belli, R. David. "Foreign Direct Investment in the United States: Highlights from the 1980 Benchmark Survey." *Survey of Current Business* 63, no. 10 (October 1983): 25–35.

Business Week, various issues.

Caves, Richard E., and Masu Uekusa. *Industrial Organization in Japan.* Washington, D.C.: The Brookings Institution, 1976.

Chandler, Alfred D., Jr. *Strategy and Structure: Chapters in the History of the Industrial Enterprise.* Cambridge, Mass.: The M.I.T. Press, 1962.

Clark, Rodney. *The Japanese Company.* New Haven, Conn.: Yale University Press, 1979.

Curran, Timothy J. "Politics and High Technology: The NTT Case." In *Coping with U.S.-Japanese Economic Conflicts,* ed. I. M. Destler and Hideo Sato. Lexington, Mass.: Lexington Books, 1982.

Curtis, Gerald L. "Big Business and Political Influence." In *Modern Japanese Organization and Decision-Making,* ed. Ezra F. Vogel. Berkeley: University of California Press, 1975.

Daniels, John D. *Recent Foreign Direct Manufacturing Investment in the United States: An Interview Study of the Decision Process.* New York: Praeger, 1971.

Destler, I. M., and Hideo Sato, eds. *Coping with U.S.-Japanese Economic Conflicts.* Lexington, Mass.: Lexington Books, 1982.

Destler, I. M., Hideo Sato, Priscilla Clapp, and Haruhiro Fukui. *Managing an Alliance: The Politics of U.S.-Japanese Relations.* Washington, D.C.: The Brookings Institution, 1976.

Doktor, Robert. "Some Tentative Comments on Japanese and American Decision Making." *Decision Sciences* 14 (1983): 607–12.

Dodwell Marketing Consultants. *Industrial Groupings in Japan, 1982/83.* Rev. ed. Tokyo: Dodwell Marketing Consultants, 1982.

Drucker, Peter F. "Economic Realities and Enterprise Strategy." In *Modern Japanese Organization and Decison-Making,* ed. Ezra F. Vogel. Berkeley: University of California Press, 1975.

Easton, David. *A Systems Analysis of Political Life.* New York: John Wiley & Sons, 1965.

Farmer, Richard N., and Barry M. Richman. *International Business: An Operational Theory.* Bloomington, Ind.: Cedarwood Press, 1974.

Flowers, Edward Brown. "Oligopolistic Reactions in European and Canadian Direct Investment in the United States." *Journal of International Studies,* Fall/Winter 1976: 43–55.

Frank, Isaiah, and Ryokichi Hirono, eds. *How the United States and Japan See Each Other's Economy: An Exchange of Views between the American and Japanese Committees for Economic Development.* New York: Committee for Economic Development, 1974.

Franko, Lawrence G. *The European Multinationals.* Stamford, Conn.: Greylock Press, 1976.

Fritschler, A. Lee, and Bernard H. Ross. *Business Regulation and Government Decision-Making.* Boston: Little, Brown, 1980.

Gresser, Julian. *High Technology and Japanese Industrial Policy: A Strategy for U.S. Policymakers.* Subcommittee on Trade of the Committee on Ways and Means, U.S. House of Representatives. Washington, D.C.: U.S. Government Printing Office, 1980.

Hattori, Ichiro. "A Proposition on Efficient Decision-Making in the Japanese Corporation." *Columbia Journal of World Business,* Summer 1978: 7–15.

Heller, Frank A., and Bernhard Wilpert. *Competence and Power in Managerial Decision-Making: A Study of Senior Levels of Organization in Eight Countries.* New York: John Wiley & Sons, 1981.

Hulburt, James M., and William K. Brandt. *Managing the Multinational Subsidiary.* New York: Holt, Rinehart & Winston, 1980.

Hymer, Stephen. *The International Operations of National Firms: A Study of Direct Foreign Investment.* Cambridge, Mass.: The M.I.T. Press, 1976.

International Financial Statistics. International Monetary Fund, various issues.

"Japan: A Nation in Search of Itself." *Time,* Special Issue, August 1, 1983: 18–88.

The Japan Economic Institute of America. "Japan's Expanding Manufacturing Presence in the United States: A Profile." *JEI Report,* April 17, 1981. (Annual updates as well.)

____. *Yearbook of U.S.-Japan Economic Relations in 1982.* Washington, D.C.: The Japan Economic Institute of America, 1983.

____. *Japan's Industrial Policies.* Washington, D.C.: The Japan Economic Institute of America, 1984.

The Japan Economic Journal, various issues.

Japan External Trade Organization. "Japanese Manufacturing Operations in the United States: Results of the First Comprehensive Field Study." New York: Japan Trade Center, 1981. Mimeograph.

____. *Directory: Affiliates & Offices of Japanese Firms in the U.S.A.* Tokyo: JETRO & Press International, 1982.

Japan-U.S. Businessmen's Conference. *Agenda for Action.* Joint Task Force Report. Washington, D.C.: Advisory Council on Japan-U.S. Economic Relations, 1983.

____. "The Industrial Policies and Practices of Japan and the U.S. — A Businessmen's View." Advisory Council on Japan-U.S. Economic Relations and Japan-U.S. Economic Council, July 1984. Mimeograph.

Johnson, Chalmers. *MITI and the Japanese Miracle: The Growth of Industrial Policy, 1925–1975.* Stanford, Calif.: Stanford University Press, 1982.

Kaigai Shinshutsu Kigyo Soran (Japanese Multinationals, Facts and Figures). Tokyo: Toyokeizai Shinposha, 1984.

Kaisha Shikiho (Japanese Company Handbook). Tokyo: Toyokeizai Shinposha, September 1983.

Kamo, Takehiko. "The Behavior of Transnational Organizations between the United States and Japan." Ph.D. dissertation, Yale University, 1977.

Kanou, Akihiro. *Sony Shinjidai* (A New Era for Sony). Tokyo: Presidentosha, 1982.

Kaplan, Eugene J. *Japan: The Government-Business Relationship, A Guide for the American Businessman.* U.S. Department of Commerce, Bureau of International Commerce. Washington, D.C.: U.S. Government Printing Office, 1972.

Kelly, Marie E. Wicks, and George C. Philippatos. "Comparative Analysis of the Foreign Investment Evaluation Practices by U.S.-Based Manufacturing Multinational Companies." *Journal of International Business Studies,* Winter 1982: 19–42.

Kindleberger, Charles P. *American Business Abroad.* New Haven, Conn.: Yale University Press, 1969.

Knickerbocker, Frederick. *Oligopolistic Reaction and Multinational Enterprise.* Cambridge, Mass.: Harvard University Press, 1974.

Kobayashi, Noritake. *Nihon no Takokuseki Kigyo* (Japanese Multinational Enterprises). 2d ed. Tokyo: Chuo Keizaisha, 1983.

Kojima, Kiyoshi. *Direct Foreign Investment: A Japanese Model of Multinational Business Operations.* New York: Praeger, 1978.

Kujawa, Duane. "Employment Effects of Multinational Enterprises: A United States Case Study." A report submitted to the International Labor Office (Geneva) for publication as Working Paper 12 in its research project Employment Effects of Multinational Enterprises, August 1980. Mimeograph.

_____. "Technology Strategy and Industrial Relations: Case Studies of Japanese Multinationals in the United States." *Journal of International Business Studies* (Winter 1983): 9–22.

_____. "Production Practices and Strategies of Foreign Multinationals in the United States — Case Studies with a Special Focus on the Japanese, Volume I: Analysis." A final report submitted to the office of Foreign Economic Research, International Labor Affairs Bureau, U.S. Department of Labor, December 1984. Mimeograph.

Lin, Nan. *Foundation of Social Research*. New York: McGraw-Hill, 1976.

Makino, Noboru, and Yukio Shimura. *Nichi-Bei Gijutsu Senso* (The Japan-U.S. Conflicts on High Technology). Tokyo: Nihon Keizai Shinbunsha, 1984.

Ministry of International Trade and Industry. *MITI Handbook 1984*. Tokyo: Japan Trade and Industry Publicity, 1984.

_____. *Tsusho Sangyo Roppo* (Japanese Laws on International Trade and Industry). Tokyo: Tsusho Sangyo Chosakai, 1984.

Morsicato, Helen G., and Lee H. Radebaugh. "Internal Performance Evaluation of Multinational Enterprise Operations." *The International Journal of Accounting Education and Research* 15 (Fall 1977): 77–94.

Murakami, Yasusuke. "Sengo Nihon no Keizai Shisutemu: Kyoso to Kainyu no Fukusokozo o Bunsekisuru" (The Economic System of Postwar Japan: An Analysis of the Multilayer Structure of Competition and Intervention). *Economisuto*, Special Edition, June 14, 1982: 38–54.

The *New York Times*, various issues.

"Nihon I.B.M. no Jinji Jinmyaku Kenkyu," (A Study of Personnel and Human Linkages at IBM Japan), a special feature article, *Zaikai Tembo*, September 1984: 105–43.

Nihon Keizai Shinbun, various issues.

The Nikko Research Center. *Japan's Direct Investment in the United States: Summary of the Study*. Tokyo: The Nikko Research Center, 1979.

Ojimi, Yoshihisa. "Basic Philosophy and Objectives of Japanese Industrial Policy." In *The Industrial Policy of Japan,* Paris: Organization for Economic Development, 1972.

____. "A Government Ministry: The Case of the Ministry of International Trade and Industry." In *Modern Japanese Organization and Decision-Making,* ed. Ezra F. Vogel. Berkeley: University of California Press, 1975.

Olmer, Lionel H. "Japan's Drive for Technological Preeminence Challenges U.S." *Business America,* January 24, 1983: 6–10.

Organization for Economic Cooperation and Development. *The Industrial Policy of Japan.* Paris, 1972.

Ouchi, William. *The M-Form Society: How American Teamwork Can Recapture the Competitive Edge.* Reading, Mass.: Addison-Wesley, 1984.

Ozawa, Terutomo. *Multinationalism, Japanese Style: The Political Economy of Outward Dependency.* Princeton, N.J.: Princeton University Press, 1979.

Phatak, Arvind. *Managing Multinational Corporations.* New York: Praeger, 1974.

Reich, Robert B. *The Next American Frontier.* New York: Times Books, 1983.

Riche, Richard W., Daniel E. Hecker, and John U. Burgan. "High Technology Today and Tomorrow: A Small Slice of the Employment Pie." *Monthly Labor Review,* November 1983: 50–58.

Robbins, Sidney M., and Robert B. Stobaugh. *Money in the Multinational Enterprise: A Study of Financial Policy.* New York: Basic Books, 1973.

Robinson, Richard D. *International Business Management: A Guide to Decision Making.* 2d ed. Hinsdale, Ill.: The Dryden Press, 1978.

Roemer, John E. *U.S.-Japanese Competition in International Markets: A Study of the Trade-Investment Cycle in Modern Capitalism.* Research Series, no. 22, Institute of International Studies. Berkeley: The University of California, 1975.

Sasaki, Naoto. *Management and Industrial Structure in Japan.* Oxford: Pergamon Press, 1981.

Schmenner, Roger W. *Making Business Location Decisions.* Englewood Cliffs, N.J.: Prentice-Hall, 1982.

Schwendiman, John Snow. *Strategic and Long-Range Planning for the Multinational Corporation.* New York: Praeger, 1973.

Seki, Kaname, and Noriyuki Watanabe. *Atarashii Gaikokukawase Kanriho* (The New Law on Foreign Exchange Control). Rev. ed. Tokyo: Zaikei Shohosha, 1982.

Shindo, Muneyuki. "Seisakukettei no Shisutem: Shingikai, Shimonkikan, Shinkutanku no Yakuwari" (Policy-Making System: The Roles of Deliberation Councils, Advisory Organs, and Think-Tanks). *Jurist* 29 (Winter 1983): 246–51.

Stopford, John M., and Louis T. Wells, Jr. *Managing the Multinational Enterprise: Organization of the Firm and Ownership.* New York: Basic Books, 1972.

Tang, Roger Y.W., C. K. Walter, and Robert H. Raymond. "Transfer Pricing: Japanese vs. American Style." *Management Accounting* 60 (January 1979): 12–16.

Tsurumi, Yoshi. *The Japanese Are Coming: A Multinational Interaction of Firms and Politics.* Cambridge, Mass.: Ballinger, 1976.

_____. "Managing Consumer and Industrial Marketing Systems in Japan." *Sloan Management Review,* Fall 1982: 41–50.

_____. *Ikareru Amerika: Nihon no Kigyosenryaku Saitenken* (Angry America: Reevaluation of Japanese Corporate Strategies). Tokyo: Toyokeizai Shinposha, 1983.

_____. *Multinational Management: Business Strategy and Government Policy.* 2nd ed. Cambridge, Mass.: Ballinger, 1984.

U.S. Department of Commerce. *Foreign Direct Investment in the United States.* Washington, D.C.: U.S. Government Printing Office, 1976.

_____. *Attracting Foreign Investment to the United States: A Guide for Government.* Washington, D.C.: U.S. Government Printing Office, 1981.

_____. *An Assessment of U.S. Competitiveness in High Technology Industries.* Washington, D.C.: U.S. Government Printing Office, 1983.

_____. *Foreign Direct Investment in the United States, 1980.* Washington, D.C.: U.S. Government Printing Office, 1983.

U.S. News & World Report, various issues.

Vernon, Raymond. "International Investment and the Product Life Cycle." *Quarterly Journal of Economics* 80 (May 1966): 190–207.

Vogel, Ezra F., ed. *Modern Japanese Organization and Decision-Making.* Berkeley: University of California Press, 1975.

The Wall Street Journal, various issues.

Yanaga, Chitoshi. *Big Business in Japanese Politics.* New Haven, Conn.: Yale University Press, 1968.

Yoshino, Michael Y. *Japan's Managerial System: Tradition and Innovation.* Cambridge, Mass.: The M.I.T. Press, 1968.

____. "Emerging Japanese Multinational Enterprises." In *Modern Japanese Organization and Decision-Making,* ed. Ezra F. Vogel. Berkeley: University of California Press, 1975.

____. *Japan's Multinational Enterprises.* Cambridge, Mass.: Harvard University Press, 1976.

Index

About the Author

MAMORU YOSHIDA, Ph.D., CPA, is Assistant Professor of International Accounting at the College of Business and Public Administration of Florida Atlantic University, Boca Raton, Florida. Formerly, he was an auditor and a tax specialist at Peat, Marwick, Mitchell & Co., an international accounting firm, in New York City. He is currently working as a co-researcher on a Japanese-U.S. joint research study on problems associated with local production of Japanese manufacturing firms in the United States, which is sponsored by the Toyota Foundation and the Institute of Social Science at the University of Tokyo.

Dr. Yoshida holds a bachelor's degree in economics from Keio University (Japan), an MBA from the University of Kansas, and a Ph.D. degree from the University of Miami. He is a member of the Academy of International Business, the American Accounting Association (the International Accounting Section), the American Institute of CPAs, and the New York State Society of CPAs.